ⓂRIGI

NEW WRITING FROM
BRITAIN'S OLDEST PUBLISHER

Risk-taking writing for risk-taking readers.

JM Originals was launched in 2015 to champion distinctive, experimental, genre-defying fiction and non-fiction. From memoirs and short stories to literary and speculative fiction, it is a place where readers can find something, well, *original*.

JM Originals is unlike any other list out there with its editors having sole say in the books that get published on the list. The buck stops with them and that is what makes things so exciting. They can publish from the heart, on a hunch, or because they just really, really like the words they've read.

Many Originals authors have gone on to win or be shortlisted for a whole host of prizes including the Booker Prize, the Desmond Elliott Award and the Women's Prize for Fiction. Others have been selected for promotions such as Indie Book of the Month. Our hope for our wonderful authors is that JM Originals will be the first step in their publishing journey and that they will continue writing books for John Murray well into the future.

Every JM Original is published with a limited-edition print run. This means every time you buy one of our covetable books, you're not only investing in an author's career but also building a library of (potentially!) valuable first editions. Writers need readers and we'd love for you to become part of our JM Originals community. Get in contact and tell us what you love about our books. We're waiting to hear from you.

Coming from JM Originals in 2022

Catchlights | Niamh Prior
An unexpected novel that sets the innocence of childhood against
the violence of adulthood, the joys of passion against the horrors of
obsession and the reality of death against the magic of life.

Nobody Gets Out Alive | Leigh Newman
An exhilarating virtuosic story collection about women navigating
the wilds of male-dominated Alaskan society.

Free to Go | Esa Aldegheri
One woman's around-the-world adventure, and an exploration of
borders, freedoms and womanhood.

Free to Go

Across the World on a Motorbike

Esa Aldegheri

JM ORIGINALS

First published in Great Britain in 2022 by JM Originals
An Imprint of John Murray (Publishers)
An Hachette UK company

1

Excerpt from 'St Bride's' from *Jizzen* (Picador, 1999) by Kathleen Jamie. Reproduced
with permission of the author.

Excerpt from 'Migration Day' from *Moder Dy* (Polygon, 2019) by Roseanne Watt.
Reproduced with permission of the Licensor through PLSclear.

Excerpt from 'The Republic of Motherhood' from *The Republic of Motherhood*
(Chatto and Windus, 2018) by Liz Berry. Reproduced with permission of the author.

Excerpt from 'The Language of the Brag' from *Satan Says* (Pitt Poetry Series, 1980)
by Sharon Olds. Reproduced with permission of the author.

A CIP catalogue record for this title is available from the British Library

Trade Paperback ISBN 978-1-529-38968-5
eBook ISBN 978-1-529-38967-8

Typeset in Minion Pro by Palimpsest Book Production Ltd, Falkirk, Stirlingshire

Printed and bound in Great Britain by Clays Ltd, Elcograf S.p.A.

John Murray policy is to use papers that are natural, renewable and
recyclable products and made from wood grown in sustainable forests.
The logging and manufacturing processes are expected to conform
to the environmental regulations of the country of origin.

John Murray (Publishers)
Carmelite House
50 Victoria Embankment
London EC4Y ODZ

www.johnmurraypress.co.uk

For my Glad Companion
sine qua non

Contents

Prologue

Bridges, Borders and a Burning

Late one night in Edinburgh a motorbike burned, down by the river. It stood on ragged grass, in a deserted forecourt half enclosed by high-rise flats whose upper floors were lost in the darkness, lower windows boarded up or broken. Wings of flame feathered the night.

The motorbike's windshield, foot pegs and mudguards had melted and lay in blubbery, earth-bound puddles. Its fuel tank had blown off and landed some metres away, scorched and grey as a meteorite. Whoever stole the bike had hot-wired it and driven to this place before flicking out the side stand, pulling out the fuel hoses and throwing a match, illuminating the high flats in blasts of orange and yellow. The police officer who had phoned said to come as quickly as possible.

'There won't be much left,' she said, condolence in her tired voice.

By the time the fire brigade arrived, only smoke, twisted metal and cinders remained in place of a beloved old motorbike that had once carried two people halfway across the span of the planet. Rage and grief flickered in my stomach, along with a sudden wish that I'd been there to see the match struck and thrown, the motorbike transfigured on that desolate bit of grass into a beacon, a glorious firework. I wondered whether the fire-strikers had felt a rush of joy at setting off that explosion of heat and light against the darkness – a momentary release from boredom, perhaps. Then, slowly but unmistakably, a sense of glee and release began to rise through the heat of my anger, the way oil bubbles up and separates from water: this fiery Viking burial was a fitting end for Mondialita the strong, the steady, the flame-red. I had learned to drive and maintain her, then to rely on her; the hardest learning was letting her go.

Still I dream of her burning, especially in seasons of anxiety and loss. Today I wake from dreams in which I watched her melt into snakes of lava that hissed towards my toes. My hands are shaking; my eyelids feel as if their capillaries are brambles. It is early morning and I can hear my children talking in the uniquely loud whispers they use when trying to be quiet. They are cooried in one bed, discussing plans to visit their cousins in Italy at Easter: our first trip outside Scotland since the UK left the European Union. I realise they are trying to decide what things they couldn't do without: what to pack 'if we can't get home because of Brexit'. Anxiety rises in my stomach, a familiar presence, and jangles me up into the weekend. I tiptoe towards the kitchen with the practised stealth of the parent hoping to maximise their chances of an uninterrupted first coffee.

A cold dawn is opening up the sky behind the Forth Rail Bridge. The Forth estuary is a dark blue shiver below. Along the shore, oystercatchers call as Edinburgh wakes up a few miles to the east. Today is the first day of February in the year 2020: the Feast of St Bride, or St Brigid, the Irish saint who protects a wondrous miscellany of things including babies, beer, poets, cattle, oystercatchers and scholars. St Bride's is also the day of Imbolc, a much more ancient Celtic celebration of Brigid, goddess of fertility, fire, poetry and spring. Both versions of Brigid are strongly associated with water – sacred wells, the waters of childbirth, rivers running after the winter's ice. I am a multitasking poet, scholar, gardener, a fire-loving and sea-swimming mother of three; Brigid in all her guises is welcome in my house. I raise my mug to her and hold on to its warmth as if it is a potion against fear.

Outside I can see signs of winter loosening, the spring whispering its approach through the softened light and the bumps of buds. The window is cool against my hungover forehead. Yesterday I was late home from a vigil outside the Scottish Parliament, where a defiant gathering of people sang and wept as the United Kingdom left the European Union and took Scotland with it, despite the fact that a strong majority of Scottish people had voted against Brexit. I had brought with me a hip flask of single malt, and an espresso cup to drink drams from: a Scottish-Italian symbol which felt both ridiculous and potent. My hybrid parting glass was raised many times, in the best tradition of wakes. This morning, with Scotland on the cusp of spring and unimagined change, the deep apprehension I feel is not just a hangover, and fresh coffee is not enough to counter it. I fear for my future as a hybrid citizen of Scotland and Italy, and, even more, I fear for my children's future. Like a bairn needing comfort, I turn to stories: memories of different times and open borders.

Thirteen winters ago I sailed under that same bridge, out across the river Forth on a ferry heading south to the Belgian port of Zeebrugge. This was BC, Before Children, or, as they themselves would put it, in the Olden Days. Below me, the motorbike, burdened and untested, waited in the hold with other vehicles; beside me stood the man I'd married just over a year before. We were on our way to New Zealand, overland, as much as geography and geopolitics would permit. I carried with me many hopes and worries, but the possibility of closed borders across Europe was not one of them. My most immediate concern was that I already felt seasick, and we weren't even out of the estuary. Out on the deck I gripped the rail and looked out on to the waters of the Firth of Forth, dark beyond the engine's churning, thin strings of distant lamps showing where the sea stopped and the land began.

As a child growing up in Italy, I had learned that this river marked the uttermost northern border of the Roman Empire; our teachers solemnly told us that beyond those waters, in what is now Fife, lived Enemy Barbarians. I grinned at my husband, blue-eyed and Fife-bred, and felt excitement win over nausea. As the ferry slid under the great red fretwork of the Rail Bridge, a train rumbled over our heads, taking commuters home to their families while we popped the cork from a bottle of fizzy wine and drank to our journey. I poured some bubbles into the Forth – a libation of sorts, to whatever entities protect travellers and their freedoms.

*

The port of Zeebrugge was a world of shuttling containers like giant, moving Lego bricks. A stern Belgian policeman waved us through customs imperiously, shouting after us: 'Careful with those French drivers, they are all insane!' I revved the motorbike and cheered at being free to go, at the thought that this land ahead of us stretched all the way to the Bosphorus. Already the air felt different, alight with possibilities.

We were soon on the wide motorways of France, the tarmac spooling out between immense fields. I edged our motorbike towards the upper reaches of the speedometer: a terrifying and magical margin where even the tiniest change in balance, or pressure on the handlebars, communicates instantly through the bike to the road, and it feels as if your mind and body are a single impulse of movement. This state of hyper-vigilance, of almost transcendental concentration and awareness, was the most awake I had ever felt. I whooped with glee as our motorbike swooped south, wheels for wings.

My Italian father drove across these same roads during my childhood summers – more sedately, in a sensible family car, my brother and I sweating in the back as we headed north towards holidays in Glasgow with our Scottish mother's family. Open borders across Europe were a given, a fact my child-mind took for granted, like how on Italian tables olive oil was always greenly waiting and on Scottish tables there was white butter instead, strangely salty. When my two grandfathers were together, I would act as translator, incredulous as they swapped stories about a time when their countries were at war with each other and they both decided to evacuate their families from the bombs falling on Glasgow and Milan. I was suspicious that they were making it all up for my benefit, these crazy stories of a time when European borders were closed. I only

5

realised it was not a joke when, one day in Glasgow, I heard stories of a distant English great-uncle who always boasted about how he was proud to have served in the RAF and 'bombed Milan good and proper!' My mum went very quiet then, as I sat on her knee, and held me tight in a way that told me this was true, and dangerous, and not funny.

I knew my dad had spent his childhood in the countryside near Pavia, escaping from the Allied bombing of Milan. His father – my Nonno – had to keep working in the city but cycled to the countryside every weekend to be with his family, a return trip of over a hundred kilometres. Nonno told stories of sheltering from Allied bombs in ditches, of passing Fascist checkpoints where dissenters hung from trees by the roads through the rice fields. He told me how one day he met his sister-in-law Tosca near the old covered bridge in Pavia; how she gave him packages for the family and offered to help him carry them the last few kilometres; how he thanked her and told her to go back home across the bridge, he could carry everything just fine; how he waved at her and cycled off, then heard the bomb that destroyed the bridge and everyone on it.

War games are developing in the next room, involving escapes from exploding bridges on flying unicorns and giant motor-bikes powered by glittery farts. At school my children have been learning about the Second World War and how it affected the Forth: the huge defences built against German submarines, the fear that the Rail Bridge would be bombed and a vital transport artery destroyed. Their attempts at quietness have been entirely abandoned and the question of what toys to pack seems settled or forgotten. I seize the moment to make more coffee, and realise that I have never told the children about Zia Tosca and the covered bridge: I have never had the courage to bring tragic family history so close to their peaceful lives. It still seems too much; but what stories should I tell to my small humans when they worry 'in case the borders close'? What stories should we turn to in times of change and shifting certainties, when fences and walls and mistrust are increasingly used as the way to deal with difference?

Stories arrive through your ears and eyes and skin; they settle among your bones as you sleep, and when the time is right, you let them out so they can be free to go and grow. My Nonno told me that, I think; or maybe I told myself. Either way, coffee and paracetamol have worked their magic and I feel ready for the day now. Anxiety has coalesced into urgency: the need to weave a story about travel and change, freedom and fear, wide horizons and frontiers – weave it like a sail for navigating times of increasing restrictions. On a beloved motorbike I had crossed borders that are now impassable, changed my understanding of freedom, embraced an adventure which did not end with Mondialita's burning. I want to share it, like all travellers share tales: a gift from the road behind for the journey ahead, whatever it may bring.

I check on the children, dig out the box of travel diaries, pour a coffee, sit down at the kitchen table and begin.

Part One

FREE TO GO

1

Free to go

Orkney to Italy

Many travel stories open with a clearly defined event, often dramatic, which catalyses the journey. Somebody dies, someone comes of age, a transformative encounter happens – and so the quest begins. Not so this tale.

Life was comfortable: I was not long married, moving through glad months filled with love and work and friends. When I was eighteen, I had met a man with crinkly blue eyes and knew he was the one for me, but conflicting desires and distances had kept us apart for years. My work and joy grew in building connections between people, in learning and speaking the languages of warm, thickly populated parts of the world. He gravitated towards remote islands and cold, thinly inhabited places. I thought that finally being together and married was the happily ever after, the end of a journey; our gladness felt like a shining lake. It took me a while to realise that something unsettling was moving beneath the surface, and that it was not a monster: it was me, it was us, a restlessness within. There was no dramatic catalysing event, but a vague sense of unease grew from deep down: *careful*, its note of warning sounded out, *careful, this is not what you need to be doing.*

Instead of listening, I took on extra work, began a masters degree and started training for a half-marathon, but the discordant feeling was still there. I saw it reflected in my husband's eyes, in the increasing frequency of his solitary walks and short-term jobs on distant Scottish islands. We were happy together, but we needed something different. I didn't want to ask exactly what that 'something' might be: I feared that the answer would involve more incompatible desires, the ruin of our hard-won life together.

The unease surfaced in an Edinburgh club, bubbling up into clear questions amidst the thumping music, like air from lungs forced too long underwater: *'Is this enough for you?'*, we shouted to each other. *'Is this the life you want?'* We walked out under the pellucid sky of a Scottish summer night washing into dawn, found a pub where we could hear each other speak, and finally, deliciously, all the unresolved fears came up for air. One by one, they were revealed as being shared, and unfounded, and useful. We wanted to leave, but not leave each other; we wanted to go away, but not separately.

With an ease that didn't feel reckless, we sketched out a journey together, and it was like a decision made long before. We would quit our jobs and spend our savings on a journey overland to the opposite side of the planet: New Zealand, where we had both long wanted to go. It was as if this plan had been biding its time to emerge, fully formed, once we knew how to find it. I understood what Patrick Leigh Fermor meant when he wrote that his plan to walk across Europe unfolded in his mind 'with the speed and the completeness of a Japanese paper flower in a tumbler'.

Deciding how we would travel turned out to be as simple as a list of pros and cons sketched on a pub napkin.

'Looks like we'll be going by motorbike,' I said.

So began the alchemy of action, hope and obduracy that transforms scribbles on a napkin into events. No plan is perfect, but this one held such enormous imperfections that all I could do was laugh and order another drink. The first flaw in our plan: neither of us could ride a motorbike. The second: we didn't own one. The third: had we owned one and been able to ride one, we had not the slightest idea how to fix anything that might go wrong with it. But in that electric moment, no such concerns mattered. I raised my glass for a toast, and grinned: 'Minor, insignificant and temporary details.'

It didn't take long for the paper flower of euphoria to sink, pulled down by the many cumbersome necessities that loomed after that initial moment of joyful revelation. Could we really drive a motorbike across the world? My sense of direction is non-existent: I am infamous for getting lost in big supermarkets. Friends were genuinely worried for us as they realised we were serious: 'You know you really could get killed,' one said.

To prove them wrong, I first needed to learn how to ride a motorbike. I procrastinated by reading, one impatient afternoon, a Yamaha motorbike manual instead. It had stern words for the aspiring rider: 'Motorcycles are fascinating vehicles, which can give you an unsurpassed feeling of power and freedom. However, they also impose certain limits, which you must accept; even the best motorcycle does not ignore the laws of physics.' It cautioned further: 'The good motorcyclist rides safely, predictably and defensively – avoiding all dangers, including those caused by others. Enjoy your ride!'

All this safety and predictability talk was tiresome. I wanted what Fermor wrote about: 'A new life! Freedom!' Abandoning the intractably severe manual, I turned to motorbike travel books to cheer me up. When in fear, read about the thing you fear, then you won't have to actually do it; at least not for a while.

I was looking for accounts of excitement and transformative adventure. I found plenty: *Jupiter's Travels*; *The Motorcycle Diaries*; *Two Wheels Through Terror*; *Long Way Round*; *Borderlands*; *Through Dust and Darkness*; *One Brit, One Bike, One Big Country* – the list of books was long, but I felt impatience growing in me again, like a weed you can't suppress. Why were all these stories by men, about men? I enjoyed all their journeys, most of their company, and some of their writing, but where were the voices of women? When I found some, my sense of relief was strong. Lois Pryce and Melissa Holbrook Pierson's accounts of riding motorbikes especially thrilled me, although I sensed a warning in their stories: it felt as if they needed to emulate the machismo that surrounded them in the world of motorbike adventuring, almost as a survival tactic. Martha Gellhorn, in her excoriating *Travels with Myself and Another*, wrote of going to China with that most macho of men, Ernest Hemingway, referring to him as 'U.C.', her 'Unwilling Companion'; but I found not one book written by a woman about driving a motorbike with a willing companion.

'I'm willing!' said my lovely man.

'But I can't call you W.C. – can I?'

'Fair point.' He grinned. 'How about Glad Companion – G.C.?'

Throughout these days of preparation, my mind filled with memories of my early impressions of motorbikes. In northern Italy, I had watched as first my male classmates and then my younger brother were given 50 cc mopeds at the age of fourteen: a normal rite of passage for boys, which was usually followed by a trip to the mechanic who would 'unofficially' increase the power and volume of the engine to 125 or 250 cc. I was not asked if I wanted one. No girl I knew was asked. Girls just didn't ride motorbikes – unless they rode pillion, of course, preferably in tight jeans or short skirts. Nobody ever said these things directly, but unspoken norms can be very loud, imposing themselves through glances and seemingly harmless comments.

Once I asked if I could try my brother's moped. With an audience of family and friends, I wobbled on to it, managed to start the ignition, opened the throttle, closed my eyes, and drove straight into a concrete gate post. *Driving like a girl.* I was aflame with humiliation, my growing anger exacerbated by well-meaning words of consolation: 'Don't worry, you don't need to learn, you'll always be able to get a lift.' I did not get a moped, nor ask to drive one again.

'Esa? *Hello?* You with us?'

A shout hauled me back to the parking lot in Edinburgh where I was astride a Suzuki 500 cc. It was the day of my motorbike driving test, the end to a week of intensive training. When I first clambered on to the Suzuki I had wobbled even more than on that tiny Italian moped. My feet felt like pebbles, miles away, unconnected to my legs. My chest was a balloon with a panicking cricket trapped inside. I was scarlet and sweating inside my helmet, which led to an intolerably itching scalp. I wanted to cry, to run away, to evaporate. Instead I swore, quietly, at whatever was generating the panic blocking me – and opened the throttle. With my eyes open this time, I managed it, grateful to Jim the instructor, who never once treated me differently because I am female.

Jim was equally abrupt with us all, only softening into smiles when he recounted past biking adventures. On the day of the final driving test, while we sat waiting to be called, he gave us a pep talk that consisted of reasons he'd seen people fail. My favourite story was of a man who opened his visor – 'to show off his sunglasses, the idiot' – while he was speeding down the motorway; a wasp flew into his helmet, crawled upwards and stung him all over his face. Jim replicated the exact series of sounds and movements that ensued. I laughed so much I forgot to be afraid. The man waiting next to me shrugged, knees spread wide and helmet dangling between them: 'Oh, I've been riding bikes since I was twelve, what could go wrong?'

There followed a concatenation of roundabouts, traffic lights, motorways, and U-turns-without-putting-feet-down-or-you-fail. I passed. I passed! The wide-kneed dangler of helmets didn't. My new driving licence, a flimsy piece of pink plastic, felt like a fanfare I could carry in my pocket, a triumphant message to the world: I could *do* this, despite the fear.

Passing the driving test gave me the confidence to put my name down for an evening course in Motorbike Maintenance: Beginner Level. I walked into the first lesson to find a room filled entirely with men, all chatting about motorbike journeys past and planned. With horror, I recognised one as a particularly objectionable ex-boyfriend. He stared at me, slowly pulling his long red hair tighter into its ponytail. Sidling into the back row, trying to blend in, I listened to the teacher explain the components of a motorbike battery. I didn't have a clue what he was talking about, but thought I'd show enthusiasm by asking a question: 'Why does it have water inside if it's electric?'

The room was silenced by the scale of my ignorance. Objectionable Ex-Boyfriend smirked. And then, just as I thought I would have to leave or melt from embarrassment, something wonderful happened: the teacher said, 'Good for you, hen,' and one of the older men echoed him, 'Aye, that's why you're here, eh!' The silence bubbled into enthusiastic explanations of how lead–acid batteries work. Teaching me became the group's collective mission, my learning curve the measure of the course's success. As the weeks passed, I became able to change brake pads and fine-tune a carburettor. Objectionable Ex dropped out after the second class. At the end of the course, the teacher and the other students gave me a compass as a gift, 'for the road ahead'. Accepting their kindness felt like scraping off the first layers of old, encrusted anger and fear.

We now needed to actually acquire a motorbike that could manage an open-ended journey across half the planet. G.C. started coming home with motorbike magazines and pored over them as if they held the secret of human happiness. Our options seemed to involve bewildering dichotomies: shaft or belt-drive, double- or single-barrelled exhaust, twin-shock or monoshock, water-cooled or air-cooled, kick-start or button start. Only one manufacturer was recommended on every site and magazine we turned to for a motorbike that was reliable and robust: the Bavarian Motor Works – B.M.W.

One we could afford appeared in a local paper. It was an 800 cc touring model, a beautiful fiery red motorbike built in 1982 and owned by only three people since then. From its condition, it seemed that all three owners had treated it like a sacred object; its service manual read like a litany of devotion. This was a bike built for days of comfortable cruising, with a high windshield, a double padded seat, and a wide fibreglass faring designed to keep both of us warm and dry. Twin cylinders of 400 cc stood out from its engine like rocket boosters: a machine strong enough to carry us and our bags across the world, up mountains and through deserts. We fitted an intercom system with voice-activated microphones and headphones which slotted into our helmets, so we could communicate without having to yell over the engine's noise.

I could see how much strength G.C. used as he eased the motorbike off the centre stand. It swung on to the ground, slamming down with the force of its own weight – a quarter of a tonne. I was scared to try. He got on, pushed the ignition and the engine coughed and growled into life as I jumped on the back and found the pillion foot pegs. It felt like being on a huge, powerful creature, a motorised beast. I was seized by absolute certainty that this was an insanely dangerous thing to be doing, and also the only possible thing we could or should do. The motorbike throbbed underneath me, its engine metronomically precise, carrying us away.

Daily I practised getting the motorbike off its centre stand, frowning with impatience, the ache in my muscles not quite translating into enough strength to manage the task. I grew increasingly terrified that this journey would find me too small, too weak, too timid; attributes so often associated with 'girly' behaviour, while their opposites add up to the figure of the macho male motorbike rider so comprehensively present in books and films. My hackles rose whenever big, strong, brash men assumed I would only ride pillion or – worse – were openly amazed to find that I 'could drive too'. I resented them with a silent, corrosive fury which did nothing to change the facts: I couldn't become a huge man; a smaller bike wouldn't carry us where we wanted to go; we couldn't afford two separate ones.

I didn't know what to do, so I threw myself into practicalities that I could control, like getting the paperwork sorted for the motorbike. Vehicles, like people, need a passport to cross international borders without being challenged. The *carnet de passage* is a customs guarantee certificate which promises that the motorcycle will not be sold in the countries it enters, and will leave within a specified time limit. If these promises are kept, the motorbike has freedom of movement – within certain limits and at a cost.

Packing was another absorbing practical task. We decided on which tools and spare parts were indispensable, bundled them into small plastic bags and put them into compartments around the bike. There were openings in the frame where we would be able to hide money if necessary, and I took note of them feeling like a smuggler. G.C. stitched sturdy canvas tool bags to the frame on either side of the bike, and in these we dropped our faithful old hiking rucksacks. There were strict limits on what we could each have: one change of clothes, one warm jumper, minimal toiletries, and one book. Before a new book could be carried, the old one would have to be left behind or posted home. The only book we would take for the whole journey was the Haynes Manual *BMW 2-valve Twins*, which we read obsessively. It was written in a style that alternated passages of sensible clarity ('be careful to avoid burning your hands on the hot exhaust pipe') with ones of infuriating inscrutability ('drop the output shaft oil baffle into the housing') which made my confusion about water in batteries seem laughable.

Last on, ratcheted down on the back of the bike, were two bright orange dry-bags that held our camping kit: tent, sleeping bags, stove, sleeping mats, waterproofs, and one shared roll of romantic toilet paper. That was it: our luggage for the undefined future.

We still have that Haynes Manual, but have somewhat lost the art of minimalist packing. One week after St Bride's, the kitchen is drowning under bags, waterproofs, soft toys, books, phones, chargers, snacks – the debris of what two adults and three

children think they need for ten days in Orkney. I inspect P's bag and find ten pairs of socks and a few T-shirts, but no pants or trousers. S has packed five variations on the unicorn theme, ranging from fluffy onesies to pencils, but no actually useful clothes. T's bag is entirely filled with comics and books. I sit down in the middle of the floor and laugh.

G.C. walks in and looks delighted, saying, 'I haven't heard you laugh for weeks!' I realise he is right: my reservoirs of glee have been clogged up by the fear of Brexit's consequences. I feel a dissolution of who I am, a fraying in the fabric made of family histories carried like an invisible cloak. My children would not exist had it not been for the European Union and Scotland's place within it: I was able to study in Edinburgh having grown up in Italy because, as a citizen of the European Union, I was not charged university tuition fees in Scotland. This left me free to study, work and find love in Scotland, eventually growing a flourishing family here. My whole life has been coloured by having two languages, two passports, two countries; my children's lives too. Does Brexit mean that we will have to choose between belongings?

I turn towards our sea of stuff – belongings, in a different sense – and try to focus on the glad anticipation of travel, the pleasure of visiting friends.

The layers of life that G.C. and I had grown in Edinburgh fell away from us like leaves as we said goodbye to friends and worked our notices in various jobs, with no firm plans to return. As we cleaned and tidied, we realised that we would not miss most of our possessions and decided to give them away over the course of a farewell weekend. According to our calculations, our savings would allow us to travel for about a year, maybe up to eighteen months if we were very frugal. We also expected to find work along the way, if we decided that we needed more money to extend our journey beyond New Zealand – to cross the South Pacific, perhaps, and drive through Latin America. 'I can teach, you can doctor,' I said to G.C., with the confidence of those whose luck and skills and passports have always brought them such freedom.

Today I feel decidedly unfree, my thoughts snagging on tiredness, worry and domestic chores. I have still not unpacked our smelly car since driving back from Orkney with the children. Our time there was filled with the hospitality and warmth of our old, dear friend Calum: a week of drinking whisky into the wee hours of the morning, laughing and making music. But now it is a Monday in the endless middle of February, G.C. is staying in Orkney for another week working as an island locum, S and T are having a ridiculous fight over the jam, and why did I even let them have breakfast in white school uniforms?, and come ON, we're going to be LATE.

The mess greets me like a scolding when I get back from school drop-off. I ignore it, make a coffee, step outside and message my Italian friends in Edinburgh. We are organising a children's party for Carnevale – carnival, Mardi Gras, Pancake Tuesday – the festival of excess and fun that sets us up for the austerity of Lent. Our talk of plans for sparklers and party food are interspersed with rumours of disease: an Italian man in Lombardy is in hospital with pneumonia caused by a new virus first discovered in China. His close contacts are being tested – it seems there is a test for this, but nobody is sure. There is talk of travel restrictions between Italy and other countries. 'This could be even worse than Brexit, guys,' texts the joker of the group. We say goodbyes and return, slightly subdued, to our various days.

I force myself to clear up the kitchen and unpack, turning away from the temptation to just pick up the kids from school and drive away from all these worries back to Orkney, that place of welcome where we lived when P was a baby and have returned to ever since; the place where, Before Children, our motorbike journey began.

Wide horizons had disappeared into a smudge of grey, with water everywhere. Late autumn gales hit our Orcadian cottage at over a hundred miles per hour. It sounded as if giant fists were battering the thick walls as we huddled inside. I was writing up my masters thesis, G.C. was at the end of a locum job; in between work, we packed and prepared and waited for the gales to ease.

We left Orkney between storms, on a ferry, just before the midwinter solstice. This, the darkest season of the northern year, is considered inauspicious by some and was most certainly a silly time to be riding a motorbike in Scotland. I tried not to worry too much about that. We had made decisions based on the urgency of enthusiasm, our desire to *just go*, rather than on logic – not for the first or last time.

As we approached the ferry terminal gate, the motorbike slipped on some ice. I couldn't manage the weight, and we keeled over; the heat of the exhaust melted my trousers and shrivelled my confidence. The bike was so huge, so heavy. I would never be able to do this: how could I, when I could only just about touch the ground with the tip of my boot, and had dropped the bike before we even left Scotland?

'It's auspicious,' G.C. said into the intercom as I struggled to right the bike. 'When Che Guevara set out from Buenos Aires, he fell off nine times.' I was grateful for G.C.'s kindness, but also felt a familiar hum of anger: whatever Che Guevara had done wasn't going to help me now. I needed stories of small women who had ridden motorbikes, not another man on a mission to change the world.

There was frost on the roads of the Scottish Highlands, and the gritters had been out. I drove for short, tentative bursts, never going over fourth gear. On our left, the North Sea shone all the way to Scandinavia while the east wind froze G.C.'s fingers on the handlebars. The woodlands of central Scotland arrived like a benediction, and the fields rolled in green waves down towards the Forth estuary.

Our last night on the island of Britain was spent with G.C.'s family in Fife, their warmth and kindness filling us up like fuel. His mum presented us with a bottle of sparkling wine, 'to celebrate your adventure'. His dad showed us how to use fibreglass and Araldite, 'just in case any cracks in the bike need fixing'. Waving goodbye, filled with sadness and impatience at the same time, I missed the wisdom of their parting gifts: celebrating adventure and fixing cracks before they got too wide would be essential for both our journey and our marriage.

Messages from family and friends in Italy are buzzing into my phones like flies, the worries of Brexit eclipsed by another escalating disaster: the spread of the new virus now known as SARS-CoV-2, also variously called Covid-19, Covid, coronavirus or the plague. My cousin in Milan supplies medical equipment to hospitals, and this is the first time I have ever seen a crack in his cheerful certainty that 'everything will be fine'. I stare at his messages showing unbelievable numbers of dead people in our region. I try to imagine each one of those people, their hands or noses, how they laughed.

Celebrations and laughter still happen, however thick the shroud of grief. Life insists on happening. The snowdrops mean that P's birthday is approaching: I must think of cake and sleepovers and presents, despite the vertiginous numbers of people dying of Covid in Lombardy, even though I feel that I am leaking grief and worry everywhere, everywhere. I ferociously mop up every trickle as soon as it wells up. It is like cleaning up soul vomit that keeps on spewing out. 'You can do this,' I mutter, clutching at lists, trying to remember that past self who learned how to drive and fix motorbikes, pushing through sticky barriers of fear to find freedom on the other side.

On the wide motorways of France, I had felt my confidence rise as I edged the motorbike to its highest speed: we wanted to get to my parents' house in Italy as quickly as possible, in time for Christmas. Soon the motorway was coiling tightly away from the Mediterranean into the Apennines, unravelling on the other side of the mountains as we descended into the vast alluvial floodplain of the Po Valley. I drove through the gates of my childhood home, stomach warm with pride, glanced down at the concrete post I had once crashed into so ignominiously and opened my visor to greet my family.

Technical Interlude

Just across the border into Italy, at Ventimiglia, the engine had started to make an unusual sound: a clattering, as if the crankshafts within the casing were limping. The plains of the Po were fog-bound in the winter, as usual. Living there is to be at the bottom of a huge geographical bowl rimmed by mountains, with no sea breeze to move the air. The hoar frost was inches deep, and black ice patched the roads: a motorcyclist's nightmare. Just as well we had planned to spend a month saying goodbye to Italian family and friends before the journey ahead. We took advantage of our time to remove the cylinder head covers to check the valve clearances.

In *Zen and the Art of Motorcycle Maintenance*, Robert Pirsig distinguishes between a 'romantic' and a 'classical' sensibility: the former is more interested in the aesthetics of an experience, the latter in rational understanding. For Pirsig, checking the valve clearances on a motorcycle is a classical problem, but one that carries all the dignity and emotional power of a devotional act. I first read the book as a teenager and recognised the beauty of the process he described, long before I'd dreamed of performing a valve adjustment for myself. Checking valve clearances was one of the things I had learned on the motorbike maintenance course. Our manual gave it a difficulty rating of three spanners, which was about as tricky as we were prepared to undertake.

My father found us as we struggled with the four-thousandths-of-an-inch feeler gauge, sliding it into the gap between the valve stem and the rocker arm, muttering instructions and the occasional expletive. The exhaust valves were too tight. This was a worrying finding: it had been only a couple of thousand miles since we'd last adjusted them. He invited us to have a coffee break and gently insisted on paying for a 'properly qualified BMW mechanic' to give the motorbike a full service, and fit new tyres.

A few days later, as we waited for the mechanic to phone us with updates, my brother Lorenzo made me a coffee and insisted that we needed to name our vehicle: 'For goodness' sake, it'll be like a third person in your marriage and it doesn't even have a name?' After more coffee and much debate, he came up with 'Mondialita'. It was perfect: here was a motorbike made in 1982, the year Italy won the Football World Cup (il Mondiale); a vehicle that could take us half across the world (il mondo); a machine that was clearly fabulous and world-class (mondiale). Mondialita. The diminutive ending belied her massive, tractor-like strength, but it expressed the affection with which we already spoke of her. My mother organised a shopping trip to buy me a pair of new trousers, 'because you need to be comfortable on the journey'. They were black, soft, tough, with many pockets and zips, and outlived Mondialita.

These gifts of safety, naming and comfort were well chosen,

although it would take me months of travel to realise their true value. Others were not so generous, and we spent a fair amount of time shrugging off questions that were more like accusations from people who were variously appalled by our choices: 'Aren't you afraid of getting robbed?' they would ask. 'Aren't you afraid of border guards?' 'Aren't you afraid you won't find safe places to sleep?' 'Aren't you afraid of breaking down?' Their questions felt like a leaden presence, an enemy to the golden, bubbling feeling that filled my stomach whenever I remembered that we were free to go.

Mondialita was declared 'fixed and ready to go wherever you want', so we decided to go on a pilgrimage of gratitude, and pay homage to the shrine of Saint Colombano, patron saint of motorcyclists. Colombano lived twelve centuries before the invention of the internal combustion engine. He was a Scots-Irish monk, a wandering scholar who left Ireland in a little leather boat and reached Europe, where he is said to have multiplied flagons of beer, given sight to the blind, and yoked a bear to a plough. He founded a monastery after decades on the roads through France, Savoy and Lombardy – the same itinerary we had travelled in just a few days.

A rare sea wind managed to cross the Apennines and lift the fog for a few precious, jewel-like days. We drove in sunlight to Bobbio, a small Apennine town where Saint Colombano is venerated in a rock-cut sanctuary beneath the cathedral, under a Renaissance Annunciation. His relics were in a marble tomb, carved centuries after his bones had turned to dust. There were no motorbikes on display, but G.C. inserted a coin into a slot machine and pulled out a wallet-sized laminated card of Colombano. He looked like a Hell's Angel with a mitre, surrounded by a blue light like the sky above the distant Alps in Lombardy's springtime. G.C. put the card in his wallet, hoping it would bring us some of the old monk's luck.

Just before New Year's Eve, we undertook something like a monastic ritual, a shedding of the past in preparation for the unknown ahead: we shaved each other's hair down to the shortest buzz cut. My brother joined in too. We grinned at each other's new faces, as brown and black fluff gathered in a pile at our feet. Putting on the motorbike helmet was now very simple, like donning a second skin. I thought of the Selkie legends from Orkney and the North Sea rim, the stories of women who were also seals and could slip from land to water by putting on their sealskins. My motorbike gear freed me to slip into speed and flowing motion, a transformation that never failed to thrill me. I was also suddenly free from tugging curls and clips, liberated from the Barbie-like standards of female beauty that still dominated Italian television and public spaces.

We rubbed our stubbly heads as we sat in an Irish-themed pub discussing all the advice we had gathered about the road ahead. Our original plan had been to drive overland to Greece through the Balkans, but every book, person and internet forum had advised against it. The roads were terrible in the best weather, and deadly in the winter. There were many border crossings, and we read of hefty bribes required to pass each one. All accounts by women spoke of harassment by the border police, and of sometimes being asked to pay for border crossings through other means than money.

We considered our route on a map of Italy drawn in beer froth on the table: white splurges marked Florence, Rome,

Naples and the port in Puglia where ferries left for Greece. I dabbed some froth at the head of our beery Adriatic.

'What about Venice?' I asked, smearing the map. 'It's carnival time there soon.' I wanted to show off the whole of Italy's beauty to G.C., but we were both concerned about the long drive ahead through some of the most expensive places of our whole journey.

G.C. dabbed his finger into the foam. 'We might have to miss out on Venice . . . unless . . .' he said.

'. . . Unless?'

'. . . Unless we sail directly to Greece from Venice.'

Today is Shrove Tuesday, or Pancake Tuesday in Scotland. In Italy it is 'Fat Tuesday', Carnival time. The northern mornings grow lighter. I watch some high clouds, mind blank for a minute, before turning back to the unbelievable news: Carnival in Venice has been cancelled due to fears that the swirling crowds would be a perfect spreading place for the new virus. Its name tumbles about everywhere in the news, in texts and phone calls and conversations; it seems impossible that only a few weeks back we dismissed it as 'some weird new flu'. I phone a friend who is a writer and schoolteacher living in Turin, and he confirms more incredible news: yesterday schools did not open across the north of Italy. Nobody knows when children will return to classes. He doesn't know if or when he will be paid.

In Scotland, our small Italian Carnival party is also cancelled, even if schools here are giving no sign of closing. I feel fear unfurl from the place where I keep it curled away, covered in lies and smiles to protect the children. I add a layer of pancakes and

*sweet spreads to my weavings of comfort. P asks me, as he wipes
chocolate off his pyjamas, 'Will we be able to go to Italy for
Easter, Mamma?'*

*'Ach, yes, sure,' I tell him. 'Don't you worry.' The fear stirs,
softly, murmuring.*

The drive towards Venice took us through the landscapes of
northern Italy in its full beauty, the road threading through a
tessellation of paddy fields. The Alps were just visible along
the northern horizon, like a rip in the sky which cut southward
towards us as both mountain range and roads converged on
the Adriatic coast where, for most of the last millennium,
Venice has been Europe's window on the East. It started as an
island refuge from plundering barbarians and evolved by
making its own harmony out of the discord between East and
West: a city built for fusing cultures; a place of enterprise,
power, and the bridging of empires. Its two principal islands
lock shapes like a yin with a yang.

We padlocked Mondialita in a backstreet on the mainland
and took a train out over the silvered waters of the Venetian
lagoon. A man at the train station, in a fedora and fur coat,
approached G.C. with the promise of 'very cheap-price rooms.
View of canal!' He had a moustache like Groucho Marx. When
he realised that I was Italian, he became friendlier, and the
price immediately halved.

From the window of our room, peering along an alley, we
could just about make out a metre of water. Plastic cups, dead
rats and cigarettes floated down the Canal Grande. It was late
February, just before Lent, and Carnevale was in full swing.

The walkways and bridges of the old city pulsed with people, many of them masked and gowned in fabulous costumes. The air smelled of cigarettes, incense, damp bricks, dirty water and hot, sweet pastries. We left our room and were carried along in the press and rush, past jugglers and fire-breathers, clowns and acrobats, to the centre of the city, Piazza San Marco.

It felt that other horizons were beckoning to us through the Carnival fabric of Venice. The Basilica looked more Byzantine than Roman Catholic, with its cupolae and domes, and on its façade were four equestrian statues looted from ancient Greece. Venice, now a glittering tourist bauble, was once a fierce city at the interface between Byzantium, the Ottomans and Christian Europe. Looking past the gondoliers and blown-glass shops, I could sense the stories of other empires and cultures edging in through traces from the past. Further on down the canal, at the entrance to the Arsenale, we found two stone lions, hauled centuries ago as booty from medieval Venetian looting trips around Athens.

Our last evening in Venice was dreamlike, a time of in-between, filled with visions and omens. We wandered by the Canale di Cannareggio as the daylight faded and street vendors lit rows of brightly patterned wax candles along dark alleyways. We passed a solitary gondolier, lanterns lit at bow and stern, punting alone through the dark waters singing a pop song about lost love. An old man and woman stepped out of their front door. There was a companionable ease about their movements, a togetherness that seemed the fruit of many loving decades.

Squinting up at the antique streetlights, the man turned to his wife: *'Carissima – è luce, o luna?'*, 'Dearest – is that a light, or the moon?'

'Luce,' she said gently, taking his arm, and helped him on down the street.

In the morning light, our ferry seemed impossibly huge, a monstrosity rising above the lagoons. The Venetian border official grunted, 'Where are you going with all these bags and this motorbike?' My long-standing distaste for his profession rose inside me, dredged up by memories of his uniform in another setting: when I was about ten, my Italian father was stopped at the border between Italy and France, accused of kidnapping me and my brother because our names didn't appear on his passport. I can still feel the fear of being separated from my family, like a paralysing flood of ice, and remember my dad's supreme calm while appeasing and persuading the guards that all was in order, that his Scottish wife was waiting for us in Glasgow.

I channelled that calm as I smiled and lied, 'Oh, just a camping holiday in Greece.'

He narrowed his eyes then said, 'Bah, on you go. But the Greeks are all liars, so watch yourselves. And their coffee is disgusting.'

My brother phones me from his flat in Córdoba as I sit down with a mid-morning coffee. He tells me he has quit his teaching job and is preparing to travel overland from the south of Spain to Italy, so he can be with our parents 'in case this virus gets any worse'. All flights in and out of Italy are now cancelled: he will take the first train he can and make his way north, then east through France and across the Apennines. We are all

practicalities and travel logistics, straight back to the tone we used when he was helping to name Mondialita in a world of open borders. I want to say, 'stay safe', but there is no point. I want to say, 'let me know where you are', but I know he will run out of phone battery. I say, 'Go well, brother,' and he says, 'Don't worry, sister.' We hang up. The weight of reality feels impossible to bear. I burst into tears.

Stars gathered in intensity as we sailed south, slowly emerging into an arc of brilliance. The Italian coast became a low constellation on the starboard horizon, feeble against the vast darkness of sea and sky. We fell asleep on the deck.

The sun came up over the bony spine of the Balkans; we had passed Bosnia, Montenegro, Albania, Epirus. After travelling on our own terms with the motorbike, it was disconcerting to be confined again to a floating metal container, with someone else steering. I gazed at the countries we had chosen to bypass, relieved and regretful at the same time. G.C. and I spoke in occasional bursts: already, after just two months on the road, we were beginning to anticipate the direction of one another's thoughts and sentences. We sat on the top deck, passing a very fine Greek coffee back and forth, gazing out across the waves.

'Not that wine-dark, is it, really,' I said, and G.C. nodded. He knew I was referring to the sea as described in Homer's *Odyssey*, the book I had brought to read in honour of our Greek travels, rather than out of a desire to emulate Odysseus and wander for ten years seeking home.

Later in the afternoon the ferry slipped around Corfu and

past the strait towards Ithaca, Odysseus's home island. For a moment, the poem 'Ithaka' by Constantine Cavafy swooped through my mind – a song of adventure and wisdom which I had fallen in love with many years before. I had made my own translation of its Greek music, to carry around in my head:

> *Once you start out towards Ithaka*
> *hope that your road may be long,*
> *full of adventures, full of discovering*

'Here's to that,' I whispered, dripping some coffee into the sea-road: another libation, to the health of poets and travellers.

2

Shifting horizons

Greece to Turkey

Driving fearlessly off a ferry, on a motorcycle, into a new country on a warm night is among the most delicious of sensations. I felt G.C.'s body tense with delight as I soaked in the feeling of possibility ahead of us. The landscape felt the more inviting and mysterious for being hidden by darkness. We drove a few miles west along the coast, in exhilaration and anticipation, and pitched our tent under an olive tree by the beach. The pop and slide of olives falling on to canvas punctuated our sleep. Black juice stained our groundsheet, and in years to come, unrolling the tent brought back memories of that blissful first night.

We headed to Olympia, whose most remarkable feature is that it still exists: there was the arch through which the athletes entered, the sprint track, the baths. A noticeboard told me that Mount Kronos, which stands over the ancient stadium, used to be the vantage point for women and slaves who wanted to view the Olympic Games but were barred from entering under the rules of ancient Greece. According to the board, one woman who wanted to see her son compete in the games smuggled herself inside the stadium dressed as a male coach, but when her son was victorious, her exuberant high-pitched whoops of delight drew unwanted attention and she was ejected. To prevent a repeat transgression, it was decided that from then onwards Olympic coaches had to attend the games naked.

The red of poppies from our campsite in Olympia joined the black olive stains on our groundsheet. The campsite owner who befriended us spoke English, Italian, French, and Russian, and passed his time singing opera while feeding a multitude of cats. His demented mother wandered the grounds in a daze, picking at her nightdress and shouting obscenities through her straggly hair. We sat swinging our legs over the river that Heracles is supposed to have diverted as one of his twelve labours, sipping Greek beer and talking about what we hoped to see of this land so full of ancient tales.

Different heroic labours carry me through a breezy March morning: I wipe away breakfast cereal before it becomes cement, gather scattered pyjamas, mentally review a paid work commitment for International Women's Day, remind myself to fix T's torn trousers, turn on the radio – and the news swells into the room: Lombardy is in quarantine. My region. My family. Nobody can get in or out. Immediately I throw up on the kitchen floor, my whole body rigid with disbelief. The morning passes on the phone to family and friends who are also in shock, even if some say they could see this coming. Nobody has heard from my brother.

Just before the school bell rings, I receive a text from Lorenzo:

he is on a train leaving Barcelona, his fourth since departing Córdoba. My children pour out of their classrooms under after-noon rain, in a swirl of smiles and hugs and wild hair. I am dizzy with uncertainty, worry, the speed with which journeys have been curtailed and lives changed. Some friends in Scotland have stopped sending their children to school for fear of the virus. Each day I reluctantly choose to let them go, not wanting to darken their days before absolutely necessary. Weeks have passed since Italy closed its schools, and still there is no indica-tion Scotland might follow, no public acknowledgement that what is unfolding in Italy could arrive here too.

G.C. comes home in the evening, sits with me at the kitchen table in silence and gently takes my hand.

'We're not going to Italy for Easter. I know. It's going to be OK,' I say, and start to cry.

The next day brings the news that the whole of Italy is now in quarantine, borders closed and all movement restricted. I obses-sively research the rules on lockdown and travel, fretting until a message arrives from my brother: he is in Marseilles, where he spent the night in a hostel full of men from Tunisia and Algeria who don't have the residence permits required by French law. They are technically not allowed to be in France, so they can't go back home to their families without the risk of being arrested by French border police for being 'illegal immigrants'. They wait, trapped.

Lorenzo can get back into Lombardy because his Italian ID card states it as his place of residence, though he will need to sign a document promising that he will not thereafter leave the region until it is legal to do so. I tell him my research findings.

43

He thanks me and jokingly says, 'Don't worry, sister, if they stop me at the border, I can always walk across the Apennines, I know the old Salt Road paths. Who knew this would happen to us, the lucky ones, eh?'

Patrick Leigh Fermor set out to write a book about southern Greece and ended up writing about just one small part of it – the Mani peninsula, where Mondialita was now threading the roads in a slow loop of red motion. It felt that there was enough in a single village or view to fill a book.

In Greece we were told for the first time that the idea of a man and woman travelling together by motorcycle was unusual. In a roadside restaurant on the way to Arcadia, we met a man from Athens who loved riding motorbikes and fell to his knees in front of me when he learned that I too drove the bike.

He said, 'Greek women would never do what you are doing; they want to stay home and have *babies*.' He stopped for a moment, exasperation stealing his words, before he turned to G.C. and said: 'Where can I meet a woman like her?'

Babies were very definitely not part of my plans, but I did find myself increasingly wanting to stay in places for a week, a month, a year – longer than a few days, lingering long enough to sense rhythms of place and time. The Peloponnese enchanted me, with its light and roads and ancient stories at every turn. It began to feel as if we were being pulled by some invisible horizon beyond the next border, despite knowing that there were no limitations on what we could do, no promises that would be broken.

I looked out over the Adriatic from Pylos and imagined the sea of New Zealand. We were in the place mentioned in the *Odyssey* as the site of Nestor's palace. King Nestor offered Telemachus, the son of Odysseus, a bath in his palace washed by his 'fairest, full-grown daughter'. Archaeologists working here discovered 3,000-year-old patches of original colour still on the walls, and a bathtub which might be the oldest still functioning in world literature. We hadn't had a bath since Italy. On the beach I stripped off and ran shrieking into the cold spring sea.

The daffodils are opening, bright defiances in the blustery rain. Their yellow makes me think of mimosa, the flowers like tiny balls of sunshine opening now in Italy. Every year in Scotland I miss mimosa, and the swelling spring in Lombardy: the liquid of vines as they wake up, the fig trees stretching out their leaf-hands to the light, the swallows arriving a full month earlier than in Scotland. This year my usual springtime nostalgia turns into something sharp and physical, a drag deep in my solar plexus, knowing that there is no way I can reach Italy unless I am prepared to swim across the Channel.

Lorenzo has arrived at our parents' house after travelling for two days on a total of nine trains. He made it home without being turned back at the border, without having to cross the Apennines on foot following the old trading Salt Path from the sea to the Po Valley. He tells me that the trains were full of people trying to get home before it was too late, packed into slow carriages, mostly without masks, many coughing. In Ventimiglia, just past the border with France, the train passed

45

huddled shelters full of people with dark skin – labelled 'illegal migrants' by certain European voices – waiting on the Italian side for a chance to get into France. He is sure, in his exhaustion, that he must have caught the virus along the way, and now fears giving it to my parents.

'Rest,' I tell him, and then send him a message which is as much for myself, something our Italian grandfather used to tell us: 'One day at a time.'

I tell myself I am lucky, my family is lucky: we are all safe. Whatever limitations Brexit might bring, even if we have to leave Scotland, my children and I have Italian passports, and surely to goodness – as my Glasgow Gran would say – this virus quarantine nightmare will be over soon. But gratitude does not diminish grief. I distract myself by thinking of the word nostalgia, its beautiful Greek roots: it means 'pain of distance, pain of home-return'. Language brings comfort, but only for a while. Missing my places and people in Italy causes me a pain that I cannot share with G.C. because he doesn't understand, he doesn't feel this shredded by Brexit and closed borders. His horizons seem the same as always. I pick myself some daffodils and pretend they are mimosa. I fulfil a work commitment, plan for the week ahead, cuddle the children. Everything feels brittle, like cracked glass about to shatter. One day at a time, my Nonno's voice reminds me.

Technical Interlude

Heavy rain met us near Sparta and our engine began to misfire. The cables which carry electricity from the distributor out to the spark plugs kept getting wet, and we had to stop the bike and dry them out with a handkerchief. Eventually we had to unscrew the spark plugs, to discover they were becoming coated inside with the sort of thick tarry stuff more usually seen on the bottom of grill pans: something in Greek petrol must have been causing this residue. G.C. scraped it off with a wire brush and reset the spark plug gaps, and the engine ran fine again.

Our intercom had also started to pick up interference from the ignition coils of the bike. The noise had been getting louder each day, and by the time we were on the road to Sparta we had to shout over a maddening 'CLACK CLACK CLACK' that beat in time with the engine, drilling into our ears from the headphones inside the helmets.

We found a lump of sheet steel by the roadside and twisted it around the intercom to shield it from the coils. The sound continued, but muted. When we came to it, Sparta was a disappointment – a modern city laid out on a congested grid. But perhaps our feeling dejected was not Sparta's fault; the frigid mountain air, the stress of driving tight curves on wet, crumbly roads, that drilling intercom din had worn us down. We were learning that exhaustion means frayed tempers, and pouring rain was not Mondialita's friend.

Near Corinth we arrived at a campsite, deserted in the low tourist season, where the owner let us stay in a cabin for free. He answered our gratitude with, 'Ah, well, maybe one day you'll do a good turn for me, or someone else instead.' Corinth was the place where Strabo looked out over the ragged Greek coastline and conceived the idea of drawing it on a map. 'The birthplace of *Geography*!' G.C. bellowed, leaping around on the summit of Acrocorinth. The city also did a brisk trade in memorabilia of St Paul, as this was the place where he may or may not have preached to the Corinthians, according to a much-photographed plaque. The Corinth of the Bible is a rich city, and Paul's letters are preoccupied with rooting out corruption, as well as the ways women should keep their mouths shut and appear veiled in public: In fact, a woman who will not wear a veil ought to have her hair cut off, Paul wrote. I thought of those words and ran my hands over my head, where the shaved hair was growing back irrepressibly.

We zipped over the Corinth canal in a few seconds, catching a glimpse of ships far beneath us taking the famous shortcut from the Aegean to the Adriatic. There would be no ferries for Cyprus or Turkey until the summer, so to go east we'd need to first drive north in a great arc around the Aegean coast. Athens passed in a fog of exhaust smoke and car horns; the whirl of congested traffic spun as if around a force field, generated from the still centre of the Parthenon. We saluted the Acropolis from a concrete flyover and headed north to Mount Parnassus, and Delphi: the mythical abode of Pan, satyrs, maenads, and, more prosaically, the haunt of rich Athenians on weekend ski breaks. We joined them on the slopes. Instead of skiing gear, we wore motorbike clothes, very effective against injuries from falling.

Meteora was a blossoming of Orthodox monasteries spread high on top of cliffs and rocky outcrops. A few of these monasteries are open to tourists, with plaques announcing that women must 'wear something to cover their laps'. I moved my bag in front of my legs while looking hopefully at the Orthodox monk barring my way. 'No, no, no!' he said crossly, and handed me a makeshift sarong, indicating that I should wind it over my trousers. It seemed that my short hair could remain uncovered, but the place where my legs met had to be hidden before I could enter these holy sites. I shrugged and complied, thinking about St Paul's pronouncements on women, my Glasgow Gran covering her head when she went to Mass, the nuns and their veils at my kindergarten in Italy, the hijabs worn by my Lebanese and Syrian friends.

Throughout Greece, the light washed me awake into weeks of wandering and dreamlike exploration that we had to deliberately cut short. I wanted to stay for months. But it was at Meteora that G.C. put on his Now Let Us Be Sensible face and said, 'We're just at the beginning! Look at the map: we've hardly covered a tiny pinkie toe of the journey we want to make.' We were yet to have a proper fight – apart from some exhausted bickering in Sparta, our desires had so far always been compatible – and I decided that this wasn't worth an argument. And anyway, he was probably right, although I didn't want to admit it. We packed up our tent and headed towards the border with Turkey.

I drove Mondialita east from Meteora, up into the sky, across high mountain passes. Her thundering engine sounded offensive, entirely out of place in that landscape of dry slopes and skyward roads. We were balanced between huge blueness above and a strip of road that seemed to move with a will of its own in tight twists. Inside my head and gut roiled an equal mix of terror and elation. As I rounded each bend, I felt as if I was going to be sick: the bike impossibly heavy, the juddering engine surely about to cut out on the upward slopes, my arms and hands cramping with the effort of keeping us upright. Then the road stretched out, I shifted gears to a soaring roar, and my skull felt as if it was lifting off under my helmet. Infinite blue space was raising me up into the heavens. Without fully realising it, I began to whisper the 'Our Father' prayer in Italian; a stream of sounds rather than distinct words: *Padre-nostro-che-sei-nei-cieli-sia-santificato-il-tuo-nome* . . . Part invocation, part incantation, part mesmerised surrender to the place my body and mind had been taken to, the words repeated themselves as we looped through the mountains towards Turkey.

Scotland's March skies are a blustery, cloud-ragged blue. I am sitting with a Syrian friend, pouring her a cup of tea and trying to find a convincing answer to her gently teasing question, 'Why do British people ruin tea with milk? Milk is for children.' Nada checks her buzzing phone and the conversation slips, quick as the wind turning, into directions I had not foreseen: her cousin has sent a message saying that she and her children have landed in Greece after crossing from Turkey in a dinghy.

'What will she do now?' I ask.

'She wants to join her brother in Germany,' Nada replies, 'but she is tired and doesn't know if she can manage to walk there.

They are in a camp: no food, no milk, no papers, no idea what comes next.'

We start talking about cousins, borders, past travels, but I can't focus. My mind is full of intense remembering of how G.C. and I arrived in Greece by driving down a metal ramp directly on to Patras's main street – no barriers, no border guards, no idea what would come next, hearts filled only with excitement. The people now travelling into Greece from Turkey without the freedom of my passport will find a very different journey. I imagine Nada's cousin and her children as future ghosts in the landscape I crossed so easily, unsettling presences reminding me that we are not all equally free to go into and out of Europe.

Mondialita was trapped in gridlock as we approached the outskirts of Thessaloniki, an unwelcome shift from the high mountain roads. I had been getting better at managing the bike in heavy traffic, but the sudden swerves required in defensive driving were too much for me to handle safely. Admitting this was about as easy for me as smiling at border officials, but I had to do it. With a twisting stomach, my face red, I asked G.C. to take over as we reached the city suburbs.

'Sure,' he said, with an easy smile, as if I'd asked him to pass me a tent peg. I sat on the back, feeling a rising gratitude for this man who navigated my pride so well.

By the time we arrived in the old city of Salonica, I needed a drink, specifically *rakia*. G.C. preferred beer. We finished our drinks slowly and wandered in silence past the Roman ruins near our bar which were sunk ten metres or more below street level. I saw a mosque that had become a covered market, another that had become a cinema. We found one of the earliest churches ever built, raised 1,500 years ago on top of the ruins of a Roman bath. Thessaloniki is a city that has seen huge changes of population: at the beginning of the twentieth century, there were 80,000 Jewish people in Salonica; almost none were left after the Second World War. Hundreds of thousands of Christians were ejected from Turkey in the 1920s and came here. We sat for hours in another bar, reading and talking about this phoenix of a city, destroyed and rebuilt repeatedly – another place we could have stayed for months instead of days. Dreamily I swirled more *rakia*, its aniseed smell rising as water turned the clear spirit into milky clouds.

The Thracian border between Turkey and Greece is defined by the river Evros and flanked by marshlands. Mondialita took us closer to the crossing point, threading past columns of parked-up Greek trucks whose drivers stood about chain-smoking in the cold air. They looked up from their conversations to grin and wave as we coasted past. When we stopped, one gave us sweet tea and plenty of advice: mainly that we should watch ourselves, as the Turks were crazy drivers and couldn't be trusted. The border guards were helpful and amused, I thought, by the idea of our journey on such an overloaded motorbike. G.C. flourished the *carnet de passage* – this was the first border at which we thought we'd have a use for that expensive document – but nobody needed to see it.

The landscape after the frontier was exactly the same, as was the pummelling wind from the north, but in the roadside villages there were mosques instead of churches. Painted plywood cut-outs of police cars were parked on the motorway sidings to fool us into driving slowly, but the stray dogs and horse-drawn carts which now abounded were more effective.

On the way to Edirne, we pulled up to buy pistachios and figs at a roadside stall and a group of people gathered round, fascinated by the bike and by our story. It seemed that in Turkey, only the police were allowed to drive a motorbike with an engine bigger than 500 cc. We communicated 'thanks' in the German G.C. had learned in school: many people here had spent years working in Germany before returning home. We were immediately offered tea, and a boy ran off to find us a funnel to top up our engine oil. A man wearing a sailor cap asked about Mondialita's age and, chuckling with mirth at how ancient she was, communicated our answer to a huddle of schoolgirls standing nearby wearing matching hijabs. I wanted to speak with them, but felt for the first time the lack of a shared language, a border which I could not cross.

This morning Nada is making tea for me and other Syrian friends – 'Sweet, proper tea, with no milk!' she teases me. It tastes like Turkish tea, I joke in return: immediately there is laughing disapproval because no, Syrian tea is better, this is nothing like Turkish tea. The banter takes on a fast, flighty quality, sharpened by an edge which no sugar can remove: I realise that most of these women waited for months and years in refugee camps across Turkey while their stories were assessed by all-powerful agencies. Nada explains the absolute and binary nature of this power: 'If they believe you, then you can go to find safety. If not, they send you back.' She travelled to Turkey

53

with her children and brother, after her husband and parents were killed in Damascus. 'I don't know why, but they sent my brother back. They did not believe him. I am here with my kids, but he is back. He is trying to leave again, to reach us.' I am worried that these memories are too hurtful to bring up and stutter an apology, but Nada laughs, not unkindly: 'No, no, we are safe now, we can talk about it. You don't have to take care of us. Have more tea!' Her voice and eyes are clear, with something inside them that feels like an unyielding, a stillness. I think, this is someone who has reached beyond any level of nostalgia or grief I have ever lived, and still makes jokes and tea. This is a woman who truly knows about impassable borders. I need to get a grip.

Edirne has one of the most famous mosques in the world – the Selimiye Mosque, built by the sixteenth-century master architect Mimar Sinan, and I wanted to see it for myself. There was a shard of moon in the sky between its minarets as we arrived. I sat in the mosque all of the following morning: harmonious and symmetrical, a sanctuary which seemed to transcend faiths and traditions. Robust but filled with light, it felt dense with prayer and filled with such a sense of calm that I had goosebumps. There were no divisions at the entrance between Western tourists or Muslim worshippers. Several people said 'as-salaam alaikum' as they walked past. Nobody asked me to cover my head. In Thessaloniki, the mosques had been overgrown or converted to other uses; in Edirne, it was the synagogue that was abandoned and dilapidated, just opposite our hotel, with an almond tree flowering just inside the broken gate. Someone was living there, in a makeshift shelter.

We left Edirne in a rush, under a rainstorm, wanting to reach Istanbul before nightfall. G.C. learned how to steer the bike to follow in the tracks of the big trucks whose immense wheels temporarily cleared the rainfall from the tarmac, along a pathway just wide enough to let our motorcycle through. I followed his example in a state of terrified focus, eyes wide on the road, aware that any distraction meant falling. When G.C. sat pillion, his arms were tight around my waist, trying to hold still, knowing how difficult it was to maintain concentration.

Istanbul's suburbs began with rows of concrete blocks, batches of identically shaped and painted apartments stacked high on every hillside, dusty beige under the springtime sun, which was already warm on my helmet. After two minutes of driving, all traces of confidence vanished from me: this was a deadly stream of fast cars switching lanes, braking with no notice, relentlessly sounding their horns. It was like a new language I had to translate, where prediction was everything in the race to guess each driver's next movement from a series of clues: their vehicle's acceleration or deceleration, the motion of an arm at a wound-down window, glances in a mirror, the drumming of fingertips. Monitoring all these streams of information as I tried to slip our weight between columns of traffic was too much for me. I pulled over, shaking, sweating, and handed Mondialita to G.C. I was getting stronger after three months of motorbike driving, but there were times when her heft was more than my small female body could manage.

P's birthday celebrations are done: my springtime baby, born with the daffodils, now a boy nearing the end of primary school. A dear friend sends me a text: 'Happy Birthing Day to you.' I smile, reliving the moments after P was born, the sense of physical prowess and exultation at having done this thing, this monumental thing; feeling as if I had jumped on a monstrous train hurtling through a tunnel of pain and fear, and clung on, and come out on the other side – a mother, transformed.

I think of Sharon Olds' poem 'The Language of the Brag', where she takes on some big male names of American poetry and brilliantly shows how giving birth is as heroic a feat as any macho achievement involving knives and fire and danger:

> I have done what you wanted to do, Walt Whitman,
> Allen Ginsberg, I have done this thing

I sigh, remembering my shame when I struggled with Mondialita's weight, how desperately I wanted to be as big and strong as a man. I would tell that past me: it's OK. You can do this as you are. You can do this thing, and many other amazing things. Keep breathing. One day at a time.

G.C. gave me a reassuring hug and took over driving. I was filled with the need to compensate for my physical weakness, so put extra vehemence into gesticulating at the obnoxious drivers who threatened to mow us down. I watched fiercely, shouting 'hazard!' through the intercom whenever a collision seemed imminent, as if this was some demented driving test. We had not anticipated the scale of Istanbul's recent expansion: after two more hours, we still had not reached the city centre and G.C. too was starting to tremble. The city's outskirts seemed to go on for ever. Just as I became convinced that we had overshot the city centre and were being funnelled on to the bridge that would take us to Asia, we arrived in Taksim Square, the heart of Istanbul.

My first impressions were of a place immensely busy, thriving with life. There were thousands of people out, walking all around us as dusk spread. The call to prayer rose up from one corner of the square; a street leading away from us was lined entirely by kebab shops, the smells delicious after hours of diesel fumes. The buildings of İstiklal Caddesi – Independence Avenue – were draped with constellations of lights, and beneath them flowed a river of moving heads. There were smart teenage girls in designer-label veils, courting couples, elderly shoppers pushing bicycles, tired-looking commuters, children on people's shoulders, groups of young men with tight jeans and slicked hair. We sat on the ground by Mondialita and held hands in stunned silence.

My mother had friends in Istanbul who had offered to host us. I called their house from a phone box on Taksim Square, and minutes later Suleyman appeared in his car, shouting greetings out of the window, urging us to follow him. We jumped back on Mondialita and drove through a labyrinth of cobbled lanes. Suddenly, around a corner, the Bosphorus was before us – and beyond it our first view of Asia. Asia! We had made it to the edge of Europe! We parked the bike behind their gate and went inside to find welcome and that supreme form of kindness: hospitality without expectation of any return. Our host showed codes of behaviour through stories, telling us of a German couple to whom he had once offered his holiday house: 'They tried to pay me!' He laughed. 'As if!' I felt like weeping with exhausted gratitude.

Suleyman poured us hot sweet tea and told us how his family's fortunes had waxed and waned under Ottoman rule over the centuries. A great-grandfather had been twice governor of Baghdad; a grandfather, having fallen foul of the last emperor, had been exiled to Saudi Arabia. 'He left one wife in Turkey,' we heard, 'and then in Saudi married my grandmother – an illiterate, thirteen-year-old Circassian girl.'

'She must have been bought from a slave market,' added Sarah, tartly. She was from North America; in the 1960s she'd been so determined to get away from her small home town that she applied to the foreign service, making it clear that she would accept any posting. Shortly afterwards she was sent to Istanbul – 'And the rest is legend,' she joked, arching an eyebrow at Suleyman.

From the windows of their apartment, we watched the lights of the Asian continent. Oil tankers passed in single file, steaming through the centre of one of the world's greatest cities. The ferries and fishing boats crossing between Europe and Asia looked tiny in comparison, minnows darting between whales. I had a strong sense of being in a hinge place, a nodal point of geography, history and culture. I stared at the water, holding fast to G.C.'s hand to steady myself: my mind felt shaky with the exhaustion of the road and dizzy with telescoped time. This was the same stretch of water that the Argonauts had rowed across on their way to Colchis, that Viking mercenaries had defended against

Arabs and Turks; it was where the Venetians had battled the Genoese, where Mehmed the Conqueror had fought, where Florence Nightingale had had her hospital.

The next day was grey, the waters of the Bosphorus choppy. Each of us knew what the other wanted to do: go across to Asia. The boat terminal smelled of fried fish and sesame ring buns sold from carts. The bows and sterns of the ferries were buffered with old tyres, and as they collided with the jetties, the passengers jumped on and off without waiting for ropes to be secured. It was a pleasure to sit drinking Turkish tea on the far side, gazing back at Europe, and marvel that continental divides could be so simple to cross.

P has crossed the threshold into double digits, and he loses no time reminding his younger sisters of this. They tolerate him, indulging their not-so-much-older brother, playful.

Watching them tumble about brings a burst of joy deep in my stomach, the feeling that first started when they were born: an unimagined widening and stretching of my capacity to love. This starburst-feeling was one of the signs that I had 'crossed the border into the Republic of Motherhood', as the poet Liz Berry writes in her eponymous poem. Motherhood: once you are in it, you can never leave. You begin a journey through a place where many others also travel, but where you are also deeply alone; where heroic feats lie in wait for you alongside drudgery, magic, exhaustion, joy and ancient rage.

59

The remains of old Constantinople could be seen from the water: ancient Roman cisterns, topped by an ill-fitting jigsaw of wall sections, palaces, mosques, and what was once the biggest church in Christendom: the 1,500-year-old Hagia Sophia. The scale of it made me feel Lilliputian. For 500 years after the Ottoman conquest of the city, it had been a mosque, until Atatürk turned it into a museum. Golden mosaics were white-washed when the Ottomans conquered the city; now the white paint had been stripped back. Robust as it was, scaffolding high in the dome testified that after a millennium and a half, the building needed some support. The space was designed to draw the human mind up into a great heavenly dome, to inspire awe.

Four huge medallions bore the names of the first four 'rightly guided' caliphs of Islam: Abū Bakr, 'Umar I, 'Uthmān, 'Alī . They reminded me of the medallion portraits of the Four Evangelists, Mark, Matthew, Luke and John, so common in the Catholic churches of my childhood. G.C. was very excited at the Viking graffiti on a marble balustrade high in the Hagia Sophia: 'Halvdan' ('Half-Dane'), which was a common enough name among the Norsemen who, 1,000 years ago, had supplied the Byzantine emperor's personal guard. G.C. touched this link back to the northern countries of Europe, a bridge to another human who had travelled far from home a long time ago. I found myself back in Orkney, before we set off on Mondialita, hunkered in the Neolithic stone womb-tomb of Maeshowe. There too Vikings had left graffiti: 'Ingigerth is the most beautiful of women'; 'Helgi fucked Thorni and carved this'. I giggled, imagining what Byzantine priests and func-tionaries would have made of such carvings here. G.C. looked at me, eyebrows raised, reading my mind with a grin.

*

We needed to confront the modern-day Byzantine ways of embassies if we wanted to go any further east; our plan was to reach Pakistan overland by way of Iran. When we finally found the Iranian consulate, it turned out to be a small house in the suburbs. The consul became flustered when we asked if we could apply for a visa to visit his country: 'No, no, impossible,' he told us, 'you must ask in Ankara.' I nodded, trying to keep the fury and exasperation from my expression, as G.C. fruitlessly tried to reason with him. The consul showed us the door, muttering something about incorrect information on the consular website.

We were back by the Bosphorus as evening fell – drained by the ordeal, we Europeans so used to easily crossed borders, and very ready for a drink. We sat with a beer each near giant cannons lined up along the waterside. They had been used by Mehmed the Conqueror to take the city half a millennium earlier. In the sunset light, we watched gaunt men climb into the cannons for the night, pulling blankets in after them.

Technical Interlude

We checked Mondialita's valve clearances: they had held up well in crossing Italy and Greece, but G.C. tore the gasket while replacing the rocker covers over the cylinders, causing an oil leak. We didn't have any spare gaskets, but Suleyman guided us down a dark lane to a basement grotto where every wall was covered in engine gaskets. There were lorry gaskets the size of dustbin lids and tiny little gaskets for scooters, sheets of gasket material and racks of glues and solvents. A man in dirty overalls, with an impressive brush moustache, sat at a stool while Suleyman explained the problem in Turkish. The man reached out to take the torn bike gasket. Laying it out on his workbench, he used it as a template to score out a brand new one by hand. We bought two – just in case.

To get our visas for Pakistan and Iran, we were going to have to drive to Ankara – just a five-hour journey, we were told. We said goodbye to Suleyman and Sarah, suited up in our biking gear, loaded up the motorbike, and G.C. wound Mondialita up through the narrow streets to the highway that led to the Bosphorus Bridge. The landscape was low swells of olive green and scattered half-built developments, under clouds heavy with what looked like snow. At a trucker's pit-stop restaurant we stopped and put on more winter layers, thinking that perhaps we were over-imagining the sky's threat, but as the road climbed higher on to the Anatolian steppe we were driving through blizzards.

Snow might be picturesque on a landscape and manageable in a car, but it is death on a motorcycle. We were exposed, out on the Turkish steppe, and it seemed we'd have just as far to drive before reaching safety whether we went forwards or turned back.

'Let's go on,' I said, regretting my words when the wheel of the motorbike went into a terrifying skid. The road by now was completely white.

G.C. managed to bring Mondialita up straight again. He inched her forwards in the snow while I sat still and erect, the only helpful thing I could do. As we struggled onwards, a car drove past and went into a full spin, its rear end just missing us as it swung around. By now we were both panicking. Should we leave the bike by the roadside and try to hitch a lift to Bolu, the nearest town? We had passed it twenty minutes before. But the snow might thicken, and what if we couldn't get back for days – we might have to dig Mondialita out. Or we could stand by the motorway in the cold, hoping that gritters and snowploughs would arrive. We stood for fifteen minutes or so trying to decide, the snow falling thick around us and on to Mondialita's red petrol tank. My lips went blue and I began to chitter. Then, cutting across three lanes, came a Toyota 4 x 4 with its hazard lights on.

A man wound down the window and shouted to us in American-accented English: 'I ride Harley-Davidsons! You guys need to get off the road!' He stopped his car and introduced himself: Fatih. 'Come on, leave the bike and I'll give you a lift back to Bolu. It's a long drive to anywhere else.'

We piled the bags into the boot and were ushered into the paradise of his warm car. For ten kilometres or so, Fatih continued eastwards down the motorway, towards Ankara, looking for an exit in order to turn back towards Bolu. A break suddenly appeared in the central barrier between carriageways and Fatih swung into a flamboyantly illegal U-turn, lorries beeping all around us. On the drive back west we saw Mondialita looking cold and forlorn on the other side of the road, and as we approached her we saw that gritters and snowploughs had come out, and the snow had begun to ease. Fatih looked at us in his rearview mirror – we were

63

whispering about whether to get out and try heading towards Ankara again on our motorbike.

'What do you think?' he asked.

'Let's go for it,' I said. We tumbled our bags out of Fatih's car, thanking him over and over for his kindness.

He laughed, saying, 'No problem! We bikers take care of each other!' and beeped a salutation as he drove off. Dodging traffic and snow-piles, we jumped the central barrier, got ourselves and our bags back on to Mondialita and headed east into the numbing cold, praying for the Anatolian sky to give us a break and let us reach Ankara. The rolling landscape became more wintry with each mile we drove, but the snow held off and the gritters stayed out.

Snow closed me in a milky confinement, the winter after S and T were born. I remember the white: of the world outside, of my anaemic skin, of milk flooding the bed at night as it leaked from my breasts, which had suddenly become huge, pale, engorged spheres.

P was eighteen months old. He was a baby himself, really, but seemed to me huge compared to his newborn sisters: he could walk! And feed himself! And talk! Or at least, I understood him perfectly. He, however, couldn't comprehend the changes happening in his life, and my days were a swirl of consoling and nourishing three small, beloved people with my body and my attention both. The snow eddied and built up around our house, reaching up to P's head on our rare forays beyond the front door. G.C. had returned to work after the allotted two weeks of paternity leave. I was on maternity leave with three children under two. Friends and family brought support, without which I would have rapidly become submerged by bewildered exhaustion – one of the 'sweet fallen' invoked by Liz Berry in 'The Republic of Motherhood':

> In snowfall, I haunted Motherhood's cemeteries,
> the sweet fallen beneath my feet –
> Our Lady of the Birth Trauma, Our Lady of
> Psychosis.

I avoided psychosis, but my body wasn't fooled by my repeated statements of 'yes, I'm managing OK, thanks'. Twelve weeks after giving birth to twins, as the snow fell and fell and it became too cold and slippery to ever leave the house with three tiny humans, my womb became infected. It radiated outrage at having been asked to gestate and deliver three babies in the space of eighteen months, flooding my body with fever and delirium. I remember seeing huge, snow-covered wellies beside my bed next to a black medical bag, and hearing an unknown man's voice saying, with arrogant certainty, 'Well, she's not managing to fight this one off.' Then nothing, beyond feeling, for the first time in my life, that I would be happy to die: to be free to go towards what seemed like a sweet falling into dark, quiet, rest, a nothingness where nobody needed me.

Surfacing from the darkness, I found that a week had passed, the world was still white outside, and my babies were weaned on to milk from bottles. As my strength returned, I knew a hunger greater than any physical craving of pregnancy and breastfeeding: a need for the smell of my children, their warmth, their relentless noisy aliveness which seemed to me the distilled essence of life itself. My need felt like a wild prayer in its intensity, as I fed and

cleaned and rocked and sang. I was crowned with motherhood,
a life-giver and a survivor, and filled with swelling desire for
more living. Each day I got up and, like Liz Berry in her fiercely
true poem, I

> prayed in the chapel of Motherhood, prayed
> for that whole wild fucking queendom,
> its sorrow, its unbearable skinless beauty

Ankara appeared from nowhere – a city of four million souls
lying out on the steppe, like a space station dropped out of
the sky. It seemed so different from the crowding apartments
of Istanbul; there was space here to build broad avenues and
huge industrial outskirts. Most importantly for us, there was
good signage on the approach road that led us to the city's
embassy district. Steam swirled around the ankles of commuters
on Atatürk Bulvarı, as fat snowflakes fell on the hot asphalt
of a newly laid road. Snow billowed and settled under the
orange sodium lamps as taxis crowded into narrow streets,
pushing and nudging bumpers. The Great Mosque was ghostly
and everything seemed muffled. We found a hotel that let us
drive Mondialita down a ramp into the cellar where she would
be safe. Upstairs we collapsed on to the bed and slept for
fourteen hours.

The next day we walked miles around the embassy district
as snow fell even more heavily. The Iranians wouldn't give us
a visa unless we first had obtained permission to enter
Pakistan. The security guard outside the Pakistani embassy
offered biscuits and grins. Inside, the visa official came out of

his office door, on a mezzanine over our heads, and glowered down at us: 'Why do you want a visa?'

'We would like to enter your beautiful country from Iran, and the Iranians won't let us in unless we have a Pakistani visa,' I said, smiling up at him.

'How long for?' he asked.

'Three months? We'd like to be able to maybe travel into China, then back again, and so if it's at all possible, it should be a multiple-entry visa.'

He gave an imperious nod to the desk clerk, a stamp thudded on paper, and that was that. At the Iranian embassy, we had to pay over two hundred dollars and have our passports photo-copied. Our Pakistan visas were scrutinised by a sneering man who gave us a phone number to ring in two weeks: 'By then we'll have heard from Tehran,' he said. 'Go away now.'

We celebrated surviving two bureaucracies in one day with a beer for us and distilled water for Mondialita's battery. We found the latter in a garage run by a gigantic smiling man called Memet who offered us sweet coffee, a seat on his sofa by the stove, and refused to let us pay. A man selling pyjamas by a hospital gate insisted on buying us sweet tea, just because we were standing near him trying to find our way back to the hotel and looked cold. G.C. had a couple of weeks' growth of beard, and the man asked if that meant he was a Muslim; when G.C. shook his head, the man patted him gently on a shoulder, then clapped with delight when he understood we were intending to drive all the way to New Zealand. The hotel manager gave us a duck mascot to tie on to the motorbike, and we reciprocated with little sticker flags of Scotland and Italy. We left the city of embassies in glorious sunshine, driving west past industrial towns ringed with shanties. The steppe country ran on ahead of us like swells on the ocean, my mood rising with it: we had a fortnight of exploring before our next appointment with border-related bureaucracy.

Ancient tumuli of Phrygian kings appeared by the side of the road. G.C. scrabbled to the top of one to take a photograph, and a hawk with white feathers took off from under his feet. There was a deep silence and a grandeur to the steppe, an openness which lent itself to imagining armies on the march: Alexander's, but also those led by Xerxes, the Ottomans, the Mongols – they all had ridden past these tumuli, which were ancient even then. The land rolled in one continuous sweep all the way to central Asia. I loved driving on these roads: hundreds of kilometres of straight tarmac heading west across the plateau, and the freedom to go very fast without worrying about homicidal vehicles. From the high steppe we dropped down through alpine mountains clothed with pine forests, beneath hard blue skies, towards Lake Iznik and the Byzantine city of Nicaea.

We put Mondialita in a shed next to a guest house with frescoes on its walls and a terrace on its roof. On either side, Ottoman houses crumbled their straw and plaster back to the earth. The calls to prayer echoed sonorously across the city's lake as the sun set. Nicaea was still entirely contained by ancient Roman walls, which once enclosed a major Eurasian capital, a nodal point of empire, though now they surrounded a small market town of farmers. Tractors rattled by and horses were led down the main street as we sat in the forecourt of the cathedral where the Nicene Creed was written in CE 325, when the four official gospels were selected and Catholic and Orthodox Christianity split. In the evening light, people came to walk by the lake shore, smoking and chatting. We joined them and marvelled at the sunset turning the mirror-still water lilac, pink, smoky blue, green and gold. Gulls and coots glided over their reflections, hills and trees rimming the picture. The Credo echoed through my thoughts, a descant to the land-scape. The dangers of blizzards seemed somewhere long ago.

I had finished reading *Snow* by Orhan Pamuk and left it in the guest house. Pamuk wrote that the only people who find scenes picturesque are strangers – aliens to the landscapes they find so beautiful. I remembered how Italian friends would visit Scotland and marvel at the 'fascinating' double-deckers of Glasgow, the 'fantastic' pubs, the 'beautiful' people with milk-white skin and fair hair. Scottish people were no different: they would visit my Lombard village and exclaim about how 'amazing' everything was – the old church, the post office, the supermarket, my grandfather – everything was 'so exotic'. I thought they were all a bit crazy.

Lombardy now is not exotic: it is a place of fear. When people in Scotland hear that my family are there, they fall silent in the way of people uncertain what to say when faced with a bereavement.

What happens when borders which you assumed would always be open are suddenly closed? What happens when, after a lifetime spent moving freely between countries, you are not free to go any more? You realise that you had no clue how lucky you have been up until this moment.

You also fall deep into grief. I find no words to lament the

restrictions of Brexit and the growing number of Covid deaths.
Tears blindside me all day, like treacherous drivers in the Istanbul
suburbs. My hugs and smiles are a little too strong, a little too
bright. After the children are asleep, I walk by the shore of the
river Forth and look at its bridges: huge consolations hanging
across the water, symbols of crossing and returning. I think of
Istanbul and the Bosphorus. You are still one of the lucky ones,
I tell myself: you have passports, safety, work. There will be
journeys again. Grief sneers at the sensible truth, but wriggles
over a bit to leave room for a brief brightening of horizons.

The calls to prayer in Troy were as beautiful as Nicaea's. They
lifted above the cries of kids doing BMX stunts in the mosque
courtyard, next to the guest house where we unloaded
Mondialita, who was looking filthy and unloved, encrusted in
the dust accumulated across the Turkish steppe. G.C. resur-
rected his high school German to ask for a cloth and found
that Mustafa, the man who ran the guest house, had lived in
Germany for a few years and then had driven back to Turkey
on a BMW in 1973. Mustafa instantly loved Mondialita and
insisted on helping us clean her.

He told us that the Turkish name for Troy – Hisarlık –
means 'the place of fortresses'. Archaeologists have excavated
nine citadels at Troy; for thousands of years, the city was a
centre of commerce and military power, perfectly placed to
control access to the Sea of Marmara and, beyond that, the
Black Sea. I was reading the *Iliad*, which is thought to describe
the seventh citadel found on the site of Hisarlık. The buildings
of this layer date back to the thirteenth century BCE and show

signs of having been burned and then left empty, which fits with the story about ancient Troy told in the *Iliad*.

The Scamander River, over the past 3,000 years, had laid down enough silt to transform a sheltered harbour into fertile fields. The ancient dead in the ground here were so many that 'I could not name or even count them,' the *Iliad* says, 'not if I had ten tongues, ten mouths, a voice that could not tire, a heart of bronze.' Lament and wonder met in my mind as I walked under the Trojan walls.

Olive and rosemary branches were being burned somewhere nearby, and I wondered if they would have smelled the same thousands of years ago. The sharpness of unburned diesel from ageing trucks and vans brought me back to our own time. We walked until we found a place where the only smells surrounding us were rosemary, wild thyme, sea breeze, warm, ploughed earth. The Aegean shone its wide curve across the horizon.

The next day we each phoned the Iranian embassy separately, and heard that for the past two months, British, Australian and Canadian passport holders had all found it difficult to get visas. They had had no word from Tehran, the office clerk said.

'It is complicated. Probably not this time. You could try again with a guided tour company and pay a few hundred dollars again. Or,' he sniggered, 'you could wait a few years and see what happens.' The visa application fees were non-refundable, it turned out.

G.C. was trembling with anger as he put the phone down. 'They cheated us! They knew, and kept our money, and cheated us!'

I had rarely seen him this furious, helpless at not being able to solve a problem. His frustration was like a moth, beating and beating against a lantern's glass. I held him. We held each other. I too expected to feel angry, but a strange, still lightness filled me. It felt as if this was the heart of free travelling: the possibility of shifting horizons and perspectives, of embracing plans which evolve as circumstances change. The road overland to the east was closed to us, but there was still land to cover south and east towards the Levant, and maybe we could cross the Arabian peninsula. Gratitude grew in me – for this freedom, for the passports and savings that made it possible, for this hinge moment in our journey.

'For years you've told me stories of Syria and Lebanon,' G.C. said, once he felt calmer; 'Let's go there together.'

3

Reading the signs

Syria

The road from Antakya to Aleppo rolled through ordered, tractor-tilled fields. As we approached the Bab al-Hawa frontier, the landscape grew drier and the traffic slower, until we were passing queues that stretched for kilometres. At the border, Syrian vehicles going west were being disembowelled on to tarmac as the heat rose and shimmered. Our Turkish customs inspector silently checked the number plate of the motorcycle, then stamped our documents and passports with a precision mirrored in his trim moustache and epaulettes.

'Enjoy Syria,' he said briskly, in English.

In the stretch of land between checkpoints, a monumental Roman arch showed that this line on the map has long been a border. G.C. pointed to the ruins of what looked like old frontier fortifications, Byzantine or Ottoman, perhaps. He was frustrated at not being allowed to leave the road to take a closer look, but I feared that entering Syria would not be as easy as leaving Turkey. I drove us onwards, towards the gateway of a country we hadn't intended to visit, already irritated by the bureaucracy of borders, my mind churning with frustration

75

at the paperwork and expense we'd encountered this far. I frowned at the mere thought of the letter of introduction we'd had to pay for at the British embassy in Ankara in order to get a Syrian visa, full of absurd capital letters and sycophancy:

> Her Britannic Majesty's Embassy presents its compliments to the Embassy of the Syrian Arab Republic . . . Her Majesty's Embassy avails itself of this opportunity to renew to the Embassy of the Syrian Arab Republic the assurance of its highest considerations.

At Bab al-Hawa, G.C. offered this letter to men at a sequence of desks which felt like levels of a vastly unentertaining game: 1) the cashier, to make payments and give receipts; 2) vehicle insurance; 3) the place to get the motorbike's documents stamped; 4) the passport desk. Other men who called themselves 'helpers' thronged around us, offering to do the queuing for us if we handed them sixty dollars instead of the going rate for crossing the border, which was forty dollars. I declined: my previous visits to Syria had taught me that it would be wise to stay in control of our passports.

We waited with no sign of progress and I began to regret not accepting 'help' for an extra twenty dollars, despite all the stories I had heard of passports going missing at checkpoints. I worried about Mondialita waiting outside, red and improbable among the trucks in the hot dust. Each desk had a portrait of Bashar al-Assad, the Syrian president, and was staffed by military guards. Bab al-Hawa means 'Gate of the Air', but it was a stifling place where movement was blocked by bureaucrats, paper and ink. No breezes came as we waited, sweated, waited. I thought of all the people who had tried to cross this border over the millennia. It didn't make me calmer. I reminded myself that we were the lucky ones, with good European passports on a journey we had chosen, with some money spare for bribes, but that only added guilt to annoyance. The first border crossing into an Arabic-speaking country was not going as smoothly as I had hoped. G.C.'s face crinkled into a blue-eyed smile for the guards as he handed over all the papers for the third time. They were slow and suspicious with him. 'Maybe it's because I'm a *farangi*, and I look like a Crusader?' he whispered, and I held back a snort of laughter: the idea of G.C. violently crusading was absurd. In Levantine Arabic, *farangi* is a word – not always complimentary – meaning a 'foreigner', usually of the fair, European variety. Lebanese friends with fair hair and light eyes often joked that they were descended from rogue Crusaders. The guards frowned at me; I shut down all smiles.

At the final desk, our passports were examined by two men in military uniform, rather than bureaucrats in shirts. They both had moustaches, and sweat stains under their armpits; one had less hair on his head, but more chevrons on his sleeve. They ignored me entirely, muttering over each page of both passports, glancing at G.C. as they speculated about the possible reasons for our journey. I assumed they were trying to see how long he would hold out before offering a bribe. At first I held back, listening in to their talk, not letting on that I could understand them, playing the quiet and polite wife. My meekness melted as the thermometer climbed, stewing us in our thick motorbike gear. I was filled with memories of all the petty people who had ever tried to stop me doing what I wanted for no reason other than because they could. Suddenly the situation seemed intolerable.

I leaned across the counter and hissed at them in Arabic, with an acid edge to my voice: 'Shame on you. You call this Arab welcome and hospitality?'

The most senior of the officials blustered back in English, 'Who here is the *chef*? Is he the *chef*, or you?' He looked at G.C. in contempt, but stamped the papers and threw them back at us.

Our bodies cooled with the wind of driving, and my fury passed as G.C.'s arms held fast around my waist, steadying me as I drove into Syria; what remained was shame. I had behaved as arrogantly as the guards, playing out just as many stereotypes. Nobody had won anything in that game.

Italy's decision to close all non-essential shops and businesses in order to stop the spread of Covid-19 was made because of typical, ingrained laziness. Or so says a British TV celebrity doctor: 'The Italians – any old excuse to, you know, shut down everything and stop work for a bit and have a long siesta.' I trade messages with other Italians in response, a mix of fury and jokes. Comedy wins out in the end, with a friend texting, 'These people, they mock us, but just you wait – it will be pasta they start stockpiling when the virus gets here. And unless that doctor starts copying our bidet habits, he'll be stockpiling loo roll too.'

I try to get on with my research, which I am being paid to write, but it slips away from my brain's grasp as if it were wet soap. I am too anxious to think, and keep getting distracted by videos sent from Italy, hilarious sketches by unsung comedy geniuses about dealing with life in the lockdown decreed to stop the virus spreading. They are little hits of relief in what feels like a landscape of darkening, encroaching horizons.

G.C. continued his valiant efforts to turn my rage into smiles with a string of silly songs over the intercom, and random comments on what he could see. It worked, and I started to laugh and notice things with him. People worked the fields here, not tractors like in Turkey. The roads were narrower and the drivers more occasional, but also more homicidal. G.C. reminded me of the midwinter fields in Orkney where we had started our journey, how I had skidded on ice as we drove on to the Belgium-bound ferry, how far we had come. Here the air smelled of warm earth and hot tarmac and ice seemed impossible. There were no roadside billboards to break up the horizons of dun-coloured scrub. The only images we saw were banners and arches celebrating Bashar al-Assad, together with his late father and brother, Hafez and Bassel. Bassel al-Assad, the eldest son and heir apparent of President Hafez al-Assad, died in a car crash near Damascus in 1994. His younger brother Bashar was recalled from a medical career in London to become president.

During my first stay in Beirut, in 2001, when Syria was effectively an occupying power in Lebanon, my Lebanese friends had taught me many scurrilous jokes about the Assad trio that they called the 'Father, Son and Holy Ghost'. They spoke with hushed voices thick with laughter and cigarette smoke as we walked along Beirut's seafront. They fell silent whenever we passed Syrian men selling sesame cakes: it was rumoured that even these street-sellers were spies, ears for Assad's dreaded secret services, the Mukhabarat. It was unwise to mock the Assad family, even on the wide sea spaces of Beirut's Corniche.

'Bassel is the Holy Ghost, of course,' said the man behind the stall where G.C. and I had stopped to buy water. In the billboard behind him, Bassel was driving a smart car. I wasn't sure if this was ironic, given how he had died, and I was even less sure that this man was not reading my mind and memories.

'God have mercy on his soul,' I said with a deadpan face. I thought I'd take up the Trinity joke and then realised it might not be a joke. This man might be a secret service agent. His face was like a closed border. All the paranoia instilled by my Lebanese friends returned: the Mukhabarat were everywhere; foreigners were followed as a matter of course; nobody was to be trusted.

'God have mercy,' the man repeated.

'Thank you for the water,' I said meekly.

'Welcome to Syria,' he replied, expressionless.

There are spring days in Scotland when the sky widens out into a hugeness of blue and you would forgive it anything, even the winter dark. Today is such a day. My cycle into Edinburgh is a rejoicing made sharper by awareness that this may be the last 'normal' day for many months: everywhere I see flashing signs of impending lockdown, even if the city around me seems to be operating as if this were just another ordinary day. I return books to the library, meet a friend for lunch, have a haircut. The hairdresser's chat is all about 'ninja hair care', and whether it will be possible to sneak into people's houses to keep working if shops are forced to shut. I smile weakly: this is exactly the kind of conversation Italians were having a month ago, before

they were barred from leaving their houses, but I don't have the heart to say it.

On the way home I bump into a Syrian friend. We exchange three air kisses and beautiful, formulaic greetings in Arabic. She buys me a coffee, refusing to let me pay. Then she looks me straight in the eyes and says, 'How are you? You look tired, my friend.'

'I'm really worried for my family in Italy,' I blurt out.

'Ah, it is hard, being far away and not being able to visit them,' she answers. Her voice is full of kindness and concern, and I remember that she is from Aleppo. Her home was destroyed with the nearby souk, her daughter was granted refugee status in central Italy, and she has no idea where the rest of her family are. She hugs my privileged, sorrowful body with the gentleness of a mother, pats my cheek, and smilingly says, 'One day at a time, my dear.'

The approach to Aleppo was better than the hell of Istanbul's traffic, but only marginally. It felt like another frontier, a physically shocking transition into the reality of modern, urban Syria. Sweating and cursing as he went, G.C. fought Mondialita into the city centre, dodging and swerving so many dangers that my throat was sore with shouted 'Hazard!' warnings. We were trembling with fatigue by the time we reached a hotel, where the smiling owner welcomed us with kindness. His warmth was genuine, the coffee he brought us fragrant with cardamom and sugar.

In our room, we unpacked according to the ritual that had evolved over the past few months: everything from our rucksacks was exploded out to cover every surface, as if six people had lived here for a week. We could then relax, look at a map of the city and decide where to go.

'I need long-sleeved shirts,' G.C. said. 'I'll burn in this sun. And sandals, too.'

'I think I want to wear a hijab,' I replied. 'We need the souk.'

What ensued was the closest thing to a fight we'd yet had. G.C. was not convinced about my decision to wear a hijab: 'It seems hypocritical to me – like you're dressing up in a costume. You're trying on an identity that isn't yours, or something.'

I understood what he meant, but retorted: 'I want to wear a hijab out of respect. I mean, I wouldn't walk about in shorts and a vest top, would I? So, isn't covering my head just the next step, since every other woman does it? And I want to blend in as much as I can do, while walking about with a pale-skinned, blue-eyed Scot.' He was silent. A very spiky sort of silent. Worried that I had gone too far with the 'pale-skinned', I said: 'There's no sense of obligation or threat: it's another side to freedom, being able to adapt as we move through countries, no?' His silence softened into a smile as we walked out together.

Aleppo's souk was a vast stone network of narrow streets, so big that it took over a portion of the city, spreading through narrow streets shaded by archways and coloured awnings. The sunlight filtered down in stripes and spots, bright with dust and swirls of smoke from mopeds, cigarettes, braziers, food stalls, cups of tea and coffee drunk by the shopkeepers. Above the market loomed a colossal citadel of golden stone, rebuilt in that form in the 1260s following a siege by the grandson of Genghis Khan. It would be destroyed again in a few years – not by a besieging foreign power, but by Syrians at war with each other.

Stalls proliferated as we walked: whole streets filled with fruit, or bread, or jewellery, pots, spices, grains, frilly knickers. The souk seemed to push itself forwards in an advancing tide of colour and smell, growing new alleyways to fill up with things and noise and people, as if the whole city would become one labyrinthine market. Last time I had visited Aleppo, four years earlier, I'd got rapidly and utterly lost in the souk, wandering alone in loops for a delighted, hallucinatory afternoon until I found myself back where I had started.

In A Field Guide to Getting Lost, *Rebecca Solnit writes that the real question is how we should get lost, because if we never get lost we have never truly lived. This makes complete sense to me, because I do not possess a sense of direction – unlike G.C., who always knows where north is, like a migratory bird. For me, getting lost is normal, and I am unafraid as long as there are signs and maps to read, people to ask for help. I have meandered gladly in many parts of the world, fully absorbed in whatever appeared in front of me, trusting that I could always chat with someone who would see me safe to where I needed to be; discovering stories, following clues which are not to do with compass points. This way of doing lostness is a freedom of discovery.*

The first days of Covid lockdown, though, bring a new feeling: a breaking of some vital internal compass which I didn't know existed until it stopped working. An invisible charge that helped me navigate each day is gone. The perimeters within which I move now are limited and familiar, like those of most people I know: home, and one permitted daily outing for exercise within a five-mile radius. I am never lost; I have never felt this lost.

It didn't take us long to find a street festooned in rainbows of hijabs. I chose a grey one with matching tunic, spangled with silver sequins like the smoky, shining dots of light falling through the awnings. G.C. found a long-sleeved shirt and buttoned it up tight. The man selling the shirts smiled and said, 'Very beautiful, very respectful.' A group of schoolgirls giggled, hands over their mouths, their hijabs pastel yellow and pink over navy blue uniforms. Two women walking behind them smiled at one other. We followed in their general direction, marvelling at a boy of just two or three walking confidently alone, looking as if he knew exactly where he was going. We celebrated our transformation with *knafeh* – sweet pastries shredded into tangles with pistachios and syrup in the centre. The tea came in tiny glass cups, thick with sugar as in Turkey. A sense of ease wrapped itself around us as we watched people pass by: it felt as if Aleppo was not trying to be anything other than itself. Unlike us, I thought – see me covering up, wandering through a country that isn't mine.

My thoughts were interrupted by the tea shop owner. He had the long white beard and clothes of a Hajj, a man who has completed the pilgrimage to Mecca, one of the five pillars of Islam. Around his mouth, his beard was yellow with tobacco. His eyes were very serious. 'Are you a Muslim?' he asked me without preamble. I chose the diplomat's way of avoiding a direct answer by answering with quotations. 'We are all People of the Book, as the Holy Qur'an says, Hajji. I wear the veil out of respect. Your tea is delicious, thank you.' His eyes lightened with laughter, then became serious again. He poured us more tea and brought us more cakes, and asked us why we didn't have children. He had three himself, the perfect number, although he had to work too hard to keep them all fed.

There was no way I wanted to have babies: I could not imagine any choice which would make me less free to go where I wanted. I smiled and said nothing. When we left, he insisted that we were not to pay: 'You are my guests, it is forbidden.'

The creases in the hotel owner's face were arranged by sadness when he brought us breakfast the next day. He tried to lift a smile as he gave us olives, cheese and bread, then left wordlessly. I overheard him speaking on the phone in the next room. He was calling his sister: today was the twenty-seventh anniversary of their brother's disappearance. It sounded as if they marked the date of his arrest every year. The hotel man talked of him as if he was still alive, still a child who would one day run in through the door. I felt terrible guilt at overhearing such grief, and distracted my mind by working out that these events must have happened in 1980. I knew of the Hama massacre of 1982, when the Syrian government responded to opposition protests with a siege that left at least 10,000 civilians dead and most of the city in ruins. I didn't know about Aleppo in 1980: more protests and violence, with air force cadets massacred, civilians shot in the city square, arbitrary arrests of males of any age. The city's beauty and peace seemed miraculous, fragile.

In the days that followed, we encountered generosity and kindness everywhere we went, but also sensed, behind the smiles and the beauty, a lingering tension, like a bitter after-taste. I overheard more snatched conversations confirming something of the origins of that bitterness: decades of political repression, fear of the secret services, grief for disappeared relatives, worry about the overspill of refugees and violence from Iraq. We talked these things over quietly as we walked the city, delighted by the people and smells and shapes surrounding us, but guiltily aware that, unlike those who befriended us, we were free to go whenever we wanted.

G.C.'s motorbike boots had been battered and ripped in our battles with Turkish traffic, so we went out to look for a cobbler. We found a tall and serious man with a glossy black moustache, about our age, with hands that were strong and hardened and scarred by work. Without a glance at us, he considered the tattered boots and nodded, once.

'Yes, I can fix these. Wait there.'

We waited as instructed, outside his shop under a light-up neon Syrian flag that said, 'We Love Syria'. Improbable numbers of electric cables threaded out of buildings, signs and shops and stretched back to thin poles on the pavements. As G.C. tried to count how many wires there were per pole, the cobbler's machine for cutting leather went quiet. I looked in the shop: the cobbler had his back to us and was sitting perfectly still at his machine, useless in the power cut. After a few seconds he stood up, his shoulders rigid. He took the leather over to a workbench where he cut and stitched it by hand, precisely, quickly. We paid and thanked him. His repairs lasted all the way to Australia.

*

The Umayyad Mosque of Aleppo had remained in my memory from previous visits as a place of calm; a harmonious space. I wanted to return with G.C. From the tumble of city streets, we walked into an immense, silent space of high arches and columns that drew the eye and the spirit up into stillness. The carpets were dotted with people praying or reading or sitting. They seemed tiny, toy people, ephemeral under the huge vaults of air. I sat there for a long time.

Outside, the courtyard was full of families having picnics; one group played with a football improvised from a ball of rolled-up clothes. It was wonderful to see a place of prayer used for play and laughter as well: my childhood experience of Catholic churches was of places where you have to be serious, as if God doesn't listen to laughter and most certainly doesn't approve of picnics. We stayed in the Umayyad Mosque most of the day, chatting and eating. A woman wearing a black niqab came over and offered us juice. Her eyes were a startling blue, and she joked with me, surprised at my Arabic, that one of her grandfathers 'long ago must have been a Crusader who looked like your husband. Who knows.' Her husband was a vet with the beginnings of a paunch. Their young daughter laughed a lot, beautifully, and liked my sparkly hijab. Wardens walked about benignly, apart from one who seemed strict and angry and told a couple off for holding hands. The call to prayer sounded from the minaret as evening arrived. A stray football briefly involved G.C. in a game. We dozed and woke to offers of sweet tea from another family whose toddler slept in a purple buggy. The father asked G.C. if we would go back home soon and make a family. We smiled and said, 'We'll see.'

April Fool's Day, and the children have been homeschooling for just over a week since the restrictions which – finally – have closed down Scotland, too. I play a trick, telling everyone over breakfast that schools are back, isn't that great! I assume that the children will be relieved when they find out that actually it's just a joke and we can all stay at home, but their little faces fill with delight at the prospect of going to see their friends, and when I tell them in a tiny voice, 'Sorry, it was an April Fool's joke,' they are close to tears. I have never regretted a joke so much in my entire life. The situation is saved, just about, by my promise that now they can play the most horrible jokes on me all day in revenge. G.C. rolls his eyes in disbelief at my tactless humour before heading out to work.

I spend the day sitting on whoopee cushions, finding slimy cucumber slices in my shoes, being brought coffee with salt instead of sugar and water mixed with citric acid. The light-heartedness is cathartic: we all need some sort of release. Already we are sick of being resilient and brave. We just want to be free to go and spend time with our pals in safety.

Many of my female friends are already struggling to manage the impossible juggle of working from home while supervising their children's homeschooling. I have asked for an extension to my research funding, citing my role as carer as the reason I need to pause my work – my socially recognised and remunerated work. The truth is that my brain has lost the ability to focus on tasks which are not immediate: making food, planting seeds, cleaning the house, helping the children with home learning, transcribing sections of my travel diaries to lose myself in remembering less limited horizons.

We would have gladly stayed in Aleppo for much longer, but bureaucracy meant that we couldn't linger: in their wisdom, the Syrian officials had given us a visa of less than a month, which would have to include our time in Lebanon. We were no closer to working out how to get to Pakistan, 'and anyway, we still want to get to New Zealand, remember,' G.C. reminded me. Every day on this journey, we wrestled with a tension between the desire to stay and explore, and the allure of what was beyond the next border. We agreed that it was time to move on and that we both wanted to visit the lands once at the heart of Mesopotamian civilisation, towards the Euphrates and the road to Iraq. As we left Aleppo in the early morning, we had our biggest audience yet for the loading of the motor-bike. G.C. did all the bundling and ratcheting down of the baggage, while I gave a running commentary to the gathering crowd. When G.C. finished, he got a round of applause.

Once Mondialita had shaken off Aleppo's traffic fumes, the morning sunlight was axe-sharp, making crisp shadows beneath the sparse trees and livestock as the landscape slowly turned to desert. On maps of Syria, the roads are bundled together between the mountains and the sea in the west of the country; in the north they skirt alongside the rivers. Only a few lines mark the deserts of the east and the centre, like spindly bridges. Trade routes crossed this land before asphalt carried wheels, and we were driving east on an old way. Our road had one purpose: to get across the dry lands and reach the plains between the great Tigris and Euphrates rivers. The rivers themselves also had a purpose, expressed by their lines leaning towards the sea. The straight borders between Syria, Iraq and Jordan date to a 1916 agreement between Britain and France, which carved up the Ottoman Empire's lands. They looked ridiculous on our map: rigid, angular lines scored in ignorance of topography, without any relation to land or water, often directly across the flow of roads and rivers.

We were aiming to reach al-Raqqa, or Raqqa, a city on the Euphrates to the east of Aleppo. On these slow roads, the distance was just about what we could manage in a day – provided we didn't slow down or break down. G.C. took over and drove with one hand on a handlebar, the other animated with delight as he talked of the empires that have come and gone there, stories of Babylon, Nineveh, Uruk and Akkad. We passed modern signs on gantries over the highway, indicating only 'Baghdad'.

The sound of Mondialita's engine was a rhythmic counter-point to G.C.'s voice. As we headed east, the heat grew, and my mind roved across the borders of language. The sun dropped lower behind our backs; I thought of the word for sunset in Arabic, *ghurūb*, which comes from a word-root meaning 'to leave, to depart'. *Gharb* – west – comes from this same root. *Sharq*, east, contains the idea of 'rising' and 'radiating light', all in the same word. *Junūb*, south, is from a root with the sense of 'being beside' and also 'avoiding'; *ajnabee*, 'stranger', shares this origin. *Shamāl*, north, also means 'left'. *Shamāl* is one of my favourite words in Arabic because it seems doubly helpful in its indication of direction and compass point.

'Esa! For goodness' sake, where do we go now?' – G.C.'s tense voice roused me from etymological wanderings, and I noticed that the air had changed, becoming heavy and charged. Grey-black clouds massed ahead over Raqqa; the rain began as we reached the city's outskirts and realised our map bore no relation to the world around us.

With growing panic, I saw that street names had been changed, parks moved, roundabouts built; or else whoever had made our map had made it up. The streets were mostly mud under the rain, with plenty of SUVs further churning up the roads amidst the usual small motorbikes and rusting cars. It was getting dark. There were very few pedestrians out, and no women; this bothered me because what I needed was someone to ask for directions. Elections were on, and a man holding a Kalashnikov, his thumb stained with ink to show he'd voted, tried and failed to help us find somewhere to stay. We drove on, the motorbike skidding in mud. G.C. was cursing, and I was looking for pedestrians rather than road signs, which irritated G.C., who wanted to make sense of the map. His irritation exasperated me – why didn't we just ask for help? Why did he always need to fix everything by himself?

The motorbike skidded, badly, and almost went out from under us. We had a proper argument in the middle of an unmapped roundabout. Then, on one of the pavements, I saw a woman standing, facing out to the traffic. I pulled my helmet off, asking in my nicest Arabic if she could please kindly help us find a hotel or anywhere we could stay the night. She looked at us curiously – it occurred to me, unhelpfully, that *gharb* is closely related to *ghareeb*, which means 'strange' or 'weird'. We were indeed strange Westerners on a motorbike covered in mud. But then the woman smiled and explained in an Iraqi accent how to get to the only hotel she knew in town. Her face was pretty in the lights of the passing cars, young under

her make-up, her long hair uncovered. I heaped all the grati-
tudes I could muster into words and we left her behind.

After more broken roads, we saw the 'Hotel' sign and
squelched into a parking space. Mondialita was dwarfed by
the SUVs surrounding us. Most of them had number plates
from Iraq, Saudi Arabia, or the Gulf States. '*Ghareéb*,' I thought.
Things got stranger: lining the lobby of the hotel were women,
many with long, bleached hair, make-up and tight clothes.
After so many days of seeing women covered by hijabs and
long, loose clothing, I stared – and the penny dropped: this
was a brothel. The woman who directed us here was a sex
worker. So were these women staring right back at me with
my hijab and motorbike gear and blue-eyed husband.

Not one phrase or greeting I could think of would have
worked. The bizarre tableau was unfrozen by a flustered man
who bustled us past the line of women to the front desk and
checked us into an extortionately priced room. We were in a
state of stunned exhaustion, well aware that we had no other
options. I was roused into the beginnings of outrage not by
the price of the room but by the 'manager' requesting our
marriage certificate – a standard practice in Syria, but so
ridiculous in this situation that I didn't know whether to swear
or laugh at him. He saw my expression and swiftly muttered,
'It doesn't matter – follow me,' and led us down a corridor,
where men in white Saudi robes were chatting. We walked
past an open room where a woman with peroxide yellow hair,
white make-up on her face, black lipstick and wrap-around
sunglasses was yelling down the phone holding a bundle of
papers in her hand.

The night passed slowly. G.C. began to vomit. He passed the
night periodically crawling through to the en-suite bathroom

while doors slammed in the corridor, women screamed, and feet pounded above his throbbing head. The morning brought a dismal breakfast of food as stale as it was overpriced. The waiter took pity on us and asked me what on earth we were doing in Raqqa.

'The river,' I said, 'we want to see the Euphrates,' and he nodded as if this explanation made sense.

As I haggled with the manager, trying to lower the price of our stay from exorbitant to merely ridiculous, a girl in a tracksuit sat crying by the reception desk, her hair and make-up dishevelled. A man gave her instructions about some 'medicines', glancing uncomfortably at the hijab I was still wearing from the souk in Aleppo. Everything felt surreal, like a painting where nothing is in its rightful place. G.C. leaned on me for support as we made our way out to Mondialita, the sun already strong just after dawn.

By April the dawn in Scotland grows markedly earlier each week. I track the growing light and try to let it seep from the sky through my eyes to my mind, hoping it might dislodge the images still coming from Italy: the faces of friends who took their coughing loved ones to hospital and never saw them again; the rows of army trucks driving piled coffins towards burials without funerals. I am hardly sleeping, waking long before daybreak, obsessively digging and redigging the garden, forgetting things, becoming resentful of G.C.'s freedom to still go out – he is an essential worker and goes to his work three days a week.

I see him hide his own tiredness and strained anxiety from me. He starts to look at me sidelong, worriedly, and I try to mask my own grief and fearful unravelling. I remember how we took care of each other when we travelled with Mondialita – how easy it was, even in difficult times, to choose comradeship and love. Now I see signs of borders forming between us which were not there before. I read back through old diaries, looking for anything to help me navigate this feeling of losing my way in our relationship – of starting to lose the relationship itself. No answers come; only memories and fresh questions.

What do you do with the rage born of powerlessness and grief? Where do you put it? How do you keep it from corroding you inwardly to resentment, or exploding out into violence? How do you exert that most lofty of freedoms – the liberty to choose your reactions to intolerable circumstances? Beyond my kitchen, the estuary shines and heaves under the widening light. The children and G.C. stir and wake.

I drove us away from Raqqa. The Euphrates was fringed by groves of date palms and small plots of carefully irrigated soil. Their lush green glared against the dusty ochre of the encroaching desert. In places, the fertile strip by the river was only a few metres wide. Forty kilometres past Raqqa, we were stopped by crowds on the road. There were no army or police, and no women in sight. A flat-bed truck was parked across the highway, its trailer creaking under a load of men and boys stamping and yelling. Their faces were rageful, slicked with sweat. A press of bodies pushed around the truck, and black smoke twisted up from a row of burning tyres.

We swapped so that G.C. was driving: I knew I couldn't control Mondialita well at slow speeds through such a crowd, and I was worried I would run somebody over, or drop the motorbike. Sitting pillion, a tirade started up in my head against my weakness and inability to help – mercifully interrupted by my better self telling me to get a grip: now was not the time. I sat up straighter, took my helmet off, tucked my hair under the folds of my hijab and called out to some of the men:

'What's going on?'

'Just some angry people,' one said, '. . . politics.' He shrugged.

'Can we get through?' I asked, trying to keep the fear from my voice. The crowd was closing in behind us.

'This has nothing to do with you,' another man called over. 'You are a guest. Carry on, carry on . . .' But still I hesitated: the air was taking on a high, rattling energy, like in a room with no doors and a fire alarm ringing. Two boys with staring, glassy eyes appeared beside us on a scooter. 'Follow us!' they yelled. 'We'll lead you!'

I held G.C.'s shoulder tightly and said: 'We have no choice – go.'

The crowd was becoming more tense and we lost sight of the scooter. I could feel G.C. trembling with fever as he bumped off the road on to a thin gravel strip at the rear of the truck which was blocking the way. Bodies pushed in on us from all sides. A boy with bared teeth and a face crumpled with rage was barring the way. He whacked a stick down in front of Mondialita's front wheel but G.C. drove over it, snapping it in two, accelerating through the only space in a line of burning tyres – and we made it to the other side.

We drove on for another kilometre or so before the road was blocked again, by a different pickup truck, this one loaded with men waving poles, lined up before another low wall of burning tyres. A bus had stopped in front of us and spilled smartly dressed men and women on to the road. Two of the men were wearing tie pins of the Syrian flag, a sign of loyalty to the Assad government. They were pharmacists from Aleppo, it seemed, on their way to a conference in Deir ez-Zor. 'It's the refugees,' one of the men explained disdainfully, 'from Iraq. They're demanding more help from the government.'

He urged us to follow them, as they'd arranged for a guide to drive them past the roadblock. I translated this to G.C., who looked weak with exhaustion and nausea. We followed the bus through back lanes and across farm courtyards, then across a bridge to the north bank of the Euphrates. This bridge was not on our maps, and was guarded by soldiers. On the other side was a turn-off, also heavily fortified. I took over driving and opened the throttle as far as the road allowed: I really didn't want us to be out on this road when darkness fell. Months later, we read that the unmapped, heavily guarded road with its own bridge led to a Syrian nuclear reactor under construction. The news got out after the site was bombed by Israeli Air Force pilots in a midnight raid.

When the road became a little smoother, I tried to distract G.C. by telling him things I had learned from our battered guidebook as he slept in the brothel: Deir ez-Zor had been a key trading point between the Roman Empire and the lands to the east, a pivotal node for goods and ideas that came from as far away as India. A matriarchal desert dynasty, led by Queen Zenobia, took the city from the Romans and it became part of the kingdom of Palmyra. It was eventually destroyed by the Mongols and then rebuilt by the Ottomans.

It wasn't working: G.C.'s arms were going slack with fatigue around my waist. I drove even faster as the sun gathered light and heat.

It is one of the warmest Aprils on record, this year when the spring sun shines on days restricted to house, garden, and one daily outing for exercise no more than five miles away from home. In Lombardy, people are not allowed to go more than a few hundred metres from their front door without a permit; having a garden is a luxury, a gift, a freedom. I see dear faces from Italy on my phone each day, and it makes the distance worse. On a video call to a friend, I wave to his uncle who is making coffee in the background; the uncle waves back; five days later he is dead and buried. The meaning of things begins to blur in my mind. Dear is one letter away from dead: my brain finds this obvious, and deeply significant. I score it three times in capital letters, upside down in a book about propagating plants from cuttings.

Thanks to our hurried dawn departure from Raqqa, we arrived in Deir ez-Zor while it was still daylight. The roads matched our map and my relief bubbled into sobs, quiet in my motorbike helmet so G.C. wouldn't worry. There seemed to be fewer round-abouts than in Raqqa too, and the Euphrates running through the town provided a welcome way of orienting our approach. There were signs for Iraq, just seventy miles to the east. Elegant pedestrian bridges crossed the river, and trees grew down to the water's edge. We drove through streets and past parks full of families walking in the evening air. The hotel we arrived at was, blessedly, just a hotel. From our window, I could see little shops on the riverfront and a sky turning bright with the sunset.

'Look, the sky is orange!' I said to G.C. He didn't answer; when I turned around, I saw he was already unconscious on the bed, still in his motorbike gear, limbs twitching in a fevered sleep. I undressed him and left him there while I went out to explore, lingering on a beautiful suspension bridge across the Euphrates, watching the river flow free of manmade borders, before going to find water and food that we could trust.

Not far from the hotel, a man was selling bottled water from a wooden crate he carried on his head. He asked me where I was from, then said he had escaped the violence in Iraq.

'Let me tell you,' he said in a quiet voice, 'thirty years ago Iraq was like a garden, now it's like a graveyard.'

He told me that in Iraq he had been a primary school teacher, and spoke to me of the tensions between Sunni and Shia people. 'I know history, and in Europe you have your problems – Protestants and Catholics slaughtering one another. But you managed to get past it. We have to get past it too.' I thought of my friends from Belfast, and the stories my Glaswegian uncle had told me of growing up in a city spiked with sectarian violence, but didn't say anything.

G.C.'s fever stayed high for a further two days during which he drank only water, despite the offerings of food I brought from my walks around the city. A stall selling falafels and juices became my favourite place because of the man who owned it. He had gentle eyes that didn't match his angry mouth or his sarcastic words, and an enormous brown moustache that reminded me of a favourite Italian uncle. After I had returned for the third time, we moved past pleasantries and he told me that the local election results would be coming out later that same day.

'Of course, the government will win – after all, this is a democracy,' he said. I tentatively raised an eyebrow. He went on: 'Yes, Assad only wants the best for this country. Like his father before him.'

'Ah,' was the profound response that I came up with. When my falafel was ready, I told him that my husband was ill in a hotel room, and explained our journey so far. The fact that I was just passing through seemed to free something within him, and he told me about the steadily worsening situation in his city. There had been a drought for many years in the surrounding farmland; refugees from Iraq were arriving in 'unstoppable waves' because 'they need to eat, and they won't stay in the camps'; armed troops had moved in following rumours of opposition protests planned around the election.

'This used to be a beautiful place to live,' he said, 'but if things carry on as they are, we will become like Iraq, or worse.' I told him about our experience on the road from Raqqa. 'Oh, *country* people,' he replied with disdain. 'Out in the villages, they fight all the time over land and honour. They rule their lives with tradition; government law doesn't touch them.' Another customer approached, and he switched abruptly to asking about my husband's health, and what type of motorbike we were riding. I paid and went slowly back to the hotel.

The next day G.C. felt well enough to take a shaky walk around the city, but was conscious of being the only fair-skinned, blue-eyed person on the streets, just a few kilometres from the border with Iraq where a war had been ignited by his country. Back in our room, he packed our bags while I went to say goodbye to the falafel stall man, but he was gone.

I remembered him when Deir ez-Zor was bombed seven years later, attacked by both government and ISIS forces. The city's bridges and parks were destroyed; its inhabitants faced starvation or the long journey across the desert. Many of them would trace our own journey in reverse, through Turkey and Greece, towards an imagined safety in Europe.

Today is May Day. I am pacing the glimmering pre-dawn garden to recover from a dream in which I woke, got up to check on the children and found them all dead in their beds. It was only a dream, I tell myself, not a sign of anything other than my anxious mind. The children are alive. I repeat this like a mantra which might help me unspool the knots of memories, dreams, stories and fears tangled in my head.

A cup of coffee is scalding and real in my hands. Consolation rises up from the memories of my Nonno, for ever associated with the smell of coffee in the morning. He taught me to make espresso, and always had time to tell me and Lorenzo many stories from his extraordinary life which spanned the First World War, the Spanish flu pandemic, the rise of fascism, the Second World War, the explosive post-war growth of Italy and more. Only one thing he was reluctant to talk about: his mother's death from Spanish flu, when he was eight years old. This catastrophe changed the course of his life – by the time he was ten, the age S and T are now, Nonno had left school and was working on a building site, pushing sacks of cement in a wheelbarrow. He died when he was 101 years old, the summer after S and T were born.

I remember Nonno's friend Toni, our communist neighbour who lived across the road. Every May Day he would play the 'Internazionale' at top volume from his apartment balcony, all day, to drown out the Catholic church bells ringing out down the road to celebrate the holy month of Mary starting. 'At least one day a year we can celebrate winning against them,' Toni would say to Nonno, laughing, as they drank espresso with generous shots of grappa in it.

The ancient Celtic feast of Beltane is also today, a festival of fire and fertility, celebrating the land and its blossoming life as winter retreats and early summer bursts out in abundance. Seagulls squabble on the neighbour's roof. Sunrise gives each leaf a halo of light. One breath at a time: in, out, alive.

Two young men on a 125 cc bike wanted to race us out of Deir ez-Zor, a laughing and gesticulating escort under the arches of the Assad Trinity. We won. Bedouin tents were strung out across the desert, with sheep, goats, and camels grazing on the thin green dusting of grass brought by the recent rains. We saw trucks, tractors and a shiny silver car parked outside the goat-hair tents. A poorly marked track split off to the north, headed towards ancient Ummayad fortifications on the Euphrates. We glimpsed rigs drilling for oil in the distance. Herds of camels ambled across the highway, dotting the landscape all the way to Palmyra.

The violence and fire we had come through felt very distant as we walked through Palmyra's monuments in the quiet evening air. In the museum, we walked through rooms full of objects from the second and third centuries CE, when the city was at the centre of trade networks that spanned empires. Everything spoke of luxury: these had been very rich people.

In the temple of Bel, we found sculpted reliefs of the Moon God and the Sun God: both young men in tunics with curly hair and haloes of rays behind their heads. The Moon God also had a crescent moon arching up from round his shoulders around the bottom part of the halo. Bel was symbolised by an eagle, and there were many human figures like angels, with arching feathery wings. I was fascinated by the haloes and angel wings sculpted long before the Christian era; the imagery I had grown up with seemed to have its origins in much older religious traditions than I'd known.

Another block of stone showed a sculpted caravan of camels, followed by women who were completely covered in veils, like the images of Afghan women in burqas under Taliban rule. We read that the women of high social class in Palmyra showed their superior status by covering themselves, long before the advent of Islam.

The wind made humming sounds among the temple ruins, bringing us the smells of dry earth and sun-warmed stone. The landscape was muted, gentle, with the silver-green of plants merging into earthy browns and greys. Hills of scrubland rolled all the way to the horizon, hazy in the dusty light. Syria seemed very peaceful from here.

Beyond Palmyra the road dipped and soared towards the coast, bringing the smell of Mediterranean pine into my helmet. From a distance we sighted the Krak des Chevaliers, an immense Crusader fortress and one of the best-preserved medieval castles in the world, a shocking bulk among the gentle hills. We were held up by a herd of cows being driven towards us by a boy no older than four. He was so short that at first we only saw the waving stick with which he thrashed the cows' behinds. We sat on the bike at a standstill in jostled wonder; it was as if we were in a river of cattle. We watched the boy until he and the cows disappeared behind a bend.

The Krak des Chevaliers, incongruous after the emptiness of the desert, was built of light stone atop a hill that guards the approach roads from the coast. It reminded me of a hunkered troll. My head filled up with adjectives: massive, looming, imposing, impregnable. No castle I had seen in Europe was as impressive. Even Saladin, the legendary general who won back Jerusalem after decades of Crusader occupation, saw the Krak and decided immediately that attempting its conquest would be too much of an effort. The outer fortress was breached once, by mining a defence tower, but the keep was never conquered: the Crusader knights only gave it up because of a forged letter urging surrender.

The moat, once replenished by an aqueduct, was now full of luminous green duckweed, strewn with plastic bottles. Past the water was 'the Mountain', a sloping wall of stone, smooth all the way to the towers of the inner keep – impossible to scale or to mine, as it was based on solid rock. T. E. Lawrence famously tried to climb it in 1907 when he was writing his thesis on Crusader castles. He only managed to reach halfway. We walked around the high walls of the outer defences, together with Arab families on holiday. At the heart of the inner keep, a colonnade led into the knights' banqueting hall and chapel; my eyes were delighted by sudden familiar arches of Gothic architecture, columns decorated like the cathedrals in Italy. I found a Latin inscription: 'You may have wisdom, beauty, and grace, but beware of pride, which alone ruins everything else.'

In the chapel, frescoes had been painted on arches against one wall. The space was filled with a yammering film crew, all extroverts, arranging a shoot for that night. Beyond, there were pillared rooms, and terracotta jars of oil just like the ones – two millennia older – in Nestor's palace. A mihrab had been added to the chapel, but it was chipped, old and dirty. A man sang in Arabic in the echoing chapter with an astonishing voice, a trembling and leaping sound. High as sparrowhawks, we looked out towards the coast and discussed the road ahead: it was already May. I wanted to visit my friends in Beirut and see if we could find any wisdom there to help solve the conundrum of how to get ourselves and Mondialita to Pakistan overland.

In the house, G.C. lies ill. Yesterday he came back from work with a headache and pains all over his body, and fell asleep for hours in the middle of the afternoon. Today he will get tested for the Virus. We will know the result within three days; until then, we all are forbidden from leaving the house for any reason. Today my work, again, is to dig deep for inner wells of care and cheer to bring my loved ones as we wait – not besieged, but not free either. I hum the 'Internazionale', then a hymn to Mary, followed by a Beltane song, and a shaky smile rises like a surprise visitor. Each to their own celebrations and labour. The May blossom is so sweet I could put it in my coffee, white flower froth. P, S and T come and find me in the garden, alive and warm with sleep on their breaths, and I tickle them until they nearly pee themselves.

We make a plan, which mostly revolves around watching all possible Star Wars *films ahead of May the Fourth, when we intend to hold a banquet of strictly* Star Wars–related *food: Wookiee cookies, green Yoda jelly, light-sabre chocolate sticks. The next few days are brightened by intergalactic epics and friends bringing us food and kindness in our isolation. Everyone comments on the beauty of the season, sharing pictures of limpid skies over cities in China and India that have not known clear air in living memory. It feels like nature is flourishing freely while humans halt and sicken. G.C. sleeps and sleeps. His test comes back negative, but he can only manage a short time out of bed before succumbing to rolling waves of exhaustion and debilitating headaches. I watch him as he breathes, scanning his body for signs of health returning, and wait.*

4

Another beginning

Lebanon and Jordan

The Syrian officials at the Arida crossing into Lebanon were buttoned-up, efficient and straight-talking. They were somehow preferable to the guards at Bab al-Hawa – or maybe I was more light of heart because I was almost back in Lebanon, and this time, finally, with G.C.

My good mood was tested when the border officials informed us that our visa, despite being 'multiple entry', would expire as soon as we left Syria. Nothing I said made any difference: if we wanted to re-enter Syria from Beirut, we'd need to pay for a new visa and apply all over again. Our passports gave us freedom to cross borders, but the Syrian government conceded that freedom reluctantly, temporarily, and at a cost.

The guards stamped our passports and *carnet de passage* and we rolled the bike, engine off, across the short stretch between barriers. I pulled off my hijab and stuffed it into my jacket. The wind from the sea felt like a welcome, like another beginning.

I remembered the first time I had arrived in Beirut, in early September 2001: looking out from the plane, I saw a white city next to the blue Mediterranean and was filled with an inexplicable feeling of familiarity. Then, too, the breeze from the sea felt like a personal greeting. I had come here to learn spoken Levantine Arabic, different from the Modern Standard Arabic which is used in official speeches, newspapers and most literature. I had spent four years learning the language of official culture, but when I spoke I sounded like a newsreel, and couldn't understand everyday speech.

I was full of optimism and certainty: Lebanon was at peace; even the south of the country was safe now that the Israeli army had pulled out. A few weeks later, I was in a taxi that was refuelling near the southern border with Israel, when suddenly the world around me erupted into gunfire. Men were running out of shops and houses and cars, shooting into the air, whooping in delight. I tried to ask the driver what was happening but couldn't make sense of his reply. He pointed to a television set propped on a chair by the petrol pumps: in Modern Standard Arabic, a man was saying that aeroplanes had flown into the Twin Towers in New York. Suddenly nothing was certain any more.

I stayed in Beirut for six months and every day learned something about the complexities which define, enrich and weaken Lebanon. I made friends who took care of me, and took pity on my foreign ignorance, explaining and teaching patiently. Each night I fell asleep exhausted by the onslaught of new words and facts, waking impatient for more every morning. For the whole six months of that trip, I was on a high of adrenaline and discovery which felt a bit like the first rush of being in love; leaving to return to Scotland and finish my degree felt like a grief. My Lebanese friends who took me to the airport and waved me goodbye were unmoved: 'You love

it here because you don't have to stay. Fancy a passport swap?'
I returned as soon as I could, two years later. By then G.C. and
I had fallen in love with each other, but he was far away in
Antarctica, surrounded by the beauties of ice and silence. 'Third
time lucky,' I thought, as we approached the Lebanese side of
the border – for the first time, arriving together.

*The May blossom burgeons and G.C.'s strength grows. Tulips
flame, as red as Mondialita. Lockdown restrictions are ongoing,
to be reviewed every three weeks for as long as it takes. The
number of people who have died of Covid in the UK is even
higher than in Italy – the worst death toll in Europe. I wait to
hear back about my research funding. Once a week, I leave the
house to go to the supermarket, get there as soon as it opens,
and buy enough food for seven days. Rotas of shopping for
friends and neighbours become established, small gestures of
care which widen the circle of interaction for a few moments
before it closes again, feeling smaller than before.*

*All the time I am tired, so tired, but I cannot rest, flitting
between tasks and thoughts. One day I decide to take stock of
all the foods which are easily found in Italy but rare and overpriced here: little milk-and-honey sweets; dried porcini
mushrooms from the Apennine hills above my Lombard village;
saffron; special biscuits; tiny, star-shaped pasta you cook in broth
if someone is ill or needs comfort. I make lists of quantities and
plan how to eke out these precious supplies over the months
ahead. As we move towards summer, I prepare as if for winter.*

The Lebanese border guards had set out plastic chairs on the tarmac and were playing cards in the sunshine.

'Hey, give us a ride!' one called out in English as we coasted to a stop beside them. His accent was American: 'Guys, look, whadda machine!'

G.C. lifted the bike on to its centre stand and laid his helmet down on the road. One of the guards jumped to his feet and pretended to take aim, as if kicking it into the sea.

'Just kidding,' he said. 'Passports?'

They introduced themselves: Marcel and Nicolas. In Lebanon, names are markers to navigate the divisions between faiths and political allegiances, not unlike Catholic or Protestant surnames in the sectarian Glasgow of my mother's childhood. French names meant 'Christian' here, and my eyes flicked over the guards for any other signs: yes, they wore tiny golden crucifixes around their necks.

G.C. told them we were on our way to Beirut and they laughed: 'So, had enough of Syria? Don't blame you.' When I explained we wanted to return and visit Damascus afterwards, they rolled their eyes. 'You guys are crazy – stay in Lebanon. You might not even get across at Masna'a.' I enjoyed chatting with these men, who slipped effortlessly between English and Arabic as they asked in growing amazement about our route from Scotland, and where we hoped the journey might end. When G.C. said, 'Maybe New Zealand,' they roared with laughter and refused to believe us. They loaned us a phone card to call friends in Beirut and I wanted to hug them. It was impossible to imagine Syrian border guards being so open with foreigners. Marcel was short and round with a wet-shaved head which he stroked as he talked. Nicolas's hair was like long black plumage; while he spoke, he preened it with an oily comb.

'Be careful in Beirut,' he muttered when I ended my phone call. 'The refugees from Iraq have brought Baghdad to our streets.'

The asphalt was potholed and overgrown as far as Tripoli. On our right, the sea shone blue and immense, glittering all the way to Cyprus. Between Tripoli and Beirut, there were fewer potholes but the roads were lined with billboards covered in women's bodies advertising jewellery, Coke, cigarettes, hair transplants, hair removal, luxury apartments and supermarkets. The half-naked models were all reclining, and struck me as vulgar after the austerity of Syria. I also felt relief, and something like homecoming, to have crossed into a place where it was permissible for women's bodies to be uncovered. At the same time, there was a deep irritation, familiar to me from having grown up in Italy: women's bodies were free to be on show, but they were also used to sell everything from coffee to cleaning products, and rarely allowed to hold any meaningful power beyond the home.

We drove south with the Mediterranean never far away on our right; the wires connecting our helmets buzzed with conversation about the previous times I had been in Beirut, the people I wanted G.C. to meet and the places we could visit together this time. But the happiness I felt in showing G.C. around and introducing him to friends became shadowed by sadness at the changes since my last visit. The former prime minister of Lebanon, Rafik Hariri, had been assassinated in 2005 by a car bomb; violent protests had followed, led by those who blamed Syria for Hariri's murder. Soon afterwards, Syria had withdrawn as an occupying power, an event unimaginable only a few years earlier. In the subsequent power shifts, the Lebanese Shia militia, Hezbollah, had gained control over the south of Lebanon and threatened Israel, its sworn enemy. The Israeli army had retaliated with devastating bomb attacks across Lebanon in 2006.

There were many more tanks than I remembered, many more soldiers and loops of barbed wire, lots of closed roads and shops, so many worried faces. It felt like a different country. My memories seemed like a poorly drawn map: the inconsistencies between then and now distracted me from being fully present to the moment.

G.C. was seeing Lebanon for the first time, and countered my sadness with enthusiasm: for the indomitable party spirit of Beirut, the sublime Lebanese food, the cedar forests in the mountains, the glad welcome we were given. He commented on how so many different sects and faiths lived alongside one another – the Palestinian districts jostling with the Lebanese Shia quarters, the Druze areas near streets full of Christian Maronites, with 'Jesus is my co-pilot' a common bumper sticker among the latter. I pointed out the signs that it was not always peaceful living. Statuettes on street corners showed the Virgin Mary trampling on a crescent moon suspiciously similar to the crescent of Islam. We passed several walls graffitied with spray-painted crosses, the long arm sharpened to a sword point dripping blood, above the legend in English 'Hallowed Be Thy Name'.

On the Corniche there were croissants and *café au lait*, pizzas and Coke, all with a backdrop of Mediterranean blue. At the American University of Beirut, we walked between courtyards that could have been transposed from Ivy League universities. Parliament Square had been taken over by

Hezbollah fighters, who had pitched their khaki tents and surrounded the public space with rolls of razor wire and their flag: a Kalashnikov made of Arabic calligraphy. It became normal to look up and see a man with a gun on a tank. Attitudes had not changed: 'You don't know what will happen tomorrow, so let's party now!' said my friend Maha, laughing. She offered me her clothes to wear for dancing in nightclubs in the Christian quarter of Beirut – a long way removed from my hijab bought in Aleppo. Emerging in a strappy pink top and tight jeans, I felt almost naked.

We recovered from clubbing with a steady stream of cardamom-scented coffee, shared with friends in a variety of cafes. We were never allowed to pay. Maha's mother gave us a beautiful glass image of the Virgin Mary, 'to watch over you on the road ahead'. A Palestinian friend gifted us a miniature Qur'an to take with us on our onward journey – it opened to show perfectly formed words in minuscule lettering, with pages rimmed in gold and a cover embossed with green and scarlet. It was smaller than the coffee spoons, and fitted into a little case which hung from a tiny chain – 'so you can hang it on your crazy motorbike, you crazy people, and stay safe', Rima smiled. Unlike most other people I knew in Beirut, she was not planning to build a new life in the Gulf States, away from Lebanon and its increasing tension and uncertainty.

'My family are coffee merchants – here, when people are stressed, they drink more coffee, so all this madness is good for us! And anyway, I don't even have a Lebanese passport, remember? I'm Palestinian, we don't count.' Rima laughed as she said this, with the tone of defiance in the face of adversity that surfaced in almost every conversation we had with friends during those weeks.

New patterns are beginning to emerge, ways of managing the unimagined. I know the way T struggles with maths, why S loses patience with spelling, how P hates unplanned changes. I know that the days are much better if regularly punctuated with things to eat and drink, and if we manage to get out for our permitted hour in the outside world. We discover new beaches and tracks around where we live, and everything seems beautiful in the sunshine. When we meet friends outside, it is a physical effort not to hug them. Spring is exploding with abandon, but as seeds yield up their promises, we humans creep about cautiously avoiding each other.

Another Lebanese friend who had no intention of leaving for the Gulf was Hammoud, a university lecturer who lived in Tripoli. We took a break from Beirut's intensity to visit him for a few days, deeply grateful for the way we were immediately included in family meals and outings. He treated us to a seafood feast in Mina, the ancient seaside citadel at the heart of Tripoli, where we sat in the warm night air listening as jokes and anecdotes flowed around us. Hammoud was from a Muslim family and had married Reine, whose family were devout Maronite Christians. They had met when Hammoud was on a package holiday to Egypt with his best friend Pierre, who ran the restaurant where we were eating. 'We were on a bus to the pyramids and these two gorgeous Lebanese girls walked on,' Hammoud told us. 'I thought, just my luck, Pierre is going to mess it all up with his mad jokes. But then—'

'But then it was my mad jokes who saved us!' said Pierre as he walked towards our table. He whacked Hammoud on the shoulder, grinning. The girls were sisters, from Tripoli, homesick for Lebanese humour; by the end of the holiday, it was clear that a double wedding was on the cards. Hammoud smiled across the table at Reine. They seemed to hold between them a happiness that was deep and strong.

The next day they took us into the Lebanon mountains to visit the Cedars, famous as the centrepiece of the Lebanese flags that flapped wherever we looked, and celebrated by the words of Kahlil Gibran. 'It's one of the few things we can all agree on in this country,' chuckled Reine, 'that these trees are amazing.' They were vast, ancient, growing on poor mountain land that still held snow in May. G.C. was happy to be somewhere cool again.

Remembering all the tales we were told by friends in Lebanon – how they delighted and entertained us – I make up new stories for the children as a distraction from lockdown worries. We look through old photographs, cycle across the Forth Road Bridge and back every day, plan for next week: it is all anyone can do, and we are lucky to be able to do even that. I wonder, where is the freedom in this kind of situation? Is there liberation to be found in endurance, in just carrying on?

Planting seeds becomes a new obsession, a way of tricking time. I find myself rolling the seeds of carrot and beetroot in my fingers like the beads of a rosary. I push them into the earth, little parcels of brightness deferred. With each seed I form a litany of distance, a lament for the dead. I have started seeing

*them in my dreams, the dear dead ones, unfurling like tendrils
from the ground. I can make the dreams stop by waking myself;
but I cannot stop them from recurring, many times, each night.
The garden is a place where I can dull grief through repetitive,
soothing labour.*

We returned to Beirut determined to find answers to our
logistical transport questions. It was hard to remain undis-
tracted: I kept on wanting to take G.C. to this pub, that club,
this other restaurant, to stay on for just another day, to show
him just one more place. I wanted to recreate as a shared story
the times I had been here without him – a foolish idea, and
I knew it. 'Maybe you need to let it go,' G.C. said gently. 'We're
here now and need to work out what's best to do next.' He
was right, irritatingly so. I went for a walk along the Corniche
by myself to dispel my annoyance and think about our options.
I stopped in front of the Pigeon Rocks, one of the famous
landmarks of Beirut's seafront, and felt the truth of G.C.'s
words: I wasn't letting the journey continue because I was
tying us both to a past that was impossible to recreate.

Everyone told us that we needed to go to Jordan, to ask about
a transit visa across Saudi Arabia or a sea passage to Pakistan.
The southern border between Lebanon and Israel was a
conflict zone, so we needed to enter Jordan via Syria.

The route from Beirut to Damascus climbed steeply into
the mountains, leaving the sea glimmering beneath us to the
west. G.C. drove, and there was a helpless sadness in me at

leaving Beirut and the Mediterranean as the road wound through beige-coloured hills. I went over all the excellent reasons for moving on after a few weeks – costs, timings, logistics – but none of them made leaving easier. I heard my Lebanese friends' voices laughing, saying, '*Yalla*, come on, cheer up, at least you are free to go! Enjoy it!' They were right. Again.

After a couple of sharp curves, the air cooled and we left the Mediterranean behind. Only ten miles to the east of the city, we summited the Lebanon massif and dropped into the Bekaa Valley. I knew G.C. had always wanted to see the colossal ancient ruins of Baalbek, but this time I had to persuade him to let that idea go: friends in Beirut had repeatedly warned against exploring the Bekaa Valley. It had been safe for me to visit a few years earlier, but now it was a Hezbollah stronghold and there had been recent reports of foreigners being kidnapped there.

As we approached the Masna'a border, we passed the last few billboards and money changers. The traffic was heavy, as this was the main road connecting Beirut and Damascus. On previous visits I had often made this same journey for weekend trips, travelling with a few Lebanese families on minibreaks and many Syrians returning home from work, in the days when Syrian workers did many of the poorly paid jobs in Lebanon. Damascus was beautiful in my memory, unspoiled by the scars of recent civil war or the capitalist advertising that marked Beirut; almost as if it was held still in time by Assad's government, which controlled most aspects of economic, political and private life. Couples didn't hold hands, buying and drinking alcohol was officially controlled by the state, and prices were much lower than in Lebanon. I liked going there, but my favourite part of the trip was the return journey, when just over the border into Lebanon the driver would stop at the first roadside kiosk. All the men would crowd out to buy cheap Lebanese lager, cheering and clinking bottles. I was free to join them – as a single, foreign woman there were no moral or family codes I was disobeying. That first beer was always delicious, slightly subversive, even though I knew that there would be at least one Syrian Mukhabarat agent on every bus, taking note of everything.

This time, with G.C., the Lebanese side was a formality, the guards polite and good-humoured. The Syrian side was different. We needed to pay for a new visa at the border crossing and knew that we could be refused with no reason. I remembered the predictions of Marcel and Nicolas at the Arida crossing, and feared that they had been right – not just prejudiced.

Just before the Syrian border post, I once more slipped on the grey hijab with silver sequins. Wearing it through Syria had brought smiles, kind interest, open conversations. It had helped in those days walking Deir ez-Zor alone, while G.C. shivered and vomited in a hotel room. I hoped it would make the crossing easier. Again G.C. criticised my cynical use of it, but after Bab al-Hawa, I was willing to try almost anything.

A high desk lay between us and the guards who'd decide whether we could return to Syria. They were raised on a kind of dais, able to look down on us from a height as we waited.

'We are the supplicants,' G.C. said. 'We just need to stay calm.' Another foreigner there, a tall Danish man with impeccable English, did not keep calm. When asked, 'What is your profession?', he answered candidly, 'I am a journalist.' 'Oh you fool!' I thought – he quickly realised his mistake, but it was too late. The following dialogue ensued, with me as interpreter and G.C. standing by, not sure whether to laugh or cry:

Syrian Official: We need a statement from the Syrian Ministry of Internal Security to confirm you are not reporting on Syria.

Danish Journalist: But I don't want to do journalism in Syria, I just want to go to Damascus and talk to the Danish ambassador and the Danish Cultural Institute.

SO: We need the statement sent here by fax.

DJ: OK, fine, so how do I get the statement?

SO: You must phone the Syrian Ministry of Internal Security and talk to them.

DJ: Do you have their number?

SO: No, of course I don't have their number, you should have their number.

DJ: OK, so do you have a phone so I can phone my embassy in Damascus?

SO: No, we do not have a phone here, you should have your own phone.

DJ: So what should I do?

SO (shrugs): This is your problem.

After keeping us waiting for over an hour, the man high up behind his desk frowned at me.

'Are you a Muslim?' he asked.

'No,' I replied.

'Is your husband a Muslim?'

'No, sir,' I answered.

'Well then, why this hijab?'

'To show respect. We are all People of the Book, as the Holy Qur'an says.'

'Very good.' He gave a smile that managed to look half like a frown, and stamped our passports. G.C. grinned, hijab reservations forgotten: we were in.

We were not given a transit visa, despite our many protest-ations and explanations that we would only be briefly passing through Syria to get into Jordan: we had British passports, so we had to pay for full single-entry visas, like the ones the Syrian embassy in Ankara had given us. There was no logic, argument or blandishment that could sway the officials. We paid over one hundred US dollars, wincing as we did so, and the man in the exchange booth tried to rip us off.

I tried to be philosophical, reflecting that we didn't know what British visa policy or border welcome was like for Syrian nationals. It didn't help. By this point we were so sick of Syrian bureaucracy that we couldn't wait to leave the country as soon as possible.

'We can always come back,' I said confidently, thinking of the beauty of Damascus which G.C. had never seen. I wanted to walk with him in the honey-coloured stone streets of the Old City, where keyhole doorways led to tessellated courtyards filled with plants and fountains; visit the Great Mosque, with its astonishing mosaics of plants that almost seemed to grow and breathe; sit in the rooftop cafes where you could drink terrible Barada beer and look out over the city as it glowed in the night. But not this time: even if we had been able to muster the energy to face more Syrian officialdom, the pres-sures of budget and time meant that we needed to move on to Jordan and the rest of our journey.

'We'll come back another time to visit Damascus, it'll still be there.' I spoke with the assured ignorance of someone brought up in a place of long peace and safety, ignoring the many signs of gathering tension that we had seen in Syria.

My brother, too, has been channelling his energy and tension into our parents' garden, creating fantastic systems of irrigation, wigwams of beans, a potato grower made of straw shaped like a huge boot. I garden in parallel, although less flamboyantly, planting fragrant Mediterranean herbs. More verses of Cavafy's 'Ithaka' surface in my mind:

> may there be many summer mornings
> when you arrive with pleasure and joy
> in harbours seen for the first time.
>
> Stop in Phoenician trading stations
> and buy the finest things:
> pearls and corals, ambers and ebony,
> and sensual perfumes of every kind,
> as many sensual perfumes as you can

In the Scottish summer mornings, I close my eyes and try to reach back, through the perfumes of thyme and rosemary, to memories of Greece and Lebanon, Syria and Jordan – times of hopeful adventure, instead of grief and death.

Mondialita took us towards Jordan through a bare, rolling landscape that ceded to dusty ochre suburbs, a skyline of ungoverned wires, the heat like a kindling kiln. To the west the Golan Heights were hazy in the dust. Bedouin tents and herds dotted the landscape.

The border awaited us just beyond the town of Dara'a; we didn't stop here for long, coasting past its Roman ruins and sun-scorched streets. Petrol was sold in old soda bottles from stalls at the roadside. I suggested that we should buy a few, in anticipation of the notoriously expensive Hashemite Kingdom of Jordan.

We approached the Syrian side of the frontier with unease, though the authorities seemed happier to let Europeans out of the country than in. A solitary guard sat fanning himself on a deckchair in the middle of the road with a gun on his lap. In the shade of his chair was a row of water bottles and every so often he would pour the contents of one over the road. The water quickly evaporated, briefly moderating the blistering heat that radiated up from the tarmac. He offered us tea and iced water, nodded with approval at my hijab and asked us to visit Syria again.

To enter Jordan there were queues almost as long as those at Bab al-Hawa, with truck drivers snoozing beneath their vehicles in the shade. I was unusually silent, caught between regret at having to move on and the logistics of our unfolding journey. We spent three hours in a mercifully air-conditioned room beneath the portraits of King Abdullah II and his father, Hussein, before being allowed through. G.C. started the motorbike and I jumped on behind, still in silence. There were soldiers everywhere, as there had been in Syria, but the roads were broader, smoother and better maintained. We drove through the dusk towards the town of Irbid, five miles from the Israeli border.

Maybe it was the heat that brought on my migraine, or accumulated tension, or having to make adjustments to yet another country. Intense nausea swayed through me, and the light hurt. I sat on the back of the bike, eyes closed, visor down, my arms wound round G.C.'s chest. Every so often I felt the strength flow out of me, my arms slackening, and I almost fell off. G.C. pulled up outside a hotel where a kind man let him wheel the bike into the lobby for the night and immediately gave us keys to a room. G.C. half carried me upstairs, helped me off with my jacket and biking gear, and I slumped on to the bed and into oblivious sleep.

The next day the headache was gone, leaving a post-migraine feeling of mild detachment from the world, the absence of pain like being washed clean, almost floating. We made straight for Amman, where we had arranged to meet up with Rania, a friend who had been able to leave Lebanon thanks to the Jordanian passport she had obtained through her mother; her father was Palestinian. She told us that around sixty per cent of the six million Jordanians were Palestinian, as a result of the waves of refugees who have escaped across the Jordan away from Israel's wars.

'And to that have been added over a million Iraqis escaping from their own wars,' she told us, shaking her head. She was buying us lunch in an air-conditioned burger restaurant in the centre of Amman, full of Westerners and Jordanians who, like her, worked for the hundreds of NGOs operating in the city. She listened to the names of shipping agencies we had found online, and narrowed them down to three trustworthy ones said to have experience moving motorbikes between countries.

'I think we should go with "Horizon Freight"; said G.C., 'just because of the name. This journey is all about widening horizons, after all.' I grinned: that was exactly my way of making choices. Horizon Freight surpassed all our hopes with their kindness and efficiency. With their help, we began to untangle the threads of possibilities, hopes and worries that had been knotting in our conversations for weeks.

Back in Italy we had promised my family just two things: that we would not drive through Iraq or through Afghanistan due to ongoing conflicts there. Honouring that promise left us with only one overland option: crossing Saudi Arabia into Oman or the United Arab Emirates, then a sea journey on to Pakistan. It became obvious that the only visas available for Saudi Arabia were for pilgrimage or business. For a few hours I seriously considered trying for the pilgrimage visa, much to G.C.'s distress, but in the end I accepted the advice of the wise people at Horizon Freight, who echoed the opinions of many friends in Lebanon: we wouldn't be able to continue overland. We had crossed the last land border open to us, from Syria into Jordan.

Pursuing a way of accompanying the motorbike by sea, we investigated every possibility: going via Egypt and Zanzibar, sailing down to Yemen and driving across to Oman, getting the bike trucked across Saudi and flying over to meet it in Oman or Dubai. But none of them would work. We were told that there were no sailings from Aqaba for 'civilians – even without motorbikes', and sea freight to Karachi wasn't possible either: the latest news from Pakistan was that martial law had been declared in the south of the country, and there was no guarantee Mondialita would be allowed in. Karachi airport was closed; forty people had been shot dead in the streets.

And so it became clear that we would have to send Mondialita to the north of Pakistan: she would be flown in a crate to Islamabad, where an old friend would be able to welcome us. I reminded G.C. of the other turning points in our journey – Venice, Ankara – and the freedom we still had to choose what to do with the many options still open to us. He crinkled his eyes at me. 'We can explore a bit of Jordan while we wait for the paperwork to come through.'

Just west of Amman is the summit of Mount Nebo, which looks out over the Jordan Valley. According to the Bible, it is the place where Moses was shown the Promised Land and learned that, although it would be given to the Israelites, he would never enter it. On the summit was an old Byzantine church, its floor a mosaic of lions, hunting scenes, and figures with black skin, suggesting a past of relatively free movement between Africa, the Levant and Europe. It showed a verdant, fertile landscape vastly different to the scorched beige of the region now. Beneath the mountain, through the haze, we could just make out the occupied West Bank: the plain of Jericho, the river Jordan, the hills of Jerusalem. Even if we wanted to, we couldn't go there: an Israeli stamp on our passports would bar us from entering Pakistan, and our *carnet de passage* specifically ruled out being able to take the motorcycle into territory occupied by Israel.

At the foot of Mount Nebo, we arrived at that stretch of the Jordan where Jesus is believed to have been baptised. The river lay across a floodplain of salt-loving tamarisks where, according to the Qur'an, the Israelites rested on the way to fight the Philistines. We were not allowed to drive up to the Jordan directly – it was a militarised frontier – but we walked under the open sky, the sunlight fierce and gleaming. I chewed some tamarisk leaves; they tasted like salty crisps.

A guide and a Jordanian soldier led us down a path to the

riverbank. It was so depleted by drought and irrigation practices that it seemed little more than a dirty runnel, not at all inviting to swim in. We had read that Jordan and Israel each accused the other of taking more water than they were due. Satellite photographs show how parched the land directly east and west of the Jordan was, but how well irrigated the lands of Israel were in comparison – luscious and green, even from space. A Russian girl about three or four years old, in a commemorative baptism T-shirt that reached her knees, was being ceremoniously dunked in the water by an Orthodox priest. She cried as her mother hauled her out; the priest swung his censer and encouraged the two of us to join in with a hymn.

Just a few metres away across the water, there was a corresponding baptism platform controlled by the Israelis, beneath a flapping Star of David. The Israeli soldier looked on bemused, gun slung on one shoulder, just in case any of us should risk a swim to the other side.

After the muddy Jordan and a week spent driving through the Jordanian desert, arriving at the sea in Aqaba was a relief of clear blue, but it felt like something of an anticlimax for me, nothing like the joy-filled descents towards the sea in France, Turkey, Lebanon. Perhaps my mind was already too preoccupied with the next stage of our journey to fully appreciate that we were in a place of ancient human settlement, Jordan's only seaport, the portal to the immensity of the Indian Ocean and the African seaboard. I was also frustrated: why couldn't we just drive south across the border to Saudi Arabia, or jump on a boat which would take us and Mondialita around the Arabian peninsula?

G.C. was elated, though, talking with amazement of how our journey had taken us from the grey cold of the North Sea to this subtropical Red Sea heat, from the Atlantic Ocean to the Indian – and we were only really getting started. He also told me that Horizon Freight had got in touch: the logistics of our onward journey were nearly arranged, and we would have time for only one night in Aqaba. The next day we'd have to drive back up to Amman and sign the motorbike over for transportation to Pakistan.

To celebrate, we rented snorkelling gear and spent the afternoon floating over coral reefs of intricate magnificence. Out in the bay there were tourist sailing boats as well as cargo tankers squeezing into the pinched Israeli territory of Eilat. As I floated above rainbows of tiny fish and extravagant sea anemones, I was filled with an impulse to swim away, to keep on going until I crossed the invisible sea border with Saudi Arabia. I imagined transforming into a fish and darting across the Red Sea to Egypt, swimming down to Dahab's snorkelling resorts, nipping back up to the Eilat across the bay.

After hauling myself back out and on to the beach, I sat in silence with G.C., at the hour when the afternoon light starts to soften and carry the first hint of evening, feeling I should have been more celebratory of our journey so far instead of fretting about border constraints blocking further movement.

'We could still drive a bit further,' he said, articulating what was in my mind again. 'The road runs on south towards Saudi for a few kilometres more.'

'Let's go now,' I shouted in delight.

*

Mondialita was so hot that it hurt to touch her. We got on gingerly and drove south as far as we could, until the border with Saudi Arabia stopped us: here was the end of the road that lay open to us on our own terms. Desert stretched for thousands of miles into a peninsula as vast as the whole of India. The sea was on our right, shining as the sun descended towards evening. The only signs of humanity were the road, the watchtowers, the lonely, sun-bleached signs indicating the border. They seemed ridiculous somehow, fragile attempts to put a mark on immensity.

'We should build a fire,' I said, suddenly filled with enthusiasm for the idea, 'to mark the end. As a thank you, or maybe as an offering.'

'We'd get arrested,' said G.C. laconically, pointing out the security cameras. 'And anyway, this is just another beginning.'

Part Two

FREE TO LEAVE

5

Monsoon and mountains

Pakistan, Xinjiang, Tibet

Our plane arrived in Pakistan through a storm. Lightning flashed in the air around us as we landed in Islamabad, and two tiny boys in the seats next to us screamed in well-attuned high pitch. The weather added drama to the surreal feeling of stepping off a plane on to Pakistani soil, knowing in my body the distances and time it would have taken us to get here overland on Mondialita.

The feeling of unreality grew when we were greeted off the plane by our Scottish friend Ali, a cheery man who had been working in Pakistan for a few years. He took us to his house and made us cups of British tea with milk, then took us to the British Club where the first thing past the door was a portrait of the Queen, hung above some cricket bats. This enclave was the one place in Islamabad where you could buy alcohol and pork: bacon rolls were the first item on the menu. We drank gin and tonic by the pool surrounded by people whose skin ranged from milk-white to purple-pink, and talked about Mondialita. She seemed to me the only solid thing in this bizarre tableau of Britishness abroad. She had been delayed in

Dubai for some reason, and we were not sure when she would arrive or what we needed to do to get her through customs.

'Don't worry,' said Ali, grinning, 'I know a guy who can sort it all out. Let me take you around town while you wait.'

Islamabad is built in grids and squares, identified by numbers and letters, such as F7/4 or G6. Traffic was on the left, another strangeness after five months of driving on the right. I could not quite believe that I could sit back and be driven about without needing to be hyperalert to the infinite hazards surrounding us. I could just watch the buzzing swarms of small mopeds, the people driving with helmets but without any other protective clothes, often with only sandals on their feet, salwar kameez like coloured flags in the wind. Mini Suzuki cars functioned as taxis, with fringes of fabric entirely covering the back window and a variety of tassels and beads dangling in the front. Bunches of cubes swung clicking into the wind-screen, each face inscribed with one of the ninety-nine names of Allah. All the trucks were exuberantly decorated with panels of concentric flowers and amazing flourishes of calligraphy. The fronts and sides of the cabins were embellished with carved borders in what seemed to me all the colours in the known universe; the back and front bumpers had dangling metal tassels that jingled over the many bumps in the roads. I immediately started imagining Mondialita decorated like that, before reluctantly agreeing with G.C. that it would not be the safest option for driving.

Ali did indeed know a guy. Getting Mondialita out would take less than a week, and not too much cash from our Bribery Fund. We celebrated by going to Aabpara market in the early morning, to avoid the fierce heat and stock up on repair tools: the number of holes and bumps in the road spoke to us of many repairs and Technical Interludes ahead. There was also the small detail of needing to find a whole new battery to fit Mondialita, because Horizon Freight had been unable to transport the old one due to 'risks'. We found what we needed, but the men in the stalls would only talk to G.C. When I addressed them, they stared past me, or a little to the side of me, or looked at G.C. as if I was not there and he was the one speaking. After a few of these exchanges, I began to feel like a ghost. An angry ghost. This had never happened so far. Was it because I was speaking English rather than Urdu? But so was G.C. I was wearing a long-sleeved salwar kameez, with a dupatta over my head like other women I had seen in the streets of Islamabad. Glancing around, I suddenly realised that there were no other women visible.

G.C. gathered up our last purchases, thanked the seller, and we returned to Ali's house as the heat grew. Afterwards we read in the news that the Aabpara market was next to the Lal Masjid, the Red Mosque, where lots of activists met to preach and agitate for the government to enforce stricter versions of Islamic sharia law. They had thrown acid at a Pakistani woman because she was wearing short sleeves, and they had recently kidnapped some plainclothes policemen, demanding the release of some activists arrested at the Lal Masjid in exchange for the policemen's freedom. The newspaper said that the government had just complied.

The table in Ali's kitchen was covered in maps opened out to show the route we might have – could have – taken in a parallel journey: east past Ankara, skirting the southern side of Lake Van, across the border into Iran, turning to go south-east between the Caspian Sea and the Persian Gulf for thousands of kilometres, keeping south of Afghanistan to arrive at Pakistan's western borders. All the names, all the places that were now a past history of possibility, to be visited only through imagination and the accounts of others. I sighed.

'But look!' said Ali, with a gesture that seemed to sweep up all the other parts of the map and hand them to us. 'See how close we are to the mountains here! And see all the other roads! Who knows what you'll find next!'

The consolations of maps are many. Today they brought us the next plan: to try out Mondialita on a relatively short drive, going to visit Peshawar, the closest we would probably get to Afghanistan and some of the many roads not followed.

Mondialita, newly released from customs and fitted with her new battery, was a welcome and familiar weight underneath me as we headed out into the most chaotic and pockmarked roads we had yet driven on.

'I bet it'll be worse in India,' G.C. said cheerily, as Mondialita narrowly missed being shunted off the road by a blaring, jangling, technicolour monster of a truck.

The heat was another hazard that I had not considered: not the dry oven-air of the deserts we had crossed, but a humid, stifling heat which made steady rivulets of sweat seep under my motorbike gear and into my eyes. I could see why none of the many people on mopeds and motorbikes wore heavy protective clothing.

The old city of Peshawar was a pattern of narrow alleys full of ornate buildings. We escaped the heat into a restaurant with a slightly worrying armed guard at the door. The walls were decorated with stuffed animals hunted in the Khyber hills, nailed and Sellotaped to wooden boards. One bore the caption '*WOODCOCK: now a rare game bird*'. The restaurant owner was called Rusul and insisted that we were not allowed to pay for the many cups of sweet tea he brought us.

'There have been troubles in this time past,' he said, with a flick of his eyes towards the guard at the door. 'It is good to be welcoming guests again.' Rusul told us that Hindu people had lived in many of the old buildings nearby, before the Partition of India and Pakistan in 1947. He was keen to know where we were from; by now we had worked out that it was much wiser to say Italy than Scotland here, because of the bad taste left by British imperial policies.

People were flamboyantly friendly to us as we walked in the old town – men and boys, that is. The shop owners smiled and waved, and from a shop selling rainbow-coloured pasta shapes came a flock of wee boys who followed us laughing, shouting, 'Pasta pizza pasta pizza!' as I grinned back at them. G.C. stayed silent, watchful. The few women out in the streets wore full burqas, which according to Ali have been a part of Pathan culture for centuries. I thought back to Palmyra and the rock cuttings of noble women veiled.

We tried to go up to the Khyber Pass, which was normally possible with an army escort, but were turned back from the border with the Khyber Agency area because it was 'unsafe for foreigners'. There had been anti-government, pro-Taliban demonstrations in the area recently, and 'just now the Khyber Pass for you is technically possible but could not be recommended'. We were allowed to take 'just only one' photo of the Khyber Agency border, the furthest we could go: more jingly painted trucks, bringing in goods from Afghanistan.

139

At a market nearby, we could have bought all sorts of American goods: combat fatigues, army rucksacks, night-vision goggles, American army food rations. Later Ali told us that it was known locally as the 'Smuggler's Bazaar'. On the road back to Peshawar, we drove past the wrecked remains of one of the massive refugee camps that were built around Peshawar after the Soviet invasion of Afghanistan in 1979. It had been levelled by the Pakistani army a couple of months before, in an effort to get pro-Taliban elements out of the country, and also as part of their contribution to the 'War on Terror'. We were told that the Taliban were born in these camps, armed and trained by Pakistan and the USA, to be sent back into Afghanistan as a counter to the Soviets. Some people were still living in shacks by the ruined camp.

Mondialita took us back to Islamabad along the Grand Trunk Road, first built by the Mughals, then renewed by the British when this was all 'British India'. Before 1947, we could have gone from Peshawar to Calcutta without being stopped by any borders. We stopped at Taxila, an archaeological site between Attock Fort on the Indus and Islamabad, which had been occupied by various Indus civilisations over millennia. A panel told us that this area was lived in by Bactrian Greeks who had entered central Asia with Alexander the Great (about 300 BCE), stayed there intermarrying with locals, and eventually built up an empire which invaded the Indus Valley 400 years later, in the second century CE. The Greeks had by then adopted Buddhism, but kept some of their old artistic traditions: I was amazed to see wonderfully hybrid Buddhist stupas with Greek Corinthian capitals on them, and a second-century CE sculpture of the Fasting Buddha complete with sunken eyes and straggly armpit hair.

We got back to Ali's house in Islamabad in the early afternoon, when walking outside felt like moving through a cave full of fire and steam. Every part of my body slowed down, heavy, expanded, stultified. It was so hot that the water in the cold taps at Ali's house came out scalding. The next day the monsoon arrived, like a period overdue, a great release of warm liquid rushing down. I ran outside screaming in delight, to the amusement of the more restrained Scotsmen Ali and G.C. Never had I felt rain like this: an abandonment of any measure, a warm waterfall pouring out of the sky.

The elation evaporated as soon as I splashed back inside and realised that G.C. was concerned: while I had been losing myself in the monsoon, he had been thinking ahead, and worked out that we had spectacularly mistimed our arrival to coincide with terrible weather for motorbikes. Driving Mondialita through this sort of rain was impossible; we tried, and didn't last five minutes. Once more, we would have to modify our plans and adapt to change. We had flown from Jordan to Pakistan, from desert to mountains, and met the monsoon: another limit to movement, nature-sent; or maybe another freedom to decide a new way.

Many of my female friends, like myself, have reconfigured their work; found new ways to cope with the suddenly exorbitant demands on their brains, time and affections imposed by pandemic lockdown. This mostly seems to involve reducing the amount of time spent on work that is socially recognised and paid, while taking on more of the emotional labour of caring for family.

I watch this happen and see, as clearly as if they were lines drawn on a map, the paths leading from past choices to our present situations: the route goes from Having Babies, surviving the swamps of Unequal Parental Leave, through Years Off Work to care for children, over the treacherous mountains of Part-Time Work, across the desert of Lower Average Earnings Than Men, reaching the enclosed city of Pandemic Impact on Working Mothers.

That evening we sat again with maps and redrew our plans. The monsoon ruled out Pakistan and India for the next couple of months, but looking north, we saw the vastness of China beckoning. We quickly discovered that the Chinese government would not allow us to travel with our own vehicle unless we agreed to pay for a government 'guide' who would accompany us at all times.

'That means government spy, believe me,' said Ali with great assurance. We did believe him, and rapidly worked out that we could not afford the extra cost of paying for a 'guide' (for more than a week, anyway). Ali offered to keep Mondialita safe for us in Islamabad until we returned: we were free to leave Pakistan and return thanks to our multiple-entry visa from Ankara. With much gratitude, we accepted Ali's offer, and began to prepare for this unexpected new adventure: overland travel on public transport, up the Karakoram Highway and through the Hindu Kush into China.

Mondialita looked diminished without all our luggage. I hated leaving her in Ali's garage, even if I knew she would be safe.

I shrugged: what else could we do? The weight of my faithful red travelling rucksack felt both familiar and unusual on my back. We said goodbye to Mondialita, thanked Ali, and splashed our way to the bus station. For the next while we would depend on public transport, free from Chinese government 'guides' but tied to other people's timetables and vehicles.

The journey to China was not a gentle reintroduction to public transport. The bus from Islamabad to Gilgit took eighteen hours, immediately followed by another one from Gilgit to Sost. The map showed that we were crawling through the very top part of Pakistan, towards a mash-up of mountains and borders. My body felt mashed up too, from the hours of sitting braced against the seat of buses driven at unbelievable speeds by drivers who were unfailingly welcoming and seemingly impervious to the deafening music they imposed on their passengers.

G.C. moaned: 'I *really* hate buses. They're malevolently designed to numb, paralyse and then torture my legs.'

'Just as well we didn't decide to reach New Zealand on public transport, then,' I replied cheerily.

'Easy for you to say,' he retorted, 'you're small and bendy and can sleep anywhere.'

The landscape surrounding the Karakoram Highway filled me with awe, hour after hour. It commanded my eyes to keep looking, even though I did not find it beautiful as much as intimidating, compelling and constantly astonishing in its magnificence of scale and colours. In the Hunza Valley, green fields and trees trickled down gravel landslide slopes, following irrigation canals. We wound round the valleys following different rivers: the Indus, the Hunza, the Gilgit. We crossed an impressive Chinese-built bridge, a cement leap between slopes. Some waters were grey-white with sleek banks of silver-grey sand; others flowed deep blue but lost their colour after pouring into larger rivers. White foam curled in the rapids. We followed a precarity of tarmac, cut through rock above distant streams, mountains rising above us. From Abbotabad to Gilgit the road was narrow and the landscape steep, enclosed, so harsh it seemed impossible to scratch a living there.

As we left the plains and rose up into the Hindu Kush, I saw fewer and fewer women outside. Those I did see showed progressively smaller areas of skin, until the only female figures visible were covered in burqas. I felt undressed in my long salwar kameez and dupatta, garishly coloured, far too visible. The places where the buses stopped in the high mountains were villages which, according to a Pakistani colleague of Ali's, had been caught up in conflicts between tribes or families for centuries. I got out of the bus in Besham and walked about, stretching my body after days of travel and slowly realising that I felt hated. There were no women out, not even covered in burqas as I had seen in other villages along the highway. Young boys followed me in silence; men stared and looked with utter disapproval. Many of them wore Afghan Chitral hats and had big, full beards. I saw features so sharp that they seemed carved, with red hair and green or blue eyes. I tried not to stare as I was being stared at.

Cutting through the mountains we saw bad earthquake damage. Hundreds of NGO signs stood by the roads beside bright new roofs that seemed made of aluminium, bright in the thinning air. Many Red Cross signs were scattered across the buildings, and I saw a 'literacy and skills development' NGO sign. All writing was in French and English; no signs had an Urdu translation. The road went on up to Pattan, through a gorge so narrow that I thought we would die with every turn. The bus driver went racing and screeching around the bends, beeping with four or five different tones at everything from herds of goats to the hundreds of beautifully painted trucks we encountered. G.C. looked queasy and awed at the same time, gazing at the mist-wreathed mountains and whispering, 'I've never seen anywhere like this, not even the Patagonian Andes.' We held hands, secretly, under a fold of my dupatta.

The Pakistani side of the border had a computerised system with three terminals. There were three border officials in the room, two of them older men with impressively florid moustaches. They all sat around one computer, the two older ones reading out numbers from our passports one digit at a time while the junior official typed on a keyboard with one index finger. We were waved through with hardly a glance up.

It was snowing as we approached the Khunjerab Pass into Chinese territory. In the cold grey landscape, we saw marmots, yaks, huge dogs that looked like wolves, and Bactrian camels. The bus had ascended quite quickly, and at one stop I walked out to take pictures of the yaks for my brother and was immediately short of breath: there was not much oxygen at that height for my unaccustomed plain-dwelling lungs. The steam-cave heat of Islamabad seemed like another world. We found shelter from the snow in a hotel where everything was made in China; more and more signs were in Chinese and Urdu, but not English.

The Chinese border guards were efficient and silent. With

a shock, I realised that two of them were women, hair pulled back tight under their green caps. Most of the people crossing were Pakistani and Chinese traders; the only people from elsewhere were us and another lone backpacker. Here too the youngest guard was given the job of dealing with us. He looked about fourteen. Politely, briskly and slightly apologetically, he emptied out the entire contents of G.C.'s rucksack, checking each item in silence and passing it with a nod. He stopped at our small packets of rehydration solution and shook one suspiciously. He opened it: white powder. His eyebrows rose. G.C. had to keep a straight face while he mimed stomach cramps, diarrhoea, drinking medicine and recovery as the young guard went increasingly scarlet, his colleagues and I bent over with laughter. My bag was hastily passed back to me without being opened, saving me from having to explain 'contraceptive pills' through miming. The backpacker behind us was not so lucky: his rucksack got the full treatment, and we hurried away to find our bus as the young Chinese guard questioningly lifted up a packet of condoms.

The bus stopped at the small town of Tashkurgan, still up at about 3,000 metres; from there we caught a taxi to Kashgar together with an Uzbek man. The Turkic languages seemed to be closely related all the way from Istanbul: the Uzbek man was able to chat to some nomadic herders we met when we stopped for a break. They were herding a type of high-altitude hairy cow they called a *katash*, which reminded me of Highland cows. There were Kyrgyz tombs behind them that had little domes on top. Further on there were Tajik graveyards with little replicas of horse saddles on the top of the tombs

146

instead of domes. This region was called Xinjiang, our taxi companion told us, which meant 'Western Province' in Mandarin. Kazakhs, Tajiks, Kyrgyz and Uighurs all had traditionally travelled over this land as nomadic herders, although China has stabilised and defined the borders. I tried to get my head around the fact that five countries almost met here: Afghanistan, Pakistan, Kyrgyzstan, Tajikistan and China. The scale was so much vaster than the borders between the tiny countries of Europe.

It took us seven hours to drive from Tashkurgan to Kashgar, and we passed hardly any settlements. The landscape's enormity made all my words spiral away into distance. Our taxi driver also spoke a Turkic language, it turned out. He said that he was an Uighur, the main ethnic group living in this province. He told us that the Uighur people lived here for a long time before the land became part of China, that they are Muslim and speak a Turkic language using Arabic script. As he drove us along, he spoke about some of the current political realities of life for Uighur people in Xinjiang. He felt that the culture and religion of the Uighurs were very much under threat by increasing domination by the Han Chinese – the ethnic group from the east, which makes up about ninety per cent of China's population. We heard stories of overt favouritism towards Han settlers, rural Uighurs becoming so disadvantaged that they left en masse to cities, young men under sixteen forbidden from going to the mosque.

Kashgar was a vibrant, busy, diverse city. People seemed to wear whatever they liked, which was a great relief after the disapproval of Pakistan's mountain valleys: in an initial burst of gladness, I spent a while counting how many women's knees and elbows I could see, but gave up because there were so many. It was very warm, with a dry desert heat. We drank cold beer in outdoor restaurants looking on to squares where children played in fountains. For our first breakfast in Kashgar, I tried my luck and asked for bread, butter and honey. These were all brought out – with chopsticks. And so I brought much hilarity to everyone by trying to use these as knives for spreading. The next day we tried the local version of breakfast: buckets of green tea and spicy noodles. I felt slightly queasy as we headed for the Sunday market.

Once one of the major staging posts of the ancient Silk Road, Kashgar's old town still heaved with people from eastern China, all over central Asia, and down into the Indian subcontinent. Many of the houses were built of mud, piled close to each other in looping alleyways, with keyhole doorways and horseshoe arches reminding me of the Uighur culture's Islamic heritage. Large sections of the old town were being knocked down to make way for new, shiny apartment blocks and shopping malls. Mao Tse-Tung presided over the great People's Square. The main mosque had a sign in English telling how the Chinese people love diversity in faith and ethnicity, and their respect of the Uighurs proves it. A Han tour guide kicked aside Uighur men as they prayed to make way for some tourists – a group of loud Italians, walking in a cloud of shouting and aftershave. I walked away from them fast, towards internal gardens with pools and people praying among groves of trees.

Many Uighur women had teeth capped in gold and a black mono-brow painted on for extra beauty. They wore gloriously coloured dresses, covered in sequins that caught the sunshine. Men wore little caps that reminded me a bit of the Ottoman fez. We saw many children wearing beautiful sparkly wee hats. Everyone munched watermelon through the heat. There were snakes for sale as food, and flayed lizards stacked on to sticks; whole stalls for dehydrated reptiles and assorted condiments transported by bicycle. It was also apricot season, so we stocked up on bags of tiny juicy fruits. Rows of little donkeys waited for their low-sided wooden carts to be loaded with Uighur bread, which seemed to me a bit like a pizza base crossed with Pakistani naan bread. It was refired after baking, making it very hard and charred at the edges; the seller told us it lasted for ages on long journeys.

We needed plenty of it for the next stage of our plan, which was to follow the southern Silk Road around the edge of the Taklamakan Desert and then across it. Armed with bags of apricots and charred bread, we left Kashgar, reluctantly, and headed for the desert. G.C. was in the mood for geographical facts and cheerily told me that the Taklamakan was bigger than the whole of Italy, and that the name was said to mean 'he who goes in doesn't come out'. It seemed to me that the Chinese road builders had other ideas: the trans-desert highway was a marvel of engineering. The discovery of oil fields under the sand had funded a smooth tarmac motorway right across the desert, planted with reeds all along the edges of the road to try and prevent sand from drifting on to it. Climate change was causing a lot of problems in the region, with sandstorms that a couple of decades ago happened only once every few years now happening regularly. The desert was growing. I read that people of this region had developed ingenious ways of bringing meltwater from the mountains down to irrigate their plains before the streams evaporated or emptied into salt lakes: over 2,000 years ago they started digging tunnels, water conduits *under* the desert, similar to the irrigation systems used in Iran and Afghanistan. My eyes delighted in the wonder of travelling along in the desert and suddenly coming across a rich vine grove, entirely supplied by water that had got there thanks to human ingenuity.

We sat on a bus for twenty-two hours, driving to Turpan through a succession of desert towns. The driver treated us to about seven hours of Uighur karaoke videos with loving close-ups of sheep and young twirling girls in yellow dresses, before moving on to kung fu movies at full volume. G.C. groaned at the sounds. He had an upset stomach and rushed off the bus at every stop, climbing back on with dire ratings of the facilities along the road. I had my period, and wished I'd carried on taking the contraceptive pill without a break, to stop me bleeding – but I didn't know how long it would be before I could get more supplies, and I really did not want to get pregnant on this journey. G.C. and I traded toilet horrors. I won, with a latrine featuring a bamboo frame suspended above an open pit. Other menstruating women squatted, dripping, as rats scurried underneath us.

Just as the videos stopped and G.C. closed his eyes, a huge sandstorm blew up. The sky went dark, and in the dust-dimmed streets of towns we saw sun awnings blow away and, once, a child lifted up and hurled against some railings. The bus crept on across the desert highway like a dying beetle until we found rest and healing in Turpan, a beautiful old Uighur town with a 250-year-old mosque built out of earthen bricks. An old man outside it welcomed us in Arabic with the Muslim greeting, *Peace be with you.* When I responded in kind, he beamed with delight, befriended us and took us on a tour. The minaret was decorated with intricate patterns in the brick-work, apparently very similar to many of the mosques in Afghanistan. Inside, the whole prayer hall was decked in wood, and sunlight fell in shafts from the small skylights in the roof. The Uighurs worshipping there invited us in, welcoming us, saying, 'You no Chinese people – very good.'

Outside the mosque we saw a little girl selling sheep offal wrapped up in stomachs.

'Uighur haggis,' said G.C., grinning. I rolled my eyes, smiling back. Opposite was a stall with one of the new James Bond movies playing, dubbed into Chinese. In Turpan we also met an Irishman called Enda who rode an expensive BMW GS. He was on an organised tour of Asia with another nineteen people; they were driving from Istanbul to Xi'an in seven weeks, spending more than our entire budget for eighteen months. I missed Mondialita, and the freedom she gave.

More buses slowly took us away from Xinjiang towards the city of Golmud, a city on the Tibetan Plateau where we planned to get a train to Lhasa. We stopped on the way at Dun Huang, on the edge of the Gobi Desert, to see the greatest repository of Buddhist art in the world – all carved and painted on to the walls of the Mogao Caves. I walked into the first cave, saw a decorated sash of colour above our heads on the far wall, and thought it was a simple fresco – until I stepped further in and it became the hem of a massive sitting Buddha's robe. My neck prickled. His feet, level with my head, were enormous. I had never seen anything like him before, his huge hands, his chubby, smiling face. Other caves showed a fusion of Indian and Chinese art from the third and fourth centuries. Some statues were in the 'Gandara' style, influenced by classical

Greece, with straight noses and chins. The colours in the Mogao Caves were still vivid – vermillion, turquoise, lapis lazuli from Afghanistan, frescoes of lotus flowers and of honeysuckle, which came from Greece along the Silk Road and is still now important in Chinese medicine. Another massive Buddha reclined, depicted at the moment of entering Nirvana, painted in real gold with a blissful expression on his face. All around him were sculpted people of many different ethnicities paying their respects: a picture of this place as a confluence of cultures, in the days when it was a pilgrimage site on the Silk Route. G.C. commented that the Buddha looked so much more serene and happy than the suffering representations of Christ in churches, bringing another shaking up of the official version of truth I had been raised to believe.

The Scottish summer keeps swelling into more light and colour. By early June, a pattern of homeschooling has become well established, carved into shape by a determination to keep our days from becoming amorphous splodges in a mess of time. G.C. and I insist that the children get up by 8 a.m., are dressed and fed and vaguely clean by 9, after which we enforce half an hour of exercise led by a variety of relentlessly cheerful people who beam encouragement from a screen before P, S and T start their morning of schoolwork. This all makes me feel like a cross between a rousing song from Mary Poppins, and some sort of British colonial envoy insisting that 'one should always shave in the jungle'. By lunchtime the children are through with schoolwork, and lunch is a relief. Afternoons combine our allocated hour of outdoor exercise with the constant push

against requests for extra screen time, although I know that now the only way for the children to play with friends is online. The official version of how we are told we should parent – limited screen time, lots of outdoor time and interactions with other people – is the opposite of this reality.

I am also discovering that the versions of homeschooling I have seen on various websites and blogs are a fiction, a story told through pictures of perfect crafting, home-cooked food, smiling children and happy homemaking mothers. This story tells of women happily staying at home to nourish and educate, but like papier mâché, it doesn't stand up to real pressure or close inspection. Where are all the men? Away earning money to support their families, presumably. In these stories, home-schooling dads are rarer than women driving motorbikes on the Karakoram Highway. What happens if the women don't want to be full-time home educators?

Our long-established pattern means that, in a normal week, I am on parenting duty for three days and G.C. for two. This shared driving, as it were, has kept us all sane and happy for years. But these are not normal weeks: now I can't leave the house, and he can, and I can't focus on my work, because even if I am Officially Busy, the children still come to me when they need something found; they call for me automatically, look for me rather than G.C. – because I am the one who is always present. Presence equals availability, in a spiral of distraction and fatigue which leaves me drained of any enthusiasm. At least my funding extension has been granted, for six months: surely by then, this will all be over.

Lots of my female friends are going through the same struggles, only with full-time jobs and male partners who are also working from home full-time. Many of these women feel that *their men are not taking on equal amounts of the domestic and emotional burden of childcare, and after nearly two months of strain, relationships are beginning to break down. They couch their complaints with variations on the theme of 'Well, at least I still have work, and he means well'. But I see through their words, to the emotional cracks widening as the exhausted lines in their faces deepen. We are all appalled at the growing suspicion that always the cards had been stacked to fall this way; the roads on the maps already drawn; the glass ceilings and walls waiting, waiting for us to run up against them in bewilderment.*

'Returning to the 1950s' is a phrase often repeated these days in the news. Whenever I hear it, rage swells up inside me and pushes me to break something, anything: snap a twig, rip up some grass, shred empty loo-roll tubes, crack eggs much harder than necessary. If it is so easy to return to the 1950s, is it not because, on many levels, we never left them? Is this the default setting for the systems we live in, with women riding pillion through their own lives because that is just the way things are? It feels like any widening of horizons was a veneer, fast stripped away by economic necessities to reveal the old, dreaded pattern: most women earn less than men, take on most of the labour of caring and homemaking, find themselves with smaller horizons, options, safeties, pensions, recognition, rewards. The 1950s lurk, leering at us, behind the official story of endless freedoms and possibilities we tell each other and our daughters.

From our hostel room in Golmud we looked out to a solid wall of mountains, the Bayan Har, which seem to form natural fortress walls around Tibet. In Golmud station, I tried out the

Mandarin I had been practising for weeks: 'Please, could I buy two tickets?', with my most polite smile. The woman behind the counter yelled at me in English, shouting that we were foreigners, and we couldn't buy tickets, ever. G.C. and I froze, unsure of what to do. Her boss came over and reluctantly told her that yes, we could buy tickets now for tomorrow. She threw them across to us, scowling.

The train from Golmud to Lhasa left in the dark of early morning. I dozed in my train seat until dawn woke me to amazement: we were on the snow-covered Tibetan Plateau, an enormous landscape, bleak, relentless in its reminder of how tiny my human body was. The land was snow-dusted, thin grass on bare brown, like the colours of the Scottish Highlands in winter. I saw a man with two black dogs and many yellow sheep, some deer in the snow, one eagle. We rolled on for hours without spotting any other sign of human presence. Vast, stark beauty contrasted with areas strewn with industrial sites, where the earth all around was blackened and torn up, pitted with green pools of what looked like toxic chemicals lying under the sky.

The Chinese central government had planned the construction of a railway to Lhasa for years. International experts were consulted for feasibility studies, and they all told China that it was a crazy, impossible plan because the Tibetan Plateau has such extreme landscapes and temperatures. Some of the experts were Swiss, who knew about mountains and snow. The Chinese government went ahead anyway and completed the railway in 2005. It's the highest in the world; there were wee oxygen canisters in the carriages in case of altitude sickness. We passed a lake at nearly 5,000 metres above sea level. A road sometimes ran parallel to the train tracks, tiny against the plains that stretched out to snowy mountains and then cloud. At one point the train stopped in the middle of the Tibetan Plateau, and the silence was huge. Cloud shadows slid over the bleak hills. Blue sky glisked out. Snow blizzards blurred the distance, and herds of wild donkeys and Tibetan antelopes moved on the plains.

Lhasa was ringed with crisp brown mountains. We walked about slowly, slightly out of breath from just walking, 3,600 metres up in the sky. The old part of the city was full of vivid colours and smells. There were stalls selling saffron and burgundy clothes for Tibetan Buddhist monks, set out in the shade of old Tibetan buildings with intricately painted windows in designs of bright blue, red, green and gold. Prayer flags flew their colours everywhere. The air was thin and clear, and the light was so vivid that streets became patchworks of stark light and shadow pools.

Everywhere in the old town Tibetan pilgrims walked, a human swell pulsing clockwise in a sacred *kora* around the heart of the old town – the Jokhang Temple. We walked among them, taking in their strangeness while they stared at us in return. It felt like a very friendly staring. Groups of Tibetan men from Kham, with turquoise and coral beads braided in their hair with red string, sat outside shops wearing soot-blackened sheepskin cloaks turned inside out. Women wore the traditional Tibetan *thanka*: a long dress over a bright shirt, with a colourful, stripey apron on top. They also braided their hair with bright wool and beads. Tibetan babies were carried tied on to their mothers' backs, wearing special trousers that were made with a clever split so that when the baby needed the toilet, it could be quickly held over a handy drain, street corner or hole toilet without taking its clothes off.

Most people held wheels with prayers inscribed on them in Tibetan, whirling them clockwise as they walked, quietly chanting. People would stop to prostrate themselves, often wearing wooden boards on their hands to help with sliding along the pavements. The traditional Tibetan apron protected their legs, though some people wore sports knee guards. We saw people prostrating every five or ten paces, others almost every step. Monks begged, debated and chatted on mobile phones. Different generations all made their clockwise pilgrimages together in glad groups. Young and old threw juniper needles into incense burners as they passed, and a profusion of stalls sold prayer wheels and yak butter for burning in sacred candles. An elderly lady wore a waistcoat with a swastika on it – an ancient symbol used in Tibetan Buddhism. I remembered seeing swastikas in Palmyra, in the Syrian Desert, carved into stones over 2,000 years ago.

The new Chinese part of town was much bigger than the Tibetan centre, with wide streets and new bridges, and looked to be constantly growing. Han Chinese people were given many incentives to settle in Tibet: I had read about tax rebates, exemptions from the one-child policy and cheap housing. The Chinese government claimed that this was in the name of 'developing' Tibet, bringing jobs, economic growth, train lines, and education, among other things. But a Tibetan friend in Edinburgh had told me of the growing concerns that soon Tibetans will be a minority in their own country, and that their culture may soon be swamped by 'Chineseification'.

We came across Chinese supermarket employees going through an early morning motivational dance drill. They all moved perfectly in time, like soldiers, dancing to Chinese pop music and responding in chorus to a manager who inspected them and shouted slogans at them. A huge Chinese food market was an expanse of raw meat and abundant vegetable stalls, pools bubbling with live fish, chickens cooped up alive by the dozen in tiny cages. G.C. looked sadly at the cages and muttered about hygiene practices and the likely spread of a bird flu epidemic. We walked on among Chinese noodle restaurants and a proliferation of hairdressers. Most of these seemed to be brothels, judging by the amount of young Chinese women who ran out and tried to convince G.C. to get his short, straight hair cut 'with extra massage', while ignoring me and my messily growing curls.

We could only stay for a week: any longer meant paying the Chinese government for an extortionate 'special foreigner permit' which we could not afford. Each day we ate breakfast in the same tiny cafe near our hostel, because the waitress there reminded me of my Tibetan friend in Edinburgh – a familiar face belonging to a stranger in this place where so much felt new and unknown. The first morning she brought me tea and I almost spat it out: it was salty, slimy, full of floating fat globules which tasted like rancid butter mixed with Mondialita's sump oil. The waitress laughed so much she had to sit down.

'It is Tibetan tea! We put yak butter in it! But look, here, you can have a foreigner tea, it is OK.' She explained that not much grows at 5,000 metres, certainly not enough grass for milk cows, so people put yak butter in their tea and eat *tsampa* – ground barley mixed in yak butter. I drank my foreigner tea, grateful, and nibbled the *tsampa*. It tasted like raw, nutty flour mixed with grease.

The cafe was on our way to the Potala Palace, a huge, magnificent building of non-symmetrical unity, with red and white portions for the temporal and spiritual rooms within. The whole perimeter of the palace was lined with big prayer wheels, which people turned with their hands as they walked past. The wheels squeaked and trundled gently. Many people prostrated themselves in prayer on the pavement in front of the white wall, worshipping the Dalai Lama even if he was in exile. Behind lay the massive Liberation Square, where a huge monument celebrated how the Chinese People's Army had liberated Tibet in 1950 from the oppressive feudal theocracy represented by the Dalai Lama, thus bringing Tibet into a shiny new era of socialism and democracy.

After a few days the waitress started to sit and talk with us over breakfast if nobody else was in the cafe. One morning she gave us a napkin with a booklet inside, whispering, 'Open it in your room.' It was a Tibetan account of the Chinese Liberation. The booklet stated that during the 'Peaceful Liberation' of Tibet, hundreds of thousands of Tibetans were killed, the Dalai Lama was forced to flee to India and many monasteries were flattened by shelling. After that, in the mid fifties, centrally enforced agricultural reforms made thousands more Tibetans starve because they were forced to grow wheat instead of barley, even if it is too cold for wheat to grow in Tibet. And then during the Cultural Revolution, many more people died, more monasteries were destroyed, and prayer scrolls were burned and used as toilet paper. I could not believe the risk the waitress had taken in giving us this booklet – unimaginably higher than the danger we ran if caught with it. At breakfast the next day, she whispered that people were reluctant to talk about this and other aspects of the Chinese presence because, apparently, there were secret police everywhere, many of whom were Tibetan. Her tone reminded me of what we had heard from the Uighurs in Xinjiang, and of the Mukhabarat in Syria.

She said, 'Keep it, hide it, show other people outside Tibet.'

Inside the Potala Palace was a succession of shrines, each one dripping with gold. The tombs of past Dalai Lamas were extraordinarily lavish, for a faith that professed reincarnation and the impermanence of the body. One was covered in over three tonnes of gold. The Dalai Lama's reception hall was painted in beautiful frescoes, with scarves of white cloth thrown by pilgrims on to the empty throne. A monk by my side wept openly. Many of the Tibetans were prostrating themselves between the groups of Chinese Han tourists, whose leaders shouted over the sounds of incessant prayer. Outside the gates, people made offerings of barley flour and juniper. The whole centre of the city was filled with the wonderful smell of drifting juniper smoke.

At the front of the palace, there was a room where thousands of yak-butter lamps were constantly tended by a throng of dedicated women. All over the temple areas, there were vats of yak butter for refilling the lamps. The ceilings were blackened with centuries of smoke and some of the eighth-century wooden carvings were smeared in the butter too. It made the rooms warm, filled with a smell I had never met before and which made me think of the colour gold.

We would need months to begin to explore and understand Tibet, but reluctantly we booked tickets for an early morning bus to take us on the massive Chinese-built highway to the station where we would get a train east to Xi'an, a mere thirty-six hours away. Turning our bus ticket in my pocket, I watched a tiny, bent old lady as she painfully creaked down to the ground and up again, over and over. A young monk passed by. He had walked the *kora* every day we had been there, prostrating himself every four steps; on his forehead was a round mark, dusty and scratched.

I could see how, to a socialist government bent on modernisation and progress, the Tibetan faith and worship might seem like an oppressive feudal superstition which kept poor people prostrating themselves before golden statues, believing that they were reborn into hardship because of past actions, while powerful monks stayed rich through the doctrine of reincarnation. It could so easily be dismissed as superstition and idol-worshipping, but a Catholic upbringing had taught me the deep importance of ritual as a way of maintaining inner focus. Lhasa felt like a place where peaceful resistance was remade daily by numberless footsteps and genuflections, countless turns of prayer wheels and flickering butter lamps – a peace which was not an abstract concept but a deliberate weaving, a way of living in defiance, a labour to be maintained in the face of decades of Chinese presence and the tensions this brought.

Flowers blaze away in the green lushness outside. My two countries, the UK and Italy, have seen the world's highest reported numbers of people dead from the virus; lockdowns persist across the planet. Close to our house, we wander and discover beaches and woods and walks new to us, and beautiful. Friends in Turin and Milan have been living for over three months with their small children in high apartments through the growing summer heat, restricted from moving more than 500 metres from their

homes without a permit. At first, people sang from their balconies all across Italy, an extravagant display which fizzled into the grinding rituals of survival. Four friends have phoned me to say they are leaving their husbands and trying to work out the logistics of divorcing during a pandemic.

I sing quietly as I make food. The kitchen fills with smells, which my sleep-deprived brain sees also as colours and sounds: olio, basilico, tiramisù. *Swirls of comfort wreath the room:* risotto, biscotti, vino, caffè. *The litany of ingredients and recipes is an incantation which I weave into the days, surrounding us all, marking time and space like a protective ritual. Look, taste, smell: this is real, this is not a façade, this will strengthen and nourish you.*

One day, during an early morning shopping expedition, I come across a shelf full of Italian food in Italian packets, like the ones in the shops back in my other home. For one still second I think I am there, before Scottish voices around me bring me back to reality. I stare at the map drawn on the rice packet: the paddy fields of the land where I grew up, here in my palm. I would give almost anything to be free to leave this place and be there instead. Tears and snot well up and trickle down behind my face mask. A kind woman stops and asks, from a safe distance, 'Are you OK, pet?' I nod, sniffing, moving on quickly so as not to block the shelves.

6

Free to leave

From Wuhan to Beijing and away

It took thirty-six hours to reach Xi'an from Lhasa, and the landscape changed precisely twice. I sat trying to process what I had experienced so far, aware that we had only just skirted the western edges of China. I keep returning to size: it was hard for my European mind to wrap itself around the vast scale of everything here. The book in my bag was *Red Dust* by the artist and writer Ma Jian, which I had picked up in Islamabad. In the early 1980s, Ma Jian left Beijing and headed west towards Tibet. His departure was catalysed by a series of difficulties: disputes with his ex-wife, betrayal from his lover, investigations of his work by the police. Ma Jian's journey lasted three years and filled me with a sense of sweeping change in China and the weight of history over millennia. He told tales of poverty and brutal rulers, as well as the kindness of people who saved his life in many ways. The book also wrote lovingly about the grandeur of China's landscapes which had already so staggered me. I started *Red Dust* looking for guidance for our own journey, but soon saw that it told of a very different journey through China, in another time, starting from the other side of the country – Ma Jian became a travel companion, not a guide, as our train jolted along.

After twelve hours, G.C. and I were both struggling with ongoing altitude headaches, our eyes too tired to focus on anything. The Chinese men around us seemed to have an indefatigable capacity for playing cards, yelling, hawking up great globules of phlegm in their throat and then dribbling them out on to the floor between their knees. I summoned my magical power of sleeping in improbable places, curled up in a ball on my seat, and retreated from the world. G.C., not blessed with a small enough body to curl up in a train seat, horrified me by trying to sleep under the seats, among the spit and rubbish, alongside some Tibetan monks stretched out on the corridor floor. I dreamed of driving Mondialita across the plains of Lombardy and eating lots of ice cream.

In Xi'an I had another shock of scale – our first arrival in 'Han' China, this town in the heartlands of the Yellow River. We walked through crowds of thousands pushing around the train station, out into a massive square full of rain pools and steamy heat. There were pulsating neon lights on huge build-ings, and more 'hairdresser' women running out of shops to offer G.C. a haircut and 'extra massage'. We managed to find a hotel with a phone shop next door so we could call home after a silence of almost a month. The phone shop man snarled at us and spat in disgust at our feet, for reasons I could not understand, before making us pay a lot of money for a few extra seconds. I was too tired to argue. We ate some noodles and passed out for twelve hours.

Like so many, we had come to Xi'an because it is where archaeologists had unearthed the 'Terracotta Warriors', thousands of individual statues of soldiers made 2,200 years ago to guard the tomb of the emperor who first united the northern and southern parts of China. On the way out to the site, we passed an impressive gauntlet of stalls selling terracotta warriors of varying size and fierceness. The real ones were amazingly intricate, and the expression and facial features of each were unique, unlike the stylised statues of Greek heroes and blissful Buddhas we had seen. An expressionless guide told us that the artisans involved in making this incredible monument to one man's megalomania were all killed when the tomb was completed, so that they couldn't give away its secrets.

A melancholy mood seeped into me among the frozen warriors, and I began to question our wisdom in coming to China: driving through the monsoon season in India now seemed like something we should have at least tried. I could find no justification for abandoning Mondialita, no reasonable excuse for throwing ourselves into the dubious enterprise of exploring a country which seemed more vast than any place I had ever visited.

'I mean, look at Xi'an, look at its history, there's so much here, and no way we'll have enough time to see or understand this city, never mind the whole of China . . .'

G.C. listened to my rhetorical crescendo with patience.

'Well,' he said, 'I think you're tired – and,' he reached out to touch my hand before I exploded with indignation, 'we've only just started. Give it a chance.'

The next day, rested and drinking my first coffee in weeks, I found the prospect of travelling further into China less overwhelming. I still felt unmoored, though: helpless without

167

Mondialita, unable to understand what I saw and heard around me, unsure about what threads to follow in our decision about where to go next.

'I miss the sea,' G.C. said apropos of nothing.

'OK, that's it, then,' I replied. 'Let's follow the river to the coast.'

A night-train journey through the forty-degree humid heat of southern China took us to Yichan. We ate hot dumplings from a market stall and looked out on the Yangtze: the longest river in China, the third longest in the world, now no longer a fact from geography books but a presence of muddy rushing noise beneath me. All I could think of was jumping in to cool down. G.C. saw my expression, took my hand, and pulled us away to find a hostel with a shower.

The Yangtze was also famous for its beautiful Three Gorges, and infamous for the Chinese government's massive Three Gorges Dam project: the world's biggest dam, improving navigation and reducing flooding on the Yangtze, able to provide as much electricity as eighteen nuclear power plants. So stated the official version of events – omitting the flooded homes of about two million people, the outrageous expense, the obliteration of the Three Gorges and an entire river's ecology. The Yangtze River dolphin was already extinct. We wanted to see the Three Gorges before they disappeared, so we took a bus around the immense construction site of the Great Dam to a little funicular that took us down to ferries ready to take us on board. It was all being built so that as the great concrete rampart went up, and the water level with it, the docks could also rise.

It was raining, and brown mud poured from the cliffs into the water. The Three Gorges were like the dream of a painting, hanging dark green in mist and refracted light. All this would be gone, with so much damage to the river and the land. The ferry chuntered on, a tiny fleck moving in the river that carried seventy per cent of all China's shipping. We passed boats carrying coal, lorries, fruit, livestock; I saw big passenger cruise boats alongside little *sampan* boats where families lived, collecting and sorting the abundant rubbish that was floating on the muddy river's surface.

After six hours we arrived in what we at first thought might be Wuhan, but turned out to be Jingzhou: a city of five million people not even on our map, on account of being 'too small', according to a man who answered my mangled attempts at Mandarin in a kind voice that made me want to weep with gratitude. He helped us get to a station where we waited for the train to Wuhan, surrounded by a growing crowd of people who stared at us and laughed when I tried to speak to them in Mandarin. They looked on with amused comments as I drew pictures trying to explain our journey. One man came up and touched G.C.'s hairy forearm, with an expression of incredulity on his face.

I was constantly amazed at the efficiency we saw in China, the sense that huge structures and systems were built and maintained for the good of the majority. The vast scale of it all was beyond my brain's capacity to understand. On a train journey I read that during the Great Leap Forward, between 1958 and 1962, up to sixty million people died of starvation. The population of Italy; I could not process it. For many nights afterwards, I dreamed that I walked alone across the Apennines into Italy and found a land devastated, with everyone dead. When I arrived at the gates of my parents' house, carrion crows would rise flapping from the garden, and I would wake up.

There were so many people in cities, so many children, and yet we also moved through immense open landscapes for hours and saw that we had edged forwards only centimetres on the map. My European sense of identity was not used to this. Ideas of individual freedom that had always seemed a given to me, growing up in the ebullience of Italy – like the freedom to leave or dissent or disobey – did not seem to apply here. International news was impossible to access, and we had to be careful what we wrote in emails to friends and family in Europe. Once, in a train station, as I was trying to use my best calm Mandarin to buy tickets from an impassively obstructive woman in uniform, a man suddenly snapped in the middle of the long queues: he yelled and yelled, under the echoing cement ceiling which dwarfed the throngs below, his face contorted by rage and frustration. He was taken away by police immediately. The crowds of people carried on as if nothing had happened, as if nobody had been there.

Mid June, and we are still in lockdown. After a long and worrying silence, I manage to speak with a friend who works in Shanghai as a teacher. She shakes her head at my anxious face and reassures me: 'I'm fine! I feel much safer here than I would in Scotland; they're already talking of vaccines and everyone is really careful. We have to be. If anyone tests positive, they get

an electronic quarantine tag on their wrist, and if they leave their room, it sets off an alarm and neighbourhood security guards come to stop them. Every block has volunteer guards. It's amazing, so organised. Don't worry!'

Now I see how the capillary state control which so confounded my European sensibilities has allowed the Chinese government to achieve effective lockdowns and mass population control in the pandemic. Here in Scotland some football players went to Spain for a weekend of partying without anyone stopping them. The news is full of how a senior advisor to the UK government in London drove hundreds of miles with his family after testing positive for the virus – allegedly to 'test his eyesight', it seems – and was not sacked. China is also in the news due to the persistent theory that the epicentre of this pandemic was a food market in Wuhan, as well as rumours of Uighur people in Xinjiang being deported to forced labour camps.

We got off the train in Wuhan, grateful to be in the right city, and found a hostel not too far from the Yangtze. Despite being still far from the sea, the river was already broad and deep. It was spanned by a huge bridge, very appropriately named the Wuhan Yangtze River Big Bridge; one of the first colossal public monuments built by the Chinese Communists in the 1950s. Now it was choked with cars and fumes, accentuating the contrast between modern Wuhan and ancient buildings like the beautiful Yellow Crane Tower, built as a military lookout tower more than 2,000 years ago.

Our breakfast was noodles and vegetables, bought in one of the many alleyways completely lined with food stalls, where men and women shouted out what sounded like prices and enticements while preparing all sorts of things under our eyes. They chopped vegetables, insects, fish, chicken, bird nests, flippers and fruit into soups. I sat drinking tea made from dried flowers that unfurled from tiny brown balls into amazements of shape and taste. Live scorpions twisted and arched on the sticks which impaled them. Their thrashing stopped in a sudden curl of heat as they were deep-fried for customers. Live bats hung, stunned and twitching, above cages crammed full of squawking chickens. I thought one crate was filled with strange round scaly stones until one moved and I realised it was a pangolin.

Friends had recommended one of Wuhan's special dishes – noodles with peanut sauce – and I tried it for lunch, pronouncing that it tasted like spaghetti with peanut butter. I immediately felt embarrassed at how Italian my tastes remained, even now, after so long. By evening, G.C. and I were exhausted, the heat unbelievably oppressive. We had planned to stay in Wuhan for a few days, but I was not sure how long we could last in the sweltering weather. In our hostel bed, I dreamed again of Mondialita, of finally managing to get her off her centre stand by myself and driving off through cooling rain.

It was endlessly strange to me that I was unable to communicate with the people we met. Most Chinese people laughed in my face when I tried to stumble out a few phrases; in some places the barrier between us was as total as if I had been voiceless. I knew that Chinese was a tonal language, and vowels can be pronounced in four different ways which carry four different meanings. 'Ma', depending on how I said it, could be 'mother', 'hemp', 'horse' or 'scold'. I carried on trying, in the dwindling hope that I was not being atrociously rude to people or their mothers. People sometimes also laughed just at seeing us, in the street or when we walked into restaurants. It was a bit disconcerting, although G.C. always gave them his crinkly smile. We were not sure if the amusement lay in G.C.'s gingery beard, my curly hair, his blue eyes, my freckled face or his hairy forearms. Or something else entirely. Who knew? I developed elaborate ways of recognising symbols for 'restaurant' or 'hotel', navigating signs using lengthy descriptions such as 'the hatstand next to a snowflake on a picnic table' or 'the stick man kicking the photocopier on top of a toaster'.

Xinjiang had seemed so exotic and strange when we were there, but I started to remember it fondly — at least there I could eat bread in some form, I could read the Uighur script and share my love of Arabic with the Muslim people who welcomed us. Since leaving Tibet for Han Chinese regions, I had felt acutely aware of being a foreigner, more than in any other place we had visited, and I had never felt more surrounded by things incomprehensible to me. In the cities, we visited supermarkets that were full of strange packets and unidentifiable foods under oil. I wandered the shelves in Wuhan's huge malls and got lost among mysterious things. I bought what seemed like a sausage but tasted of sugar and strangeness; chocolate raisins that somehow didn't melt in tropical heat. Any bread I found was packaged in plastic and tasted of chemicals.

'Nobody asked us to come here,' G.C. reminded me, happily eating his noodles for breakfast.

'Nobody cares if we live or die!' I retorted, pining for proper coffee.

'Why should they, though?' he answered. Why indeed.

*

G.C. was the one to point out, repeatedly, the things he found generous and interesting. Everywhere in hotels and on trains there were vats of boiling water that people used to top up glass flasks of tea. In cafes and stalls, our cup was always refilled when it was only half empty. At almost every table, there were wee bowls of fresh, raw garlic, which people chewed and swallowed before eating their meal. Women carried babies in cloth slings on their backs; like in Tibet, small children had trousers that opened in the middle, so they could be held out to squat in the streets if they needed to pee or poo. The efficiency of this system never stopped pleasing me. And nowhere did I get harassed or stared at because I was a woman; nowhere did I need to cover parts of my body to avoid opprobrium. G.C.'s blue eyes and hairy tallness attracted more attention than I did.

My chopsticks skills were improving, too, and I no longer slobbered noodles all over the place like a baby. We found one dish which became our staple, because we liked it and could also pronounce it reliably: *hongshao qiezi*, red-fried aubergines, with *mei fan*, white rice. This was our evening meal on our last day in Wuhan, as we planned our onward journey across China's immensity towards the ocean.

The light grows towards midsummer, and with it an amorphous seething inside me. After more than two months of reduced horizons and immensely expanded demands, my inner landscape is losing coherence and shape. There seems to be a barrier between the world and my ability to process it. Time feels formless, and yet I persist with pushing through its swampy jungle, for fear of what might happen if I stop trying. Days are only

loosely demarcated; the weekend means special breakfasts and family sleepovers in the living room. The children's ongoing happiness is my single marker of success: even if I spend all of myself, even if nothing is left, at least the children are OK.

After they fall asleep, I turn to the Odyssey again, this time because I want to listen out for the story of Penelope. While Odysseus fought, won and wandered, she waited at home in Ithaca with their son, who was a grown man by the time her husband returned. What did she think of over those decades of separation? I read about how she was cunning like Odysseus: not fooled by the many suitors who sought her hand, assuming she must be a widow as the years passed, but instead tricking them into fruitless waiting by promising to choose a new husband when she has finished weaving a tapestry which she unpicks by night. She is famous as a paragon of wise wifely fidelity, a metaphor for faithful waiting. This version of her I find boring, irritating and difficult to believe, but the Odyssey doesn't tell us much about her inner world. Did she ever feel lost, despairing, angry? Did she ever feel that she was unravelling along with her weaving?

A friend's son is born, one of many pandemic babies. His arrival propels us all towards joy and new life, like a springtime fully unfurled in the space of hours rather than months. I walk in the woods as I wait for news. The flowers surrounding me seem impossibly beautiful, like jewels in the clear light. I send photos of them to my friend, message-pictures like talismans as he paces outside the hospital where his partner labours without him: a rainbow of May blossom, California poppies, wild borage, pink campion, forget-me-not.

Images of China reeled through my mind as I held G.C.'s hand in Hong Kong. We stood by the ocean, silenced and replete with stories, after a concatenation of journeys which had taken us over hills covered in subtropical jungle, past vastnesses of terraced rice fields, through groves of rubber trees whose sap smelled like fish, into cities where old buildings survived, squatted here and there at the feet of the huge new ones that rose up like glitzy giants, out into landscapes of conical hills and sudden gorges, across rivers swollen and heavy with brown silt, until the last train spat us out here. We had made it, together, from the North Atlantic to the shores of the South China Sea.

Just a few days in Hong Kong had been enough for us. Its profusion of skyscrapers had caught me unprepared: an astonishment of soaring glass and steel surfaces reflected each other up into the sky, vying to find the most bizarre architectural variations on the skyscraper theme. One looked like the Tower of Sauron, one had round porthole windows, another had a slanting top like a knife. As the daylight faded, the buildings blinked on their neon and the lights competed in brightness, designs, size and shifting colours. Everything was suddenly too expensive for us. In Kowloon we were accosted by an Indian man who ran one of the many cheap hostels in Chungking Mansions: a huge block of seventeen floors, grey cement stained with damp. AC units dripped above basement shops selling drinks, cheap clothes, random tourist tat, porn magazines and pink dildos. There were only two lifts for the entire building and a permanent queue of people waiting to use them. We stayed for a few nights in a room hardly bigger than the sweaty single bed that filled it, with a ceiling lower than my height. Bright neon signs were strung across the road, so by night it was bright as day.

We joined the shoals of people navigating the streets, noticing the sudden presence of European languages around us for the first time in over two months. We saw black fungi for sale that looked like fossilised ammonites, and swallows' nests for making soup and medicine. At the back of the shops, people sat around a table piled high with grey-black nests covered in feathers, cutting off the best parts and passing them on to men who picked out smaller bits of dirt with tweezers. Coiled, barbed, dried deer penises seemed to be in high demand. We found an Irish pub where we spent a day's food allowance on cold draft beer and chips. The sweltering alleyways, tired cement buildings, sagging wires, rubbish bags, sewage smells – all this felt far removed from the cool, clean world of the malls and luxury skyscrapers towering above us.

There were remnants of British Empire everywhere in Hong Kong: double-decker buses, red pillar postboxes, traffic suddenly driving on the left. Many streets had names like Edinburgh Place, Sutherland Avenue and Queen Street. Old colonial buildings squatted among the forest of skyscrapers – the old courthouse, the old western market building, St John's cathedral, incongruously whitewashed and gabled, built in the mid nineteenth century and the second-oldest building left standing in Hong Kong. Wooden pews and chairs welcomed us inside under whirling ceiling fans. Leaflets about the church's history explained Christianity as a religion 'started 2,000 years ago by Jesus who lived in Palestine, an obscure country which was then part of the Roman Empire'.

Chinese temples curled their green roofs among jungly trees. Inside, through air foggy with incense, I saw statues of deities and red cloth hangings covered in beautiful calligraphy. Huge pyramid coils of incense hung from the roof porches too, sometimes with special plates under them to catch the falling ashes. The religion of much of China seemed to be a synthesis of Buddhism, Confucianism, Taoism, and reverence for ancestors. These temples were no exception. But the true religion of Hong Kong was the making and spending of money. Few spaces, other than churches and temples, were free of adverts.

Escaping on a boat across the Pearl River estuary, we reached another ex-colony: Macao, granted to Portugal as a trading concession from China in 1557. For hours we wandered the hot narrow streets of the old town, and stumbled across a beautiful old temple to A-Ma, the Cantonese goddess of the sea. Supposedly the name 'Macao' comes from her name: when the Portugese arrived, they found a temple to A-Ma on this site and when they asked the name of the island, they were told 'A-Ma Gau' – the Place of A-Ma. Offerings to the sea goddess had to be underwater: at one altar, under hanging coils of incense, a plastic bowl of water had been filled with flowers and coins. Not far away, in a Catholic church, the statue of a blonde Caucasian Mary, the 'Queen of the Air', stood with money offerings at her feet. Street corners and shops sheltered shrines, where people made offerings of incense, fresh flowers and fruit.

We walked past baroque Catholic churches and seventeenth-century buildings so similar to ones I knew in Italy that I was suddenly in tears of grateful, homesick relief.

'I'm fine,' I sniffed to a concerned G.C., 'I just didn't realise how much I'd been missing Italy.'

'I did,' he answered gently. 'It's OK. Let's see if we can find some food.'

Around the corner, a tiny Portuguese restaurant awaited us

like a desire revealed. Its equally diminutive owner told us that it had been in his family for 'two hundred years! At least! Yes!' He brought us crusty bread, white wine, olives (OLIVES!), fish from the South China Sea cooked according to a 'secret family Portuguese' recipe, and freshly made coffee in tiny cups. My joy felt outrageous: what was I doing, travelling across the world, if all I wanted was the food and buildings of home?

'I think you're right,' I admitted to G.C. 'I've missed home a lot. Not just Italy and Scotland – I mean home as in Europe, feeling like I know what's going on around me, where I don't think about leaving all the time.' It felt like confessing a secret, hoping that G.C. didn't think less of me for it.

It turned out that he too had been having doubts about our journey: wondering what the point of it was, whether we were just being selfish wandering about China. The desire to travel for the joy of it was shifting into something else; or maybe we were just tired. I was certainly exhausted by the daily realisation of my limitations as a traveller: in China I had reached the limits of my ability to learn new languages, limits to my tolerance of different ways of doing. I had been so proud, so sure of myself, the intrepid linguist explorer, and here I was, almost in tears of joy because of some crusty bread and a coffee. And olives.

'Neither of us has even been to Portugal,' G.C. remarked. This seemed absurd. And from that comment, like a knot that unravels once you find its end, a conversation unspooled, whereby we decided that we would not travel on indefinitely. Our original plans, with the possibility of stopping to work if we wanted to keep going past New Zealand through Latin America and wherever else we fancied – these felt as if they belonged to different people. We now wanted to leave China and head back to Mondialita, work out how much energy and money we had left, somehow make it to New Zealand – and then return home, to Europe.

Walking back to our hostel, we saw a bicycle whose owner was clearly dreaming of one day owning a motorbike as great as Mondialita: it had panniers like motorbike box ones, a BMW symbol and faring fashioned out of cardboard and metal on the front. I couldn't believe it: *an omen! A sign!* G.C. nodded in agreement and smiled.

As the sun went down, we saw what made Macao go round. Beyond the streets of the old town, a horizon of neon lit up, pulsing and strobing: a row of casinos, enormous with luxury hotels and restaurants attached. There was a gigantic round building fashioned like a squat lotus flower with 'petals' in glass and steel, flashing and blinking. A huge pool suddenly started spouting fountains in the middle of a sound and light show, with a high-speed chorus blasted from enormous external loudspeakers: 'Money makes the world go round'. It was like the huge, demented offspring of a Christmas tree and a fireworks display. On the Portuguese fortress walls, a man slowly practised t'ai chi with a fan, silhouetted against the flashing lights.

The summer solstice means that in Scotland the sky is hardly ever dark. In the abundance of light, all the seeds I planted in early spring have become a flourishing. I have watched them, happy in their place, growing and thriving. They don't want to go anywhere; that is not a freedom they need. For eighty days I have not left this place for more than an hour at a stretch, and

my dreams are always of Mondialita: I set off on her, alone, and not long afterwards there is a falling, a skidding, and I watch her go up in flames.

G.C. is away, working for a week in Orkney. His freedom to leave still outrages me. The seething inside me solidifies in the days of his absence, and becomes recognisable: a rage akin to despair, a seeping dullness which has nothing to do with the flaring of anger that lights up the soul like a lantern. In the worst moments – the early morning hours when the children are asleep and another brief summer night edges into dawn – the rage feels like an acid inside me, burning me wider awake with questions.

How did it come to this? From the days of travel as equal companions, from the tent under the Greek olive tree, from that restaurant in Macao – to this broken balance? It came along a path of your own choices, I answer myself; choices which led here, to beloved sleeping children who need looking after, so that G.C.'s freedom to leave means that you have to stay. That's how.

Against whom should I rage? Not my children: they did not choose this. Not G.C., with his strained face and attempts to fix my hurt, which he senses, like a bruising in the air around us, even if he can't understand it. I read and re-read Soraya Chemaly's book Rage Becomes Her, *where she writes of how women's anger so often turns inwards to become depression or a corrosion of the soul. Chemaly calls on women to recognise their rage as legitimate and useful; to embrace it, use it, see that it is not a shameful thing which must be hidden but rather a vehicle for transformation. This seems impossibly hard. I lie awake and berate myself for all the paths I chose, thinking I was doing so freely, ignoring the signs that pointed towards these restricted days. Another season of confinement returns in*

181

memory: the time of three-babies-under-two. That passed because the children grew, their needs changed, our horizons slowly widened. My imagination fails to see a future beyond this present, this tangle of restrictions, resentments and fears.

I make a coffee, giving up on sleep again. A message arrives from a female friend who is also awake, angrily, far too early. She is one of the many women I know who have decided to leave their marriage, joining the growing ranks of pandemic divorces. I hear these women's anger, like an echo handed down across the centuries. What can help me try to feel a way through its dark and sticky mass? Lines from 'St Bride's', a poem by Kathleen Jamie dedicated to her daughter, whisper themselves in my head:

> So this is women's work: folding
> and unfolding, be it linen or a selkie-
> skin tucked behind a rock.

Perhaps I do have a choice now, as this long midsummer unravels. I could fold away the hot tar of my rage and tuck it out of sight – or I could follow Soraya Chemaly's advice and embrace rage as a woman's powerful discovery, unfold it like a mantle which will bring me strength, like a selkie skin that can return me to where I need to be.

Looking out at the dawn-lit sea, I think of the selkie stories, which are so tied to these northern waters. Very often in these tales, the selkie is female – a woman upon the land and a seal in the water – not half of each, but fully both. A man comes across her as she dances on the shore in human form. He secretly takes her sealskin and hides it away, so she is forced to remain a woman. She chooses to marry him, on condition that after a set number of years, he will return her selkie skin so she will be free to leave and go back to her sea home. Babies arrive; he doesn't keep the initial promise; the selkie woman becomes ill from staying away from the sea for too long. Very few versions of the story feature a happy ending for everyone.

Before leaving China, we wanted to visit Beijing, where some old friends were waiting to host us. An overnight train took us to Shanghai, on the mudflats of the Yangtze Delta. Once famous for fast deals, opium dens and gambling, it is now the financial centre of China, where people come to get rich, work all the time and spend their money. A young woman who worked at the hostel we could afford welcomed us, delighted at the chance to practise speaking English.

'Hello! I am Alien!' she said, beaming, coming over to shake our hands very formally. 'This is my English name. I chose it to show I am a friend to aliens! Like you!'

In our hostel, floors thirteen and fourteen were missing because these numbers were believed to bring bad luck. We took the lift to floor 12A instead. The first room was rapidly closed when Alien realised there was no AC. The second had no working key. The third had problems with electric sockets, but we asked to please just have it. Once we had sorted our room, Alien offered us some green tea downstairs and became a well of information. She told us that the land where tall buildings now stood used to be a swamp fifteen years earlier. The architects didn't take into account the buildings' correct weight together with the ground's sponginess, and the city's water consumption has almost emptied the water reservoirs under the ground, so now the buildings are sinking lower every year. This all seemed hilarious to her, like a joke told about somewhere else.

We walked by the shore, watching huge barges transport sand down the river to make cement to fuel the city's building frenzy. I wondered what Shanghai would be like in another fifteen years.

Adam and Marie met us off the train in Beijing. I had first met them in Edinburgh; they were now living here to learn Mandarin because Marie loved China, and Adam loved Marie. Seeing their friendly faces was a gift. They immediately took us out to see the sights, starting in Tiananmen Square – the biggest public square in the world. A combination of square Communist architecture and historic Chinese buildings, it seemed impossibly immense. Under Mao's orders, hundreds of houses had been levelled to make a space worthy of a great nation. Now people walked Pekinese dogs and flew fantastic, elaborate kites under the watchful eyes of police, secret and not-so-secret. Parades of soldiers marched up and down.

Marie explained that *Tian An Men* meant 'Gate of Heavenly Peace', and the ancient gates still standing in odd places around the city marked where the old city walls used to be, before they were demolished in the 1960s to make way for big ring roads. Much of the centre of Beijing was also being knocked down and redeveloped for the impending Olympics, but near the Forbidden City we found a neighbourhood where things were kept looking as traditional as possible, for tourists like us. I found my two all-time favourite signs in the same restaurant, prize examples of mysteries made in translation: 'The temple explodes the chicken cube' on the menu; and 'Mega

Cheerful Business Travels Reserved Flourish of Legend Street Recurring' on the wall.

Huge crowds surged around us on the metro. Amazingly cheap flashing neon toys were sold on every pavement and underpass, as well as lotus flower seed pods to snack on. Even though this was the furthest north we had been in China, it was still hot. Men stood about wearing white vests rolled up to show their stomachs, the better to disperse heat. We cooled down walking around the lake in Bei Hai park, where some early Ming palace buildings were still standing. This was the centre of the city when the Mongols were in charge, and there was a massive jade urn decorated with dragons that was allegedly the only remnant of the court of Kublai Khan.

Adam and Marie were wonderful guides, and I had so many questions to ask. Adam explained how Chinese ideograms express concepts but not necessarily words, so the same ideogram could hugely change meaning depending on context, collocation and what other ideograms are next to it. Marie said that after a year she still felt unsure she could communicate properly in Mandarin, understanding all the shifts and nuances expressed in the language: although the basic constructs were put together without tenses or conjugations, there were so many shades of tone, concept and meaning that advancing past a certain level felt very hard. I felt saddened listening to her, aware of the fact that here I was in Beijing learning about China through the filter of another European.

G.C. sensibly brought the conversation around to travel logistics: we needed to get back to Pakistan before Mondialita's temporary import licence expired. Ali had emailed to say that there had been bomb attacks on the Karakoram Highway: our only real option to make it back in time was to fly.

Adam and Marie took us to the airport, and we sat in an aeroplane for four hours, crossing over the Gobi Desert, back westwards to Urumqi.

G.C. returns tomorrow, in time for our wedding anniversary. My dreams have evolved so that when I start driving Mondialita she suddenly becomes immensely, impossibly heavy; I fall over, her weight crushing my left knee, and she becomes a blue car which I struggle to lift before it catches fire.

A very similar car ran me over, in real life, a few years earlier. I was on my way to pick up the children from school, waiting on my bike at a T-junction just outside our local shop where I had filled my rucksack with their favourite biscuits for snacks, feeling very smug after a day of good work. Hubris? Maybe. Like a chariot driven by a demented goddess, a blue car swung across the T-junction towards me. I yelled, backed off, tripped over my own pedals, landed on my right side with my rucksack under me, and the car drove up on to my left leg. My entire being was charged with a rage unlike anything I had ever felt before. It filled my bones and muscles with fire, with a strength that helped me wrench upwards, bending my left knee sideways at ninety degrees, until I was hammering my fists on the bonnet of the car, screaming, 'HOW DARE YOU!!! THE CHILDREN! THE BISCUITS!!! STOP! STOP!!!'

The mass of metal stopped on top of me. I heard the hand-brake crunch on and felt the car jolt to a standstill: parked, on my knee. I heard feet running and a man yelling, 'You're parked on her leg! For God's sake! Reverse, reverse!' The car lurched. Its blue weight rolled off me on to the road and stopped again.

An old lady got out. She wore red slippers on her feet, and her dark trousers were dusted with short light hairs. Her hair was white and scraggly. Wispy hairs grew out of her chin. Silent, shaking slightly, she stood there. One of the Fates!, *a part of my brain whispered.*

'Let's get you into the surgery, dear,' said one of the GPs who had rushed out of the nearby health centre with a wheelchair.

My rage still coursed strong. I felt like a goddess.

'I can't do that!' I snapped at the doctor. 'The children! I have to phone the school, call a friend to pick them up, tell my husband!' She looked at me in that assessing way GPs have.

'OK. You do that. I'll get this other lady in first.' I saw the red slippers shuffle on to the wheelchair. By the time I had made my phone calls and submitted to being wheeled away by mere mortals, the fire had abandoned my body, and with it all strength. I shook as the doctor cut my trousers open and gently took off my boots. One week later I allowed myself to cry.

I remember that rage power as I make coffee the day of G.C.'s homecoming. How could I channel that again? I turn to Cavafy's 'Ithaka' once more:

> Don't be afraid of the Leistrygonians and the
>   Cyclops,
> or angry Poseidon –
> you'll never find them on your path
> if you keep your thoughts high,
> if a rare excitement touches your soul and your
>   body.
> You won't meet the Leistrygonians and the Cyclops,
> or the wild Poseidon –

not unless you carry them along inside your soul,
not unless your soul places them in front of you.

*My soul has been filled with a wild and monstrous anger which
has become an enemy, corroding me from the inside out. I want
the path of my days to involve rare excitement again instead of
acid rage. The coffee goes cold as I remember all the times when
G.C. and I were equals, comrades in adventure, neither of us ever
left behind; how he took care of me when I was unable to walk
for months after the old lady ran over my leg.*

*When G.C. returns, he is quiet. I am quiet. In the silence he
turns to me, puts his hand on my shoulder and asks, 'Do you
still choose this?'*

We were about to leave China after ten weeks of peregrinations.
In Urumqi airport, we walked around parking lots, looking
for a bus to the city centre. We'd been told it would cost only
one yuan, a few cents. Our flight to Islamabad, to reclaim
Mondialita, wouldn't leave until the following morning. A taxi
stopped, and the driver held up his hand with five fingers.

'Wu?' I asked him. 'Five?' Could he really be charging us
less than one US dollar each to reach the city centre? Yes, he
nodded. Five and five, indicating each of us in turn.

We reached the centre, got out by the hostel that had been
recommended to us, and handed the driver ten yuan. He was
furious and started yelling; G.C. looked at me, shrugged, and
offered a further ten. The driver wouldn't accept it, so we
walked off, but he followed us, still yelling, then he began
pulling at the bags on our backs, and violently seized G.C.'s

shoulder. Something in me snapped almost audibly when I saw his hand on my man. A cataract of rage poured through me, and I stopped thinking. I slapped his hands from G.C.'s shoulder; he kicked me in the leg; I punched him in the face; he punched me in the throat. So I kicked him in the balls.

He collapsed to the ground, groaning. The crowds around us flowed on. No one had tried to intervene. I crumpled up forty yuan and threw it at him.

'I've *had it* with China!' I yelled. G.C. stood back, breathing hard.

'Remind me not to piss you off,' he said.

We dragged our bags to the hostel, but a bouncer on the door wouldn't let us in. Then a man outside the gate tried to take us somewhere else, for a fee, but after the fight with the taxi driver I was suspicious and refused. Despite all our careful budgeting, we were going to have to withdraw more Chinese currency and find a room at one of the expensive, state-backed hotels. But at the state hotel, a receptionist took all our money for a room, then said we needed to give her the same again as a deposit.

'I don't have that. *Mei-yoh-lah,*' I said, repeating back to her one of the phrases that had followed us around China. G.C. showed her both our wallets and pulled out alternative currencies that could stand as a deposit: dollars, sterling, euros.

But she shook her head and pointed first at the two of us, then out of the door, and repeated, 'Go Bank of China.' At this, I picked up all the bank notes from her desk and treated her to a brief discourse on how I'd travelled half the span of the world and lived in many countries, and in my humble opinion, China had, without a doubt, featured the most difficult experiences I had ever come across – an exhausted tirade of which

189

she seemed to care nothing. But it made me feel marginally better. Only when we picked up our bags and walked out the door did she run after us and offer us the room after all.

I lay on the chintzy bed, mulling over the events of the day. Had the taxi driver meant fifty yuan each, not five? Had my attempts at Mandarin numbers confused things? Either way, I knew that we probably could have settled the matter without getting into a fight – but as I thought of him grabbing G.C. and punching my throat, rage filled me again. This vast, complex, beautiful, infuriating country had been the nemesis of any pride I had in my ability to learn new languages and adapt to different cultural norms. I lay, feeling completely empty, staring at the electric sockets in the walls that hadn't been wired to any power supply and the cheap plastic doors of the wardrobe which were screwed shut.

At the check-in queue the next morning, the airline tried to make us pay extra for our ticket; G.C. argued, and they relented. Then we were told our Pakistan visa was expired; I argued, and they let us on the plane. G.C. sat glued to the window, gazing down over our route through the Taklamakan Desert and the mountains which for centuries had been such an effective barrier between different cultures. In minutes we hurtled above the Karakoram, covering hundreds of miles that had taken us days to cross overland. I put my seat back and lay listening to the murmur of Urdu all around me, feeling light with the relief of leaving China.

At the passport desk in Islamabad, an immigration officer with a glossy, trimmed moustache flicked through our passports while I gave what I hoped was a sweet smile. His expression didn't change but, looking straight from the passports to some chairs by the wall, he pointed across and said, 'Sit.' A colleague caught his eye, with an enquiring look.

'No visa,' he said, and looked beyond my sweet smile to the queue behind me. 'No visa, no entry. You will be returned to China. Next!'

7

God laughs at borders

Peshawar, Ladakh, Kashmir

The immigration officer was a kind man. He reassured us: 'Do not be panicking, all will go OK,' and let us phone Ali at the British High Commission. It turned out that the Pakistani embassy in Ankara had falsely said that our visa allowed us to re-enter Pakistan any time within three months of first arriving there. The Islamabad immigration official explained, very courteously: 'You have been misled by my fellow countrymen. I apologise for these scoundrels.' Our visas apparently were only valid for three months after they were *first issued*, way back in Turkey. I nearly cried. Not only were we about to be deported back to China without a valid China visa, just as I thought we'd managed to get out – but we would then be sent back to the UK at our own expense, minus Mondialita, whose import visa for Pakistan was only valid for another week and who would therefore be impounded in our absence.

Ali talked to G.C. and calmed him down; spoke to the kind border official and vouched to him that we were not enemies of any state; and then, somehow, miraculously, we had a landing permit which could be converted to a short-term visa. It meant extra expense that we could hardly afford, on top of the costly original visa which had turned out to be useless, but we had no choice. Border bureaucracy ruled supreme.

Being reunited with Mondialita was like returning home. My muscles immediately slid into familiar movements, a litany of actions: left hand hold down the clutch, right hand press the ignition, left foot find neutral gear then flip into first gear, right hand turn the throttle, left hand release the clutch, and then the moment when everything comes together into the miracle of motion and – in the words of Melissa Holbrook Pierson – it becomes obvious that 'the motorcycle cannot be steered, but it can be willed to follow you'.

I could see that G.C. felt the same. I remembered how the Yamaha manual that had so annoyed me with its caution had also said that 'Motorcycles are fascinating vehicles, which can give you an unsurpassed feeling of power and freedom'.

'Maybe it's ancestral memory,' G.C. said, continuing my thoughts. 'Jumping on to a motorbike and skidding off in a cloud of dust is now the closest most of us can get to galloping on horseback into the sunset.'

'Maybe that's why in Italy motorbike riders are called centaurs,' I said.

'Taking things one step further, as usual,' G.C. said, grinning.

Technical Interlude

Mondialita's front brakes had been dodgy since getting off the plane from Jordan, with the hydraulics losing pressure without leaking fluid. G.C. emailed his uncle Chris in New Zealand, who is a motorbike genius, and he said we had to overhaul the brake master cylinder.

We had never taken one apart before, and were a bit scared of breaking it – but we managed. We were glad not to lose any spring-clips or washers. The rubber seals on the piston of the old brake cylinder were all worn, with a bit broken off at the back, so the hydraulic brake system didn't seal properly and the brake fluid didn't pressurise. Now it worked perfectly again. Mondialita was healed.

It was time for us to head towards the border, as our temporary motorbike import visa was about to expire and we really didn't want any more border hassles. Ali had organised a surprise bonfire in the hills for us with some of his friends, as a goodbye gathering. Islamabad's grids glowed below us to the west. Eastwards, beyond a contested mountain border, lay Jammu and Kashmir, claimed by India.

The Grand Trunk Road swept us towards Lahore, capital of the Punjab before Partition. It was considered the cultural capital of Pakistan, famous for its glittering parties and arts world. We parked Mondialita safely at a hostel and took a taxi through Lahore's crazy, heaving traffic to see what we would find. The taxi driver was a young, smiley and very bearded Afghan Pathan who kept saying, 'Afghanistan, Taliban, Alhamdullilah!', which we took to mean, 'Thanks be to God for the Taliban and Afghanistan!' We told him we were Italian and I spoke to him a little in Arabic, quoting the Qur'an. He was delighted and refused to take any money from us for the drive because we were his guests. His eyes were bright green and full of certainty.

Lahore Fort was slightly dilapidated, but it was once one of the grandest palaces of the great Mughal Empire. In those days, the English and the Portuguese used to shuffle around court hoping for favours from Mughal rulers, long before Europeans started taking over. Just outside the fort complex we found a drain cover made in Kilmarnock, Scotland. As we marvelled over the networks of empire that had brought it there, a man walked over and befriended us by saying, 'Come! You will now taste the best roasted corn in the world!' His name was Rahim, and he was right. He took us to a stall where another man was roasting sweetcorn on what looked like sand but turned out to be hot salt. It was delicious. Rahim insisted on paying, then took us on a tour of his city.

He showed us a golden-white *samadhi* monument to Ranjit Singh, a warrior-king who carved the Sikh Empire out of the Punjab, taking it from Mughal and Afghan warlords in the eighteenth century. The Punjab saw some of the worst violence at the time of Partition, when thousands and thousands of Sikhs, Hindus and Muslims massacred each other as they tried to get to the 'right' side of the newly created border. Rahim said that there are hardly any Sikhs left in Lahore.

'But now! No sadness! You must come to have food with

my family!' And so we did, meeting his wife and their three children, sharing more food, marvelling at each other's different life paths.

The next day we drove to the Wagah border, where a white line between two gates separates Pakistan and India – the border drawn by a British civil servant on a piece of paper decades earlier.

'Do you still choose this?'

G.C.'s question lies heavy between us.

'What is "this"?' I think to myself – this spiky border between us? Marriage? The possibility of joy we might still hold together? The promises we made each other?

We are sitting outside. The children are asleep. I can smell cut grass, the sea, rain coming. Swifts scream through the Simmer Dim. The horizon glows with the greenish blue I have only ever seen in Scotland at midsummer. Its colour transports me to another translucent night sky under which I stumbled away from a deafening club with G.C., minutes away from deciding to travel to New Zealand on a motorbike we didn't have and couldn't drive. Thoughts fill me, flocking like birds, of the many times we have again and again chosen each other and trusted: trusted that borders can be reached across, that each other's freedom to leave is counterbalanced by the desire to stay.

'Yes,' I answer.

The Pakistani and Indian border guards were clearly friends and chatted to each other in Punjabi while they checked our passports and let us take photos of Mondialita by the gate. Our visas were in order! We were free to leave! A Sikh border official on the Indian side showed us a shiny new Harley-Davidson which had been impounded because its owner didn't have the proper temporary import documents, which made us feel smugly virtuous.

We were now in Sikh country, and saw many men with spectacular beards and turbans. Two of them befriended us and talked us through the evening flag-lowering ceremony at the Wagah border, insisting we stay to see the magnificent spectacle. The ceremony happens every day, and apparently it is an excellent opportunity for Indians and Pakistanis to vent nationalist feelings without resorting to violence. The ceremony draws massive crowds on both sides of the border gates.

We watched the Indian flag being paraded up and down by soldiers and any members of the public who wanted to participate. The crowd went wild over two young Indian girls racing each other holding flags. The Indian soldiers – all very tall and handsome, with fantastic fans on top of their turbans – marched towards the closed border gate and then strutted in front of their equally gorgeous Pakistani counterparts. The two cohorts exchanged theatrical glares across the border line, stomping their feet and flicking their head-fans at each other. The whole ceremony built up for about an hour, with nationalist songs and chants, to the moment when the Pakistani and Indian flags were lowered among much cheering and pomp. In what struck me as a slightly deranged carnival of nationalism, it seemed that the Indian people had by far the best time: while the Pakistani side played readings from holy texts, the Indians played Bhangra and Bollywood music, and young people jumped down to dance on the parade ground.

As we said goodbye, the two Sikh men insisted that we visit Amritsar, only thirty kilometres away from the border, and gave us the name of a friend who ran a hostel there.

For the first time in months, the nights bring consolation: in my dreams, I hear my Nonno's voice, vivid and real, as if he were in the kitchen making coffee. He says, andrà tutto bene, *everything will be OK. I wake up filled with warmth instead of dread.*

Nonno taught me about freedom as well as coffee. I was probably about three when I insisted I could cross the busy roads of Milan on my own.

'No, you can't,' he said.

'Yes, I can! I can! I'll show you!' I replied, and started across a street. His massive hand shot out, grabbed my wrist, held me up until it was safe to cross. Then he carried me, still wriggling, still lifted up by a wrist, to the other side. I cried, more from a sense of defeat than from a sore wrist. He sat me gently down on a park bench.

'Listen,' Nonno said, 'you're like me. You think you can do everything on your own. But if I'd let you go free, you'd be squashed dead. That would hurt more than your wrist. You need to listen to other people.'

I make a coffee and scribble this memory in a notebook. Then I manage to write the first vaguely coherent sentence of my own in months: 'You may not be free to go where you want, but you're free to look for consolation and power inside you – from your family, from your own life.'

The hostel turned out to be next to Amritsar's Golden Temple, the holiest Sikh shrine in the world. We went there early in the morning and found a beautiful atmosphere, with pilgrims bathing in the holy lake around the marble building whose stones were allegedly looted from Mughal monuments in Lahore.

People walked clockwise around the water while loud-speakers broadcast a group of musicians singing prayers from the Sikh holy book inside the temple. A huge kitchen served free food to whoever wanted to eat – we were told that the idea of community service is an important part of Sikhism, and the temple kitchens symbolise this. Everyone was barefoot, and we felt completely welcome even though we were clearly not Sikhs. There was a feeling of happy celebration, with plenty of space for people to sit quietly by the water, watched over by the temple guardians with their orange and blue outfits and big spears. Many elements of Sikhism also seemed very warlike; this was explained to us in terms of self-preservation by an elderly man who took us to see the temple museum. It was full of bloody accounts of the persecutions Sikhs have suffered over the centuries.

The monsoon had passed, but the heat of the Punjab was still intense. Water buffaloes lowered themselves into squelching fields by the road, massive, dignified creatures with black oily skin and milky-blue eyes. We couldn't imitate them, so instead we followed the British tradition of heading to the hill stations to cool down. The nearest was the town of Dalhousie, named after the man who annexed the Punjab for the expanding British Empire. The Indian Himalayas have a chain of these hill stations, built for the Brits to escape from the heat of the plains in the summer. Dalhousie was the hub for the colonial administration of Lahore, now an international border away.

'Lovely and cool!' G.C. kept exclaiming, like the Scotsman he was. We walked through pine forests covered in cloud, and in the evening the sky cleared, showing views out towards the plains. In the slanting light we found the old British graveyard, clearly once a beloved place, built into the hillside in careful terraces joined by bridges with each gravestone looking out towards the mountains of Ladakh. But the gate was blocked off with piles of rubbish, and most of the gravestones had been broken or used as toilets. There was a doctor buried there who was from the same part of Scotland as G.C. His gravestone said he 'made a great contribution to the understanding of Himalayan Botany'.

We liked these mountains and wanted to see more. Over sweet milky chai the next morning, we decided our next step: to drive up into Ladakh, before the high Himalayan passes closed for the winter.

I have started distilling the Mondialita travel diaries into a story. One page stops me, from back at the beginning when G.C. and I were planning our journey despite fearful warnings:

There is one other kind of fear that we can't dismiss so easily – fear for the future of our marriage. Well-meaning friends told us of a couple who had lived happily together for ten years and then divorced after one year of travelling together. 'In their normal married life, they weren't together enough to annoy each other, see? They calculated that in one year of travelling, they'd actually spent more time together than in the previous ten years.' I'm not too worried: extreme proximity seems like a welcome and fitting counterbalance to the many months of extreme distance when G.C. was in Antarctica and I was in Milan and Beirut. We longed to shared everyday things then, even the really annoying ones. We'll be fine.

Hah, *I whisper to my pre-Mondialita, pre-mother self.* But you didn't imagine a pandemic lockdown together, did you?

Small Technical Interlude

Although not exactly a mechanical part of Mondialita, our luggage racks were falling apart, and we didn't want to lose our bags off mountainsides. A mechanic in Dalhousie welded some new ones for us, maskless and bare-handed. He gave us cups of intensely sweet, milky tea and coached us in 'useful Hindi words': *do chai*, two cups of tea; *mera naam Esa he*, my name is Esa. I could feel my mind stretch out with delight, like a cat that has found the best sunny place: here was another language I could try to befriend, and it didn't seem like an impossible task.

And so we set off east to Manali, where the road then turns north towards Ladakh. The town was full of Israeli kids, just out of the army, getting high on cheap cannabis. The place was full of it, a very stoned boy told me.

'Yeah, the valleys around Manali send a lot of cannabis to the West, and the stuff grows everywhere by the side of the road. Hey, are you Israeli? Wanna join us?'

We left quickly, and Mondialita proved her worth by climbing us up towards the first pass of the trip: Rohtang Pass, at about 4,000 metres above sea level. A scrap of grey snow had survived in a shady hollow. Indian tourists from the south had come to have their photos taken, holding ski poles, in cotton saris.

After the pass, the change in landscape was abrupt – from humid, temperate jungle and thick green hillsides to bare, grey scree, glaciers and no towns or villages to speak of for hundreds of kilometres. This was hard, hard driving: balancing the weight of Mondialita against the crooked camber, measuring her strength against the risk of going too fast around treacherous bends, and navigating the road, which was often shredded by landslides. I could barely manage, shaking with fatigue and fear. Increasingly, unspokenly, G.C. took over driving, and I was glad that he did.

At Keylong we stopped for the night – the only town on

the 500-kilometre stretch from Manali to Leh in Ladakh. Although we were still very close to the plains of India, the principal religion already was Buddhism and the people looked more like the Tibetans of Lhasa than the Indians we had met so far.

Cryptic warning signs began to appear – 'Don't be a gama in the land of the lama'; 'If you are married, please divorce speed' – as the roads became more and more precipitous, sometimes blasted into the side of a cliff. Huge convoys of army trucks drove along on their way to Kashmir and the Ladakh border with Tibet, carrying weapons and soldiers to the disputed frontier regions. Shepherds and their flocks didn't seem to worry too much about the army trucks. We did.

An army checkpoint made us pause in Darcha at the confluence of two rivers. We had to sign ourselves officially into the foreigners' book, so that the Indian authorities could keep a record of all travellers going in and out of Jammu and Kashmir, one of their more troubled provinces. It is actually three provinces, with Ladakh to the east, Kashmir to the north-west, and Jammu to the south-west.

Past Darcha, Mondialita climbed up and up, over terrible roads. Most of the time she only went at around ten to fifteen miles per hour, weaving between the potholes and big rocks. We passed many groups of low-caste Bihari and Nepali migrant workers, who lived up in the mountains all summer in little camps, fighting an endless battle against erosion by breaking rocks with sledgehammers and pouring tar out over the road.

After an eternity of high passes and soaring mountains, we reached another army checkpoint with a tent encampment: Sarchu. The roads were so slow-going that these tent encampments were essential for travellers who needed shelter at nightfall. We stopped for something to eat and chatted to a couple of guys from Mumbai up on a sightseeing trip, and a Kiwi cyclist who was biking all the way from Delhi to Ladakh. Past Sarchu we came to a broken bridge; trucks were waiting in queues for it to be fixed, but the road workers showed us a way to drive down and across the dry riverbed. Mondialita just managed it, thanks to G.C.'s determination and strength. The embankment on the other side was too steep for her, though, and we had to get a push from the guys from Mumbai, who thought this was hilarious. G.C. was less amused.

Mondialita climbed up, higher and higher, into the border places between India, Pakistan and China. The light was harsh without the gentling filter of dust which cloaks lower lands. Air moved through my lungs but didn't hold enough oxygen. No plants grew by the roadside, no birds called. I sat pillion all the time now: we had agreed that it was safer for us all, including Mondialita. G.C. was silent, focussed on navigating the crumbling track and the thundering military trucks that drove past us. I wondered if he, too, was developing a pulsing headache as our bodies protested the growing altitude.

We were looking out for a place that a fellow traveller in Manali had marked on the map for us: a caravanserai in the sky, a huddle of tents pitched at four and a half kilometres above sea level. I was not sure how much further G.C. could manage driving in this rocky, broken land. His arms and back were trembling; his silence spoke of exhausted pain. Now and then he reached his left hand back to touch my knee, as if checking I was still there. I sat on the back, making myself as tiny as possible, willing us on. We had come too far, too high: turning back was a worse option than going forwards.

The ragged peaks surrounding us, like shattered teeth

around a mouth of sky, became infused with gold as dusk approached. Mondialita was heading downwards now, and my head ached slightly less as the air thickened. Each star shining out among the darkening mountains was a flickering warning: *night is coming, the dark is growing, you have no shelter, you tiny humans.* Just as I was about to give up hope, G.C. shouted out – a gleam of fire showed ahead: tents, people, shelter. An army truck barrelled towards us as if we weren't there, clipped a saddle bag and sent Mondialita skidding off the road. I heard a crunching sound, the truck engine roared away, and I jumped off just in time. The bike was on top of G.C.'s leg. He was lying on rocks, breathing fast, alive.

'That BASTARD!' I screamed, my voice sounding tiny in the mountain night, as thin as the air and the starlight. I put all my rage in throwing rocks at the receding tail lights, which neither noticed nor slowed, and turned to help as G.C. pulled himself out from under Mondialita. After a few attempts, she started up again and we limped together up on to the road and towards the tents. All I wanted to do was to lie down next to G.C. and sleep for ever.

The caravanserai was called Pang, which my frazzled brain heard as Pain. It was set up by nomadic people who came up from the Zanskar valleys for the summer, and offered shelter to travellers who were foolhardy enough to attempt the road to Ladakh. G.C.'s muscles were so sore that he could barely move. An old woman came out to meet us, carrying a lamp which shone on her wrinkled face, grey braids, and colourful Tibetan robe and apron. She put gnarled hands together against one cheek, then pressed her fingertips together to her lips: *sleep? eat?* I nodded dumbly, still trembling with rage and shock, and she led us inside.

Our noodle stew was prepared and brought to us by an Indian boy with dark skin and bright eyes who looked about fourteen. He moved like a bird, cleaning and cooking and fetching. The Ladakhi people, like the old woman who had greeted us, had paler skin and sat wrapped in their blankets as the boy served them. They spoke a language which sounded like Tibetan.

The boy smiled at us and said, 'My name is Arjun,' in Hindi, his right hand flitting over his chest.

'Mera naam Esa he,' I replied, then continued in English, 'but I do not speak Hindi well, I am sorry.'

He grinned and said, 'It is OK. I am not from this place either.' His kindness was a gift. Later I heard him speak rapid Ladakhi.

The butter tea was rancid, a reminder of Lhasa and the courageous girl in the cafe there, and a welcome warmth. Arjun took our bowls away and showed us a space at the back of the tent, behind filthy curtains, where we could sleep. He shook two blankets out from a grey pile in the corner, and dust swirled in the lamplight. We thanked him and lay down wearing all our motorbike gear, rolled up in the blankets, scarves over our faces against the dust and the cold.

Just as he drifted off to sleep, G.C. murmured that all through that day his exhausted and oxygen-starved brain had been stabbed by certainty that I had fallen off Mondialita.

'Your silent lightness,' he slurred into the darkness. 'Don't leave, Esa. Don't fall off. Don't leave.' I squeezed his hand and felt him already twitch in sleep.

The darkness was so complete that there was no change if

my eyes were open or shut. My lungs were seizing up into a concert of dust-induced wheezes, gasps and pops. I tried to calm my breathing, and focussed on the sounds beyond my body: the hiss of a stove, people murmuring, wind-ripples on canvas. We had almost died that day, knocked off the road by a murderous army truck, and nobody we loved even knew where we were. The awareness of being alive brought a deep peace, like a surrender, a softness. I slept.

Brief Technical Interlude

The next morning, with frost on the ground and the air so thin at 4,500 metres, Mondialita was reluctant to start. She spluttered, coughed and gasped like my lungs had done. Eventually we managed to fix the problem by removing the air filter and getting a little bit more oxygen into the cylinders. I felt like hugging her and saying, 'I know, I know, it's OK, we're heading back down soon.' From then on, at high altitudes we stopped to clean her spark plugs every hundred kilometres or so, because they got so covered in soot in the thin air.

After Pang the landscape changed to become like a desert, with the porous rock all eroded away over the centuries, leaving weird columns like stalagmites standing in the sand. A wide plateau opened up at around 5,000 metres, with no road to speak of and everyone making their own way across the sands. Trucks stirred up dust clouds in the distance. At high altitude Mondialita ran fine, she just wouldn't idle – but since we were having to rev our way around potholes and over landslides, it didn't seem to matter too much. We were relieved to make it to the top of the highest pass, Taglang La. A sign there excellently summarised our very feelings:

> *second highest pass*
> *of the world*
> *Unbelievable is not it?*

Some Sikh guys had been stranded for eight days with a terminal oil leak in their motorbike. They had the whole engine out on the road and were dismantling it piece by piece. They cheerily waved us over to share some sweet tea with them.

As we got closer to the Indus Valley, small houses began to appear, and scraps of cultivated land. The architecture was Ladakhi, and to me seemed very similar to the Tibetan buildings we had seen in Lhasa. Apparently the whole area now is controlled by India because the Sikhs wrested it from Tibet in the nineteenth century, and then the British inherited it when they defeated the Sikhs.

We stayed in Leh for a few days, recovering from the road. Mondialita rested in a chicken shed. The town had a stunning setting, with the old fort looking south to the mountains of Zanskar, which are a national park. Walking, surrounded by mountains and golden light, it felt as if we were in a parallel-universe Tibet, where China had not taken over. A lot of Buddhist monks lived in Leh, and all over Ladakh. One of them grinned at us and waved as he got on his motorbike outside the Leh Palace, which looked more like a fortress. The actual fortress was up on top of the hill, wreathed with prayer flags billowing in the wind. There were monasteries built in the same style as the Potala Palace in Tibet, some of them perched on rocks overlooking the river.

The maps spread out on our bed showed just how close we were to the Karakoram Highway. It also reminded me of how high the mountain passes were, and how difficult it was to drive these roads. We were both ready to leave the mountains, and being in Leh had made us want to spend more time learning about Tibet, so we decided to head towards Dharamsala in the relatively low Himalayan foothills. But these high liminal lands also fascinated us both, so we decided to leave by a slightly roundabout route: along the river valley towards Kashmir.

The late June woods are swelling with rowan berries, blackberries and rose hips – not ripe yet, but growing towards the day when we cross over to autumn and harvests begin. I can almost taste lush green in the air as I walk between trees and beach, slowly, realising that something has shifted inside me: the folded away tar is less sticky, less hot, not quite changed into something else, but almost. I have started to swim in the sea as often as I can, depending on the movements of the tides and my children. There is a moment, as I step from land to water, when fears are left ashore like an old skin and all my focus is on forward motion into cold liquid. Gasping, splashing about, with the bridges huge over the estuary, I see why this is a good place for G.C. and I to have settled in for a while: a liminal place, between

river and sea, forest and coast, city and country. From here, it is easy to reach different places. For the first time since February, there is a gladness in me at being here, and nowhere else, in my skin floating between sea and sky.

The mountains of Ladakh and Kashmir are very far away, but I remember how their high passes and borders drew us on and in. Borders can mean war and tension, but liminal places can also hold magic: the sparks made when the edges of different things rub together. They can be where change happens, when people drop their guard and reach across to each other. I dry myself and head home.

Leaving Leh, we saw more cryptic road signs: 'Heaven hell or mother earth – the choice is yours'; 'Better Mr Late than Late Mr'. After that there was no other trace of humans apart from the road and some little settlements, really just monasteries with a few houses around them, high in the mountains. We headed on further west and dropped down towards Kargil, where the road runs right next to the India–Pakistan line of control. The side of the road was littered with memorial stones for Indian soldiers. Huge mortars pointed up at Pakistan's army positions in the mountains opposite. Signs said, 'Caution, you are under enemy surveillance'.

Soon we experienced the force of nature that is the Kashmiri truck driver on the rampage. On a straight part of the road, an overtaking truck on the wrong side forced us off the road, and although we swerved off on to the gravel, it still hit our baggage a glancing blow, ripping open my bag. At least it wasn't my leg. The truck driver didn't stop. I thanked whatever luck or angels had protected me, remembering our visit to San Colombano in the docile hills of Lombardy.

Technical Interlude

Maybe motorbikes do have guardian saints, because it was a miracle that we didn't destroy Mondialita on the road to Srinagar. She was not made for the rubble tracks of the Himalayas. When a sharp rock did finally pierce the bottom of the sump, we were only seven kilometres from Kargil. There were only three places on the whole route that had mechanics, and this was one of them. The oil started leaking out immediately; we coasted into town and found a mechanic just as the oil level reached the critically minimal amount. He patched up the hole with epoxy resin and found us the only 20/50 oil available in the town.

People we met had the same pale skin and green eyes as the inhabitants of the high Karakoram Highway. The mechanic told us that 'We were all part of the same state with the Karakoram people', until the war between India and Pakistan over Kashmir. He said that soon after the Partition of India, the Pakistani government sent hundreds of Afghan Pathan mercenaries to invade Kashmir. The Maharajah of Kashmir decided to accede to India in order to drive them out. The Pathans, he told us, were so busy looting and raping that they didn't reach Srinagar until the Indian army had already arrived and secured the airport. And so the Indians 'got the foothold that they are still holding on to'. Legally, they had the right to be in Kashmir, as the laws of the day allowed the Maharajah to decide who should rule. But India also reneged on a promise to hold a referendum for the people to decide themselves, which still has not been allowed. The mechanic was friendly, eloquent and generous with advice and milky chai, but Kargil had a tense atmosphere, with many hundreds of soldiers on the road in and out. We left as soon as we could.

To my delight and G.C.'s disbelief, an hour and half later we were in Srinagar. This was the summer retreat of the Mughal emperors of India. The Brits loved it too, but were prevented by the Maharajah from owning property, so they built beautiful houseboats to retreat to instead. One was called *Venezia*. We spent a blissful few nights in an old, ramshackle one covered in creepers, waking up each morning to the sound of the 'Chomper': a machine that floated up and down the lake chomping up water weeds. It then spat them out on to the road where people collected them in wheelbarrows to feed their animals. G.C. saw a kingfisher flying about the lake, and there were magnificent views of the mountains towards Ladakh to the east and the mountains of the Pakistani line of control to the west. It was strange to think that, a few weeks before, we had been in those hills above Islamabad, around a bonfire with Ali and his friends; that people used to cross over, before two armies had put a stop to that.

Posters for the Kashmiri Liberation Front were pasted all over town, and an air of tension hung around the soldiers with machine guns – they were at every junction in the city. While we were there, a truck driver was shot, caught in cross-fire between these soldiers and people accused of being

Kashmiri militants. The old town enchanted me, though, with wood and brick houses leaning at all angles, and the fort in the background whenever you looked up. The architecture was a mix of Indian, Persian, and central Asian: when the roads to the north were open, this was a major trade centre between India to the south and the caravan routes to Kashgar and Samarkand in central Asia. The main mosque was very beautiful too; it seemed to owe a lot to the Turkic and Mongol culture of central Asia, the cultural heritage of the Mughal emperors.

An old man sat outside the mosque and saw me admiring it. He greeted me with the Arabic salutation of Islam: *peace be with you*. I answered, *and also with you*. Delighted, he invited us in and made us some tea. When I explained to him about our journey together, he clapped his hands, whacked G.C. on the back and said, beaming: 'God laughs at borders!'

8

Kaleidoscopes

From north to south India

Dharamsala is an old Hindi word meaning 'pilgrim's resting place'. This was where the Dalai Lama chose to base his Tibetan Government in Exile when he arrived in India, escaping the Chinese invasion of Tibet in 1959. His residence is set in pine trees, on the top of a hill. Monks and nuns and devout Tibetans made ritual *kora* pilgrimages around the building, just as we saw them making circuits of the Potala Palace in Lhasa. Many Tibetan people lived here – some descendants of refugees, some newly arrived, having walked across the mountain passes from Tibet. A Tibetan hospital was set up to care for these people, staffed by Tibetans and volunteers from other countries. G.C. had a friend who had worked there, and found out that someone had cancelled at short notice and the hospital really needed another doctor for three months; a voluntary post that offered room and board. The Tibetan Women's Association also needed someone to help organise a conference and run English lessons. In our hostel room we looked at each other with sudden glee: shall we stay for a bit? Why not?

The next day our bags were already exploded all over our

volunteer accommodation: a room with a door on to a long balcony that connected up to a shared kitchen and the rooms of the other volunteers. By now we had been on the road for ten months, and the realities of settled life proved delightful: buying a whole packet of flour to cook with, going back to the same place each day to work, meeting people and having conversations that unfolded over weeks rather than minutes. Within a few days it seemed as if we had been here for years, and I felt slightly removed from the crowds of backpackers and Western tourists who also came to see the Dalai Lama – although we were still firmly in the category of foreigners, of those just passing through, whose passports meant they could leave when they wanted to. I was also aware that the Tibetan people who lived and worked here all the time saw us as fleeting presences.

Dharamsala was also a major Enfield motorbike centre. Old Enfields were still made in India, and it seemed that a favourite backpacker thing to do was to hire or buy one cheaply to drive around the country for a few months. They were too loud for us, in our loyalty to Mondialita. She was parked in a garage in our building and on weekends we would take her out to explore the nearby hill villages, giggling at the novelty of going back 'home' to the same room week after week.

Another major fixture of life in Dharamsala was stray dogs. The Indian authorities occasionally poisoned all strays, but the Tibetans were all devout Buddhists and didn't approve of this at all. They would scatter the dogs away before the 'poison patrols' passed, and also feed them, so there were hundreds of yellowish, mangy, barking strays everywhere. My daily walk was a steep uphill trek to the offices of the Tibetan Women's Association, on paths often blocked by snarling packs of dogs. I learned always to carry stones in my pockets.

A bright, fierce woman called Wangmo worked with me, organising an event which came to fruition as a joyful, exhausting five-day celebration of young Tibetan women: their talents, strengths, desires, plans. The association also ran English lessons for Tibetans. Many of the students were monks who had walked over the Himalayas to escape Chinese rule. G.C. spent his days at the hospital, where lots of Tibetans were treated for tuberculosis, which was made worse by the exhausting refugee trails over the mountains and became endemic because of the damp cement houses prevalent in Dharamsala. Many also had ruined digestions because of stress and being unaccustomed to Indian food. In the evenings, over the three months we stayed in Dharamsala, we would sit on the balcony with the other foreign volunteers and the Tibetan nurses, exchanging stories, watching the dusk spread its haze on the huge valley stretching out below us. Wangmo often asked to see our photos of Tibet, staring at them in silence. Only once she said, quietly, 'My country, where I can never go.'

Lots of the European volunteers said they were looking for 'spirit' in India, something beyond themselves. At first I ridiculed them, but then wondered if my mockery stemmed from recognition, and a fear of becoming a soul lost in the vastness of the world – restless always, drifting from one place to the next, discovering that you can only function while travelling, but are bored both by travel and by the prospect of settling. Were G.C. and I any different? Why had we travelled so far across the planet, if not searching for something special beyond our own selves? And finding it: strength in each other, awe in the stretch and size of the round earth beneath Mondialita's wheels, beauty in the places we passed through.

I began to recognise a certain type of traveller: people who were full of tales of adventures, journeys, and movement, but were unable to listen to the stories of others; their eyes held no rest. Watching them, I saw kaleidoscopes that never stopped long enough for the beauty of patterns to shine through. Fun for a while, but not something I wanted to become. Or maybe I too had been like that - before this change which tempered my desire for indefinite travel with recognition of the value of stopping, of being still for long enough to hear and see what waits beyond the whirl of onward motion. As the weeks of settled work and living passed, I saw with huge relief that G.C. too had shifted his perspective, moving away from the horizon-hunger which had filled the first part of our journey with Mondialita. Towards what we were shifting, I was not sure; but it was enough that we were changing together.

On the door of the shared kitchen was a postcard with a Taoist saying: 'Without leaving his front door, he knows everything under heaven. Without looking out of his window, he knows all the ways of heaven.' Below it I added lines from Cavafy:

> *Don't rush the journey at all.*
> *Better if it lasts for many years:*
> *then when you reach the island you'll be old*
> *and wealthy with everything gained on the way,*
> *without expecting Ithaka to make you rich.*

Today the shops reopen on our high streets for the first time in what feels like years. I take the children out for an ice cream

cone to celebrate. We sit by the sea, and I suddenly realise that we have managed to navigate the past few months: we are still here, afloat together, this crew I co-pilot. Right now, it feels that there is no more important thing, even as a rational thought inside me warns that women down the centuries have been kept at home and stopped from steering their own lives by the expectation that they should sacrifice everything for the sake of their children's happiness, that 'most important thing'. Flickering anger accompanies that thought, but I manage to hold on to it, unfold the rage, feel its colour: a red of warning against being left behind, taken for granted, stranded ashore.

The children, noisily unaware of all these emotions, garland themselves around me under the sunshine. We watch the waves in a huddle of gladness, of richness.

Our time in Dharamsala was ending: the arrival of winter meant that we needed to leave soon if we were to avoid difficult road conditions and reach the south of India before our visas expired. Packing up Mondialita again was both strange and exciting, like our brief settling had been. The Himalayas faded behind us. We crossed potholed bridges over the five rivers of the Punjab. The Indus and Ganges plains lay beneath sunsets thick with the smoke of a million kitchen fires. Everywhere were people, trucks, mopeds, free-ranging cows. I felt my mind fill up with newness: uncountable varieties of lives, languages, sights, sounds, smells.

We followed trails of pilgrims to Varanasi, a holy place for Hindu people, who go there to bathe in the sacred Ganges River. Beautiful ghats – embankments – were built all along the riverside, paid for by endowments of rich Hindu rulers over the centuries. Boats ferried pilgrims to the far bank of the Ganges. A man took us out at sunrise in his little skiff, rowing. He explained that this was the most auspicious time to bathe and pointed out all the sadhus – holy men – praying in the water. Many of them had made long pilgrimages on foot to reach here. The ghats were packed with people performing ritual baths, pouring the water over their heads and, in some cases, drinking it. Candles were lit and set free, floating on small beds of leaves and petals down the river among the ashes from burned bodies.

The boatman told us that if you are cremated here, you are released from cycles of reincarnation. The burning ghats, where wealthy and important people could afford to be cremated, were just below our hostel room. Here there was a choice of different woods to help incinerate you, with sandalwood for the super-rich. Low-caste men sifted through the ashes to find pieces of melted gold jewellery or tooth fillings. Just downstream, women washed clothes and spread them to dry, a kaleidoscope of coloured fabrics.

In this holy Hindu city there was very little sign of the Mughals, the Muslim rulers who controlled this part of India for over 200 years, but we did see the mosque built by Aurangzeb, the most violently anti-Hindu Mughal emperor. He was also the last one before the British control began to extend up from Bengal and towards this city. The mosque here had an armed guard, as there had been increasing anti-Muslim violence in this region. The day after we left, three bombs exploded in Varanasi.

Ultrasonically excited, the children are splashing on the beach with their friends without having to stay two metres apart from each other. Adults still have to keep a safe distance, conveniently measured out by the massive breakwater rocks. I sit in the sun with a friend and we watch our small people pelt each other with seaweed and splash about in delight. There is a sense of relief, of relaxing. Beer gardens can open, and it seems that schools will go back towards the middle of August, although nobody seems sure of the details. Soon we might even be able to travel more than five miles.

Delhi gave me a sort of empire-related indigestion: there were too many layers, so many amazing shifts in its history, with myth merging into fact. The ancient Hindu city of Indraprastha is mentioned in the Mahabharata, and so was over 3,000 years old. The remains of the vanished British Empire seemed modern by comparison. New Delhi was built for British colonial rule, but they only governed from here for about fifteen years. The Rajpath, a huge central mall of New Delhi, ran for almost three kilometres from the viceroy's residence down to India Gate in the distance. It was covered by pollution haze. Now the official residence of the President of India, the viceroy's residence had, in its heyday, about 400 gardeners, and 50 boys employed solely to scare away the birds. Apparently the Prince of Wales, on his official visit in 1921, said that he never really understood what 'royalty' was until he saw the way the Viceroy of India lived.

The traffic in Delhi wasn't as bad as we'd anticipated. En route to Delhi's Qutub Minar monument we met a celebratory procession: hundreds of Sikhs in full battle regalia, some mounted on elephants and some on horseback, in honour of Guru Gobind Singh. One man made his elephant wave its trunk at us when he saw Mondialita.

Qutub Minar was an area of the city in use during the time of the Delhi sultanate, founded by Muslim Turks who took over from Hindu Rajputs around the twelfth century. To complicate matters further, the Turks invaded from modern Afghanistan, and many of their generals were Afghans, so their culture is sometimes thought of as Turkish and sometimes as Afghan. They built a mosque in the twelfth century that was called 'the might of Islam', with a colossal minaret. An inscription said that it was made with the rubble of '27 idolatrous temples' – Hindu and Jain. The carvings of Qur'anic sayings were very beautiful, a strange fusion of Turkish, Afghan, Persian and Hindu style; according to historians, Hindu craftsmen made most of them.

Cold winter fog was rising on the Ganges plain, not unlike the weather in Lombardy one year ago, making driving Mondialita more dangerous. We joined throngs of people gazing at the Taj Mahal's marble symmetry and then headed south, towards Mumbai. I don't remember much of that journey – by then I had been ill for weeks with stomach cramps and nausea. Everything had become a blur of sore fatigue. G.C. took an executive decision and booked us on a train to Kerala; Mondialita was put in a box packed loosely with straw, and travelled in the goods compartment. She emerged with new cracks, stinking of fish: a box of frozen sardines had exploded all over her.

In the warmth of Kerala, G.C. insisted on taking me to a clinic where he got me on some scales and was shocked to see that my weight was down to forty-five kilograms: in a month I had lost more than fifteen kilograms. My abdomen felt like burning liquid and sharp nails. Tests showed that I had picked up a flourishing variety of intestinal parasites. A nurse told me, not unkindly, that I needed to eat very spicy food to kill the bugs. By this point I could hardly manage plain rice. G.C. picked up some pills and steered me out before I burst into tears.

In Kochi, G.C. found a guest house run by Mr Krishna, who took pity on my 'too very skinny body' and who liked Mondialita very much. He wore a cotton cloth wrapped around his waist. It was very white, and almost reached his ankles. Mr Krishna told us that this was a *lungi* and you could tell what caste a man belonged to from its length. I listened, trying not to giggle, because in Italian *lunghi* means 'long' and this coincidence seemed impossibly hilarious; but I knew I wasn't well, and Mr Krishna was very serious. A long *lungi* meant that a man didn't have to do much hard labour, so he was of higher caste. The fishermen and builders outside all wore very short *lungis*; Mr Krishna was a retired banker. He welcomed us into a quiet, light room that felt like rest made place.

After a few hazy days, the pills from the clinic started to work: I was hungry again, and to G.C.'s delight, devoured a whole plate of curry. Kochi was a kindness of healing. We walked among old houses dating back to when the Portuguese and the Dutch used this place as a trading post in the seventeenth and eighteenth centuries. I marvelled at fishing nets called 'Cheena', wide squares of gauzy weave suspended on tall, lever-like poles in rows along the shore. Mr Krishna said that they were introduced by Chinese traders back in the thirteenth century, when Kublai Khan was in power. Arab traders also settled here, and we visited a synagogue built in the early fourteenth century. Like the nets, the synagogue was still in use.

Kerala had a high proportion of Christian people, who trace their history back to the apostle St Thomas. He seemingly landed in Kerala and converted lots of people here. We found old Dutch gravestones next to Portuguese ones in the church of St Francis, and smiling angels brought from Portugal 400 years ago.

I left Kochi reluctantly, but my strength was returning and it was time to move on before our visa ran out. Roads in the south of India were much better than in the north, although drivers were just as insanely dangerous. Mondialita took us on an amazing drive down the Keralan coast, with the blue ocean to our right and Kerala's backwater canals to our left. We sang karaoke through our intercom, feeling very pleased with ourselves.

It's official: the children will return to their classrooms in a few weeks, after almost five months away from school. None of us can quite believe it. Looking too far forwards or backwards in time feels wrong, like using a telescope the wrong way round, so used have I become to living 'one day at a time'. Each day still seems unbelievably long, while weeks pass by like geese in autumn – a skein, a flicker, and gone. Friends refer to this phenomenon as 'pandemic time'.

Thinking too far back also casts into painful relief how long it has been since we were last in Italy, and nobody knows when international travel will be possible again. For so many months I have steeled myself to accept that I cannot go, that if my brother or parents get ill then I will have to say goodbye to them on the phone; now the possibility of returning is almost real, but I am scared to reach out for it in case it disappears.

Earth helps: I bury seeds and my hands in soil, returning to the levels of obsession with plants that I first developed when the children were all tiny, and miraculously slept at the same time. In those moments of quiet I didn't sleep, but planted and dug and healed myself by growing green things. In among the griefs of pandemic living, I feel again the shadow of an older loss, of finding my life suddenly and irrevocably changed by motherhood – filled with more love than I imagined possible, but with horizons suddenly restricted to my house, my bed, my breasts and the tiny mouths always hungry for more.

Kanyakumari – the Land's End of India – held a particular resonance for me. I had journeyed with G.C. to Land's End in Cornwall and Finisterre in Spain, where we stood high on cliffs and squinted into the vast sunset horizon across the Atlantic; Kanyakumari was the furthest south we had ever travelled together, the bottom tip of India, a point where you could sit all day and watch dawn and sunset from the same spot.

Kanyakumari was a sacred place for Hindus, garlanded with temples. Pilgrims splashed about in the water. We found a church there, too, where Our Lady of the Sea wore a sari. The next landfall was Antarctica, where G.C. had been and I would probably never go. We looked out, holding hands.

From Kanyakumari we headed north again, further into Tamil Nadu, and stopped at Madurai, famous for its temple, which is over 1,000 years old and a World Heritage Site. It was built by Dravidian people who were driven south from the Ganges plain by Aryan invasions 3,500 years ago. The temple was covered in elaborate statues of gods and demons and inside we found huge, ancient pillars, also beautifully carved. The complex pantheon bewildered me, and I remembered with a smile G.C.'s Protestant amazement at discovering that in the Catholic calendar, every day of the year is the feast of a different saint. There were many stalls selling religious items, which had a quality strongly reminiscent of the Catholic kitsch sold outside St Peter's in the Vatican. My attempts at Hindi were met with English, and polite explanations that 'Here we are not in the north, madam. We have our different Tamil language'. The writing was different, too: a script with round, looping shapes, whose words did not hang from a line like Hindi. Tamil, I learned, was an ancient Dravidian language. Its sounds rolled about in my clumsy mouth, my enjoyment of this new learning a sure sign of returning health.

The road curved us towards Rameshwaram, where a narrow spit of sand becomes a series of atolls almost linking India to Sri Lanka. It's called Ram's Bridge: according to the Ramayana, it was built by the monkey god Hanuman and an army of monkeys, to help the god Ram get over to Sri Lanka to rescue his wife Sita from the clutches of an evil, kidnapping demon. Recently the Indian government had wanted to dredge the sea between India and Sri Lanka to create a shipping channel, but devout Hindus blocked the streets of Delhi in protest and the holy Ram's Bridge stayed undamaged. Rameshwaram was full of Hindu pilgrims, in buses covered with ropes of yellow marigolds. Happy goats ate the flowers off the sides of buses, leaning up on their hind legs, dainty and determined.

Tamil cooking seemed more spicy than in the north, the tastes and smells of food lingering longer; or maybe it was the warm air that held perfumes more. People ate their food off huge banana leaves. Many Tamil women tied garlands of jasmine in their hair, and the scent waited in clouds to be walked through. In the tropical heat I remembered Himalayan snow, realising that I was storing up the months spent in India to carry away with me as we prepared to drive towards Chennai: from there we would travel across the Indian Ocean to Australia.

In an oppressively humid warehouse, in a corner of Chennai Port, we stripped Mondialita of all luggage and took a scrubbing brush to her. Even a spot of mud would mean not getting through strict Australian checks: there could be a seed of a new invasive weed hidden inside her, and Australia had had enough bother with foreign species like the cane toad and the rabbit.

Thankfully, friends in Dharamsala had recommended Mr Kumar, Master of Knowledge of all things to do with shipping out of Chennai Port. From his desk, he seemed to control a whole world of minions who ran around doing his bidding. I felt that Mondialita was in safe hands and hoped that she would get to Perth, Australia, around the same time as us. Still, it was strange and slightly worrying to see a crate being built up around her. She disappeared behind wooden planks like a prisoner walled up.

Part Three

FREE TO RETURN

9

Roads reopening

Western and South Australia

Strapped into a metal tube, high up above the clouds, we crossed the equator: a strange, anticlimactic sensation, being hurtled through a barrier present in my mind but intangible. A few hours later I got my first glimpse of Australia's north-west tip: lots of red earth and dried-up lakes, and long strips of white beaches. G.C. pointed it out at the same time. I knew we had to drive up there on Mondialita as soon as we liberated her from the shipping warehouse.

We were met at the airport by old friends of G.C.'s, Dan and Pat, who had emigrated from Scotland with their three children. They cheerily informed us that we had arrived on Australia Day, a national holiday, which meant all customs offices were closed.

'Everyone's at the beach,' they said. 'That's where we're taking you now.' Their youngest child screamed with piercing glee as soon as he saw the ocean. We made sandcastles and sunbathed, surrounded by white bodies under the dazzling, relentless sunshine.

Mondialita arrived in Fremantle, the oldest part of Perth

and its main commercial port. 'Freo' was where the first British settlers to Western Australia landed in the early nineteenth century. The old streets of Fremantle were lined with white colonial buildings, dazzling in the painfully bright sun which felt harsher than any light we had travelled through before. My brown eyes hurt if I didn't wear sunglasses; G.C.'s were furled into deepening crinkles by constantly squinting. We escaped for some shade into the Round Tower, where a sign told us it was the oldest intact edifice in Western Australia – a prison, built in the early 1930s. I raised my Italian eyebrows at this definition of 'old'. G.C. found a display of comments by travellers from England in the nineteenth century; one said, 'The glare is unbearable, the heat fierce, the land barren – I cannot imagine a worse place to found a city.'

That seemed a bit harsh: Perth was beautiful, with its green parks and laid-back beaches, although to my eyes it seemed incomprehensibly profligate with water: sprinklers were left on in public parks under the blazing noon sun, half of the water sprayed out over tarmac and evaporating before it touched the ground. It felt like a city that should not have been there, somehow, a place scraped out of cultural memories from the other side of the world and made to grow in a climate in which it did not belong.

G.C. wondered aloud, 'Maybe in another hundred years, Perth will have disappeared back into sand.' He musingly added, as a seeming non sequitur, that the closest big city to Perth was actually Singapore, and Western Australia had its own separate time zone. I suddenly longed for the tiny distances of Europe.

The timescales and costs involved in releasing Mondialita from quarantine were escalating: we were going to have to wait nine days and pay seven hundred Australian dollars in port, admin, immigration and customs exchange fees before being able to return to the road. We even had to pay to get the wooden crate she came in destroyed, even though it had been fumigated, because the official said there was a piece of bark on the wood. I was annoyed by not being able to cajole our way out of this: here we no longer belonged to the privileged minority of the 'rich white foreigners to whom different rules apply'. Here we were just two skint, scruffy travellers worried about their motorbike.

We had great fortune of friendships, though, which helped us through yet again. Dan and Pat said we could stay with them as long as we needed to. Spending time with their family was a wondrous change for us, their life different in almost every way to the one we had been leading. I saw their settled happiness, like a deep current, under the swirling demands of their kids and work and house. They took us to a cricket match, which felt like standing in an oven to watch some men dressed in white waiting about in the sun, as a sparse, overheated audience gave bursts of applause. I drank lots of cold beer, wore a wide hat, and marvelled at how this was considered an entertaining sport.

Our first Australian supermarket stunned me by how expensive one modestly filled basket was, and confounded me when the bored teenager at the checkout said, by way of greeting, 'Wannaplikkybeg?'

'W–what?' I stuttered.

'WannaplikkyBEG?' he said again, louder, as if I was stupid.

'Sorry, I don't know what you mean – I—'

'Wanna PLIKKY BEG?' he yelled, waving a plastic bag in my face.

'Oh! Oh, yes, please, thanks, sorry,' I said, flustered, and to make things even worse, I added, 'I'm not used to Australian English yet, you see.'

His sandy eyebrows almost reached his long blond hair as he shot back, 'It's not Australian *English*, it's Australian AUSTRALIAN!'

A few days later Mondialita was out, whole and healthy, so we were free to hit the road again and head north to find the beaches we had seen from the plane.

To celebrate, we went to a pub, a wildly expensive choice given our diminished budget. We were saved from our own profligacy: apparently I was 'wearing thongs after 7 p.m.' and therefore was not allowed in. I was about to protest in outrage at this presumptuous interference in my choice of underwear, when I realised that the massive blond bouncer was gesturing at my feet. Flip-flops – thongs – were banned for being too informal, though tiny crop tops and very short shorts seemed fine. We went to the beach instead and drank cheap beer from tins, barefoot on the sand. I lay back and took in the night sky with its new constellations, realising, with a jolt, that Orion was upside down. We discussed the advice we had been given about our travel plans. Many people had warned us that 'it gets bloody hot out there, mate'. But how hard could it be with good Australian roads and brand new tyres?

Harder than our inexperience had assumed, it seemed. On the first day out of Perth, we immediately had a—

Technical Interlude

Our back tyre – the hardest one to fix, because to get to it we had to remove all our luggage – went flat twice, with an awful skidding sensation when the rear wheel slid out of control. We stupidly tried to mend it using our spare inner tubes that were still patched from the roads of India, where we had never gone faster than a cautious trundle, always ready to weave and dodge the many hazards in our path. Australian roads were clear, unbroken, fast, and the tarmac was so hot that our patched wheels couldn't take the combination of speed and weight that was suddenly possible again. We ran out of solutions and were stuck, in the heat, in what felt like the middle of emptiness. Every car that passed by stopped to offer help. All were driven by men, loud in their kindness, but there was nothing we could do without new inner tubes. Each man checked insistently that we had enough water with us, and cautioned us against leaving our motorbike unwatched by the roadside.

We were just about preparing ourselves to camp for the night near Mondialita when a lorry covered in pictures of multicoloured jelly beans pulled over. I blinked, thinking that the heat was giving me hallucinations, but it was real, and driven by a kind man called Mike. Word had gone out on the truckers' CB network that two mad Brits were stranded, and he had made time to find us, greeting us jovially with 'Are you the crazy Poms?' I didn't mind being called that, and anyway, everything did feel a bit crazy by then. Mike winched Mondialita on to the back of his truck and drove us to the nearest town – more than an hour up the road. We thanked him over and over again. He just shrugged and said, 'Well, if you can't do a good deed, you may as well not get out of bed.' He shared some more nuggets of wisdom: in the outback, avoid driving at dawn and twilight, when animals are on the move. And remember that kangaroos never jump into the sun. Thanks to Mike, we managed to get new inner tubes, fix Mondialita and set off again the next day.

The ban on travelling more than five miles in Scotland has been lifted. For one hundred and seven days, I have moved no further than that distance from my house. Today I could go to Glasgow, walk with my friend and meet his baby. G.C. is full of enthusiasm for this plan. I am beginning to feel ill at the thought of driving a car, alone, for forty miles or so of motorway.

All day I focus on playing games and making food to avoid the panic I feel rising. G.C. gets back from work and cheerily says, 'So – will you leave this evening? I think it would be good for you to leave this evening,' and I stir the risotto as if it were the only stable thing in the universe. My heart is loud and fast, high in the back of my throat, my breathing is shallow, my stomach sore. I observe these symptoms with detachment, noting that they seem to be in line with a panic attack, and calmly serve the tea.

'Maybe,' I tell him. 'Who wants more?' I can imagine no other way to cope than to anchor in these rituals of providing, to avert fearful thoughts by intense focus on the present needs of others.

All through the meal, G.C. watches me, and I can tell he knows. The children, when told that I might go to Glasgow for the weekend, are not bothered in the slightest, more interested in what other food is on offer once the rice is eaten. I have no excuses left.

G.C. says, gently, 'Why don't you let me take you? The kids can come too, and we'll come and collect you' – and that does it. I am returned to those first motorbike lessons, the day of my test, the smirking red-haired ex, the doubts I had every day I drove Mondialita – and the knowledge that I managed to push through the fear. A stubborn pride rises up, and I say, 'No, thanks, but I have to drive myself. If I don't, I might never drive again.'

And so I do drive, feeling sick all the way down the motorway to Glasgow, tensed up as if the panic that tries to stop me is a living enemy beneath the wheel of my car. All that night my dreams are of escaping from under crushing weights, but I wake up to silence, solitude and the green shoots of courage returning.

Australia was a sudden freedom of space and speed: the release of bipeds transformed to a streak of motion. Limitless road. The smooth, empty tarmac meant that I was able to drive again without fear of the potholes, technicolour death trucks, buffaloes, landslips and other assorted hazards we'd encountered in India and Pakistan. The first time I sat in the front again I felt terrified and grateful in equal measure, holding the weight of Mondialita between my knees and trying not to think about what would happen if I dropped her. Muscle memory took over after a few minutes. My body moved me past fear, climbing up the gears without thinking, stopping or slowing. A grateful humming started up in my throat and spread all over my skin in the speed of our moving.

We were not much north of Perth, but already the land was a vastness seemingly empty of humans. It smelled of dust and eucalyptus. When it started to rain, the eucalyptus smell became stronger, alongside the smell of wet sand and sea. My enjoyment lasted for about ten minutes: the shower was changing into a tropical cyclone, after fifty-five days of drought. In all our monsoon travels, I had not seen rain like this: it was like moving through a wall of water. A huge sign proclaimed, 'Limited H_2O beyond here.' We kept driving, but soon felt that all the forces of this land were trying to push us back south. The rain and wind were so fierce that Mondialita was skidding and we had to stop, just past Geraldton. In disbelief, we got off, conferred and hastily decided to cut our losses, head back to the shelter of Dan and Pat's house in Perth and then follow the coast south. We were learning our lesson: never underestimate the Australian weather, heat and distances.

The journey south was much easier. We travelled through the Swan Valley, a landscape of chocolate factories and signs advertising Pilates lessons, driving over gentle hills covered with vineyards and fruit orchards, until we reached the forests of the southern coast: the 'Valley of the Giants', named after the giant red tingle trees that grow there. We climbed a tree which was fifty metres high. Tingle trees are a type of eucalyptus that evolved a million years ago, when continents were joined together in an über-landmass called Gondwana. When Gondwana split up and Australia moved to its present position, the tingle trees died out everywhere else in the world, apart from this corner of Western Australia. I stood, expanded by delight, surrounded by huge living beings from an unimaginably distant time.

Being in Australia also meant the freedom to use our tent

again. Whenever we could we camped wild, setting up somewhere hidden, leaving no traces of our presence. We put up our tent in a grove of peppermint trees, an enchanted cave of scented air and flickering light; under eucalyptus trees and gum trees; among bushes that I had never seen before with strange and resiny smells. It slowly became chilly enough at night to need sleeping bags, and G.C. relished the feeling of not overheating. We were travelling across the southern edge of Australia, heading east. Each day we covered many kilometres, but when we checked our progress on the map, it looked as if we were crawling, snail pace, along the bottom of this huge island continent: like travelling in China, but infinitely more enjoyable because Mondialita was back with us.

On Mandalay Beach I stood astonished by such an expanse of beauty, and in the early morning light spotted my first kangaroo. I was more amazed than she was. My European eyes couldn't quite process the strangeness of her face, like a cross between a rabbit and a deer, her front paws with sharp claws, the pouch in which she carried a baby. I mused that kangaroos and aliens are equally improbable, therefore if kangaroos exist, so might extraterrestrial life. So many things here were real which seemed impossible: later that day we stamped about on the spur of rock that once joined Australia to Antarctica, amazement juddering up through my boots.

July brings the summer school holidays, although the children have not been in class for over three months now. We have come back to the little tin caravan on the Fife coast where we spent a weekend just before lockdown began. It feels important to be

back here, to mark the fact that we can travel this far – even if it is not very far at all, even if everything feels muted and cautious and strange. For the first time in many months, the children wake up in a place other than the house. We are all quiet, glad to be in this tiny space of consolation which carries no associations with the frustrations and fears of the past months. I can't quite believe we are allowed to come here.

Across the globe, Melbourne has returned to full lockdown because of Covid infections. I wonder if we will ever again take for granted all the freedoms we had before, and wonder if this season of reopening will end with the summer's ending. We watch the sea in silence, the Bass rock white in the distance. The children don't venture far from the caravan to play, as if they are unsure of what to do with the possibility of roaming free again.

Leaving the coast behind, Mondialita followed the road into the outback. At first, near the Stirling Range, we drove under huge skies past vast sere fields. The land became increasingly dry: sand, there was always sand, on the roadside and burrowing up through the ancient topsoil. Then farmland gave way to dusty red earth, scrubby bushes and the occasional eucalyptus tree. We were increasingly unsettled by what seemed a vast discrepancy between the Australian land as it had evolved, and the way it was being used by people who farmed it according to practices which had originated in Europe and belonged to a different climate, a different hemisphere. The names of the farmers were carved into arched signs over the long driveways – we never saw the farmhouse from the entrance, it was always over the horizon, the landholdings were so huge. Some of these farms were bigger than European provinces. Somehow it felt that the landscape would seem less arid if there were no cattle trying to graze as if we were in Devon.

We reached Kalgoorlie, a city that grew in the middle of a desert because of gold mining: Western Australia's riches are all buried under its immense outback. The 'Super Pit' at Kalgoorlie is one of the biggest gold mines in the world – some 500 metres deep – and as I stood on the edge of the pit, I realised with a feeling of sick dizziness that the tiny dots on the bottom were in fact massive diggers, so big that they could easily have scooped us up along with Mondialita. It was a deeply unsettling experience, like watching a violation, something brutal and unnatural, and yet so many of the objects we depended on daily were made through processes like this. G.C.'s fingers twisted and turned his gold wedding band.

The gold mines left us in a sombre mood, and that evening we left our hostel to find a drink and shake off the Super Pit's spell. We wandered, unaware, into a 'skimpy bar': a pub where all the bartenders were women wearing tiny shorts and nothing else, apart from tassels to cover their nipples. It was full of men who drank beer, watched television and seemed not even to notice the skimpies. I got stared at, though, a woman all bizarrely covered up by motorbike clothes. Laughter bubbled out of me at this new level of human strangeness. An old photo by our table showed that this had once been a brothel, where Italian women worked so that the Italian men who had emigrated to make their fortune hunting gold could 'make love in their own language'. All my laughter turned to sadness: at the loneliness we make for each other, our desperate attempts to find consolation.

We could have decided to stop and work in Kalgoorlie, saving money to keep on travelling: teaching and doctoring were very much in demand, and our British passports meant that work visas would not have been a problem. There was a sense in everyone's conversations of being in a frontier land, with so much empty space to occupy, money to be made, futures to be built. Posters in the shops called for 'skilled migrants' to 'come and build your life here!' But it was abundantly clear that neither G.C. nor I wanted to do that: the desire to return home to Europe was too strong to be delayed by more than a few months. We had just about enough money left to reach New Zealand. And anyway, I didn't feel that this land was empty. Underneath our feet, it was full of things people wanted, greedily, and around us, the fruits of that want spilled out under the sun.

Below me, the English Channel looks tiny, little more than a river between lands. I am on a plane, returning to Italy, and I cannot believe it. The sense of unreality is heightened by the masks covering everyone's faces: it feels like being in someone else's story, one of the post-apocalyptic novels I was obsessed with as a teenager. I look again at the ticket G.C. booked for me: more tangible proof that this is actually happening.

'I thought you might not do it otherwise,' he said. 'And you need to go back to Italy or you'll get ill.'

The plane is full. It is the first flight to Milan from Edinburgh, and all passengers are Italians going home at the first chance to visit family. People's eyes are guarded above their masks and there is hardly any conversation. Our usual abundant gesticulations are also diminished. I wonder if everyone else is also thinking: what are we returning to? It is almost impossible to imagine being in Italy without effusive greetings, kisses, exclamations, without exuberant hand gestures. We are lucky to be here at all, in our freedom to go back – but this is a return to the unknown, to a beloved place we fear will be profoundly changed.

Next to me is the only child on the entire plane: a toddler, maskless, who cries and coughs, spluttering crisp crumbs for most of the flight. Some things don't change. His dad is clueless, a Gucci-clad guy from Milan who alternates between telling the boy off and offering him ineffective bribes. The dad also gives me beseeching looks and says loudly to his son in Italian, 'Maybe the kind lady here can play with you? Maybe she knows good plane games! Maybe she has a little boy of her own! Maybe she is missing him and wants another little boy to play with!' I am suddenly and deeply grateful for the mask that hides most of my face. I pull out Lois Pryce's stories of motorbike adventures across America – in English – and start to read. My stomach rumbles with hunger, but there is no way I am taking my mask off until I am out of this plane.

Thinking of food reminds me that today is the first day of August – Lammas. The word comes from the Anglo-Saxon for 'loaf mass', the festival when loaves made from the first wheat harvests were taken to churches as grateful offerings. It is also Lughnasa, a Celtic festival also associated with the first harvest and named after Lugh, the warrior-craftsman god of light. We are halfway between the solstice and the autumn equinox: today is a celebration of light and abundance before we turn back towards winter.

When I arrive in Milan, the summer heat is like a huge living thing throwing itself around me. The tarmac is spongy under my feet. With every step I feel my veins dilate and my muscles slacken into slowness; I sense the knot of disbelief and worry deep inside me loosen. My brother is waiting for me past the airport gate, and our dance of greeting is relief made manifest.

The road south was lined with signs showing the levels of fire risk, all set to the highest danger. An ongoing drought, untouched by the distant rains in Geraldton, made the threat of wildfires even higher. Water was rationed, and the distances between towns were vast. The sun hurt my eyes as I drove towards Norseman, past solitary, corrugated iron houses with windmills like those in Dorothy's Kansas from *The Wizard of Oz*. I was urging Mondialita on fast; each day we covered hundreds of kilometres, but on the map it seemed as though we were hardly moving, like in those dreams where you run but don't go anywhere. I imagined our motorbike as a red beetle under the huge blue sky, creeping between impossibly vast fields. Sheep and cattle grazed over sparse, brown stubble.

We needed to get to Norseman because that was the nearest place with a garage where we could fill up with fuel and water before driving the long, dry roads of the Nullarbor Plain. By the petrol pump there, we were greeted warmly by Bob, who invited us in to a hut-like shop and offered us cold beers. He told us in a cheery Cockney accent that he had been working in Australia for over thirty years and 'loved it, mate, every day'. His blue eyes were bright in a sun-reddened face, a bit like G.C.'s, twinkling at the people leaning on the counter.

We commented on the scale of the landscape, how vast it seemed to European eyes. He told us that 'here you need 6,000 acres for 600 cattle, not like back in the UK', because the land was so poor. In the same factual tone, he told us that he also worked as the assistant to the undertaker. Quite often they had to drive out across the Nullarbor to pick up the bodies of people who 'just drive out off the road a little then gas themselves. Lots of 'em remove the number plates first. Once we found a van with a body that had been there for YEARS. NOBODY drives off the highway if they want to live. Don't you drive off into the bush, OK?' We promised we wouldn't.

Norseman, Bob informed us, was named after a man from Shetland called Laurie Sinclair who was clearly very proud of his Nordic ancestry. He came here to seek his fortune in the early nineteenth century and started a gold rush, which led to Kalgoorlie as we had seen it.

Another man broke his beer-drinking silence to say, 'Nah, nah, it was named after his HORSE who was called Norseman.'

I nodded, slightly warily. Either way, the settlement was also famous for being the beginning (or end) of the only road that connects the states of Western Australia and South Australia. Bob showed us a photo of the first white settler women, immaculate in starched white blouses and big hats, each holding a huge rifle. I tried to imagine being one of them, and failed completely. To me, this dry land looked impossible to survive in, but I knew that Aboriginal people had lived here for many thousands of years before white people arrived.

A man with dark skin and black, tightly curled hair came in. Bob's shoulders stiffened as he joked in our direction, 'I have to work right hard to get a tan like that one.'

I put my beer down, slowly.

'What?'

Silence. G.C. was tense beside me. The man didn't acknowledge Bob, but greeted us with a smile and told us that we had to go to the head of the Great Australian Bight and see if we could spot whales. He paid and left. The shop had gone very still.

Someone said, as if talking about the weather, 'Got to watch them folks.' We left, edging around unspoken tensions.

Sitting around a fire by our tent that evening, I felt dwarfed and squashed by how little I knew: of this land, its history, the names and languages of people who had lived here before Europeans came. The next day, in the cool of early morning, we drove past tin cut-out camels glinting in the sunlight at a roundabout, in memory of the camels and camel drivers brought over by the British from Baluchistan to transport goods and gold. A sign dustily announced the 90 Mile Straight. In true Australian style, this was exactly as its name described: an almost impossibly straight arrow of road, shimmering in the heat as far as I could see, like a rope stretched taut across oceans of outback. The muted grey, brown and green tapestry of the scrub bush on each side of the tarmac was interrupted only by occasional red gum trees. Warning signs told us that the fire hazard continued to be 'extreme'. Dead kangaroos rotted by the roadside under the burning sun. I thought of Perth's city lawns being watered in the midday heat. Our pale skin, that had brought so many freedoms, fried.

We stopped for water in an outback garage and another blue-eyed, red-faced man told us that kangaroos went to lie on the roads at night, enjoying the heat released by the tarmac from the day's sun, and were then crushed by the immense trucks that thundered across the continent day and night with metal 'roo bars' welded on their front bumpers. These trucks were so huge they were called 'road trains'. In South Australia, he told us, there was a truck whose only job was to patrol the roads, picking up kangaroo carcasses. In Western Australia there was no such service, and I began to regret the way that motorcycling bathes you in the smells of the landscape around you. Our zooming past raised black rags of crows that circled and sank back down in our wake.

Kangaroos still seemed strange. They were the first marsupials I had ever seen, creatures of strength and grace. An elastic power in their muscles produced huge, smooth bounces forward without any visible effort as they moved alongside the tarmac road, which cut through the bush like a sharp grey line of human business. G.C. drove and I was lulled by the unchanging road and the heat into a reverie, imagining what it must have been like to arrive here on a ship from Britain to find no roads, no towns, plants and animals all unfamiliar. I thought of how many Europeans had disappeared into the outback and never been found, long before the time of Bob's stories.

Near the end of the 90 Mile Straight, the kangaroo carcasses became fewer. We stopped under the only object that gave shade for hundreds of miles: a huge rain-catcher which was built to drain water into a concrete tank. It was empty. Someone had spray-painted 'Blackfellow's Dreamtime, White Man's Nightmare' in big black letters on its side. I didn't understand what these words meant, and they circled round my mind long after we had driven past them.

I spend a brief week in Lombardy, absorbing the smells which are Italy in summer, willing them to become part of me to take back north to Scotland: mosquito repellent, fig trees hot in the sun, ripe tomatoes bigger than my fist, the first raindrops falling on hot earth. The sound of Italian everywhere is like a warm sea where I float, finally back in my other home again. But every conversation is infused with tales of death: oh, we didn't tell you, dear, because we didn't want to upset you, but the neighbour / the priest two villages away / the barber's dad / your old primary school teacher / the supermarket lady died. *Litanies, lists of names, meanings impossible to take in.*

I listen to stories of narrow escape from the virus, which always imply that someone else died. A friend persuaded her father to stop playing bocce *with his pals at the pensioners' club. He was deeply reluctant to listen to her because a regional tournament was coming up soon. Ninety elderly men attended the final round of* bocce. *One month later, seventy were buried. An old classmate who worked for Lonely Planet was stranded in Latin America due to Italy's sudden lockdown; by the time he got home, both his elderly parents had been found, dead, in their flat. The local priest insisted on wearing gloves and a mask to dispense communion, but many of his colleagues didn't; they all died.*

After lunch my parents rest. I go for walks around the village in the forty-degree heat, trying to comprehend the enormity of what has been happening. The village noticeboards can't hold all the announcements for memorial masses. Black-rimmed papers drop and scatter, the names of the dead like leaves on the ground. I lie on the hot summer soil among sunflowers that rise above me, three metres tall, heavy with bees. Their yellow shimmers against the sky's deep blue. I imagine souls rising like invisible bees, away from the heavy clay earth of Lombardy, away from all of us left here to miss them. My brother calls me back inside for a coffee.

Heat gathers into magnificent thunderstorms which rip lightning across a grape-dark sky. Lorenzo and I whoop and yell in delight, opening the doors and windows to let in the charged night air. The next day I have to leave: back to Scotland, to sea smells and cool winds, to my family there. No annoying men are beside me on the plane, no spluttering toddlers. I look out over the Alps, my bag full of Italian food and my heart full of stories, aware as never before of the fortune that I have taken for granted: the freedom to cross borders and return to see loved ones without challenge or fear.

Crossing into South Australia was entirely uneventful, another mile driven under the scorching sun on shimmering tarmac, but now we were in a different time zone and about to enter the Nullarbor Road on the Nullarbor Plain. This too is aptly named because absolutely no trees grow here for hundreds of miles. The Nullarbor is the world's biggest karst formation, with uncounted caves and underground lakes deep under the surface, but above ground it is flat desert that goes on to the horizon. Mondialita streaked eastwards. Rusty land stretched to our left for hundreds of miles, thousands of years. As the light waned, we set up camp in the bush, meticulously clearing the land of anything other than dusty earth for many metres around a deeply dug pit in which we lit our tiny camping stove, watching the little blue flame with fear and impatience.

The Nullarbor was named with the same pragmatic approach to language that produced 'Great Sandy Desert' and 'Blue Lake'. I reflected that we had absorbed at least some of that no-frills attitude as we ate our standard-issue breakfast: one apple, one slice of bread with Vegemite, one cup of tea with powdered milk for G.C., and for me, one cup of reconstituted milky coffee squeezed into boiled water from a tube that looked like brown toothpaste. We had quickly settled into what we called the 'Australia diet': food bought on the basis of being cheap and light, and only as much as we would need until the next shop. Lunch was always bread with sweaty cheese and another apple; dinner was pasta with onion and tomato sauce. Food felt relatively unimportant: hydration was key. We needed to have at least five litres of water on the bike at any given time or we would join the nameless multitudes of desiccated outback corpses. I threw away such thoughts with the dregs of my questionable coffee and started the Great Shaking Out of boots, helmets, and jackets – another practicality adopted as a precaution against Australia's many poisonous creeping creatures.

Despite our parsimony, we were running low on water. Everything was red earth and searing heat.

G.C. said, 'I feel the sun desiccating my eyeballs'; his eyes were sore despite his darkened visor. I drove, squinting, whispering to the universe, 'Please, somewhere we can stop and find water, somewhere, please, anywhere.' I regretted that 'anywhere' when we reached a little roadhouse motel and found the petrol outrageously overpriced, the water almost salty, and the food grim. A monosyllabic woman with short peroxide hair and a pink vest, her eyes dull, defrosted a pasta dish in a microwave and plonked it in front of us. The pasta swam in grease. I ate, silently noticing that every surface was covered with small plastic models of whales.

At sunset the sky became a bowl of flames above our heads. In the night the land spread around us like a silence. Orion somersaulted above, a glittering acrobat. I had read that to our left across the bush was Ooldea, a place on the Nullarbor Plain where Aboriginal people had met and rested for thousands of years because it had a reliable source of water. White men were led there, then took over and used up all the water to provide steam for trains on the new railway. We slept among scrubby plants I'd never seen before, the air filled with their sharp scent.

About halfway across the continent we nearly died. G.C. was driving and spotted a scene so uncanny it looked like a painting of a dream: bleached trees standing in a hollow of the land, yellow hills behind them, and above them all, a cupola of blue sky. He tried to pull over but the bike's wheels hit gravel. G.C. struggled to correct Mondialita's tilt but we were going down, skidding out of control just as a road train roared towards us. There was a moment of complete calm as I saw the huge truck bear down on us, with everything moving in slow motion. I thought, quite clearly, 'OK, we die now,' in a mind-flash that sliced through my brain, much more bright and real than any words. Then the world gathered speed again, somehow G.C. managed to wrench us into a 180-degree turn, Mondialita wheeled back and fell down on to her side, just escaping the wheels of the truck, and we scraped to a halt. The road train roared past us.

We checked the bike and each other for damage, then found a place to pitch our tent for the night. Enough driving for one day. Once we had unpacked, we both became shaky and clumsy; my knee was cut and G.C. had hurt his back straining to pull us towards safety. Mondialita was, amazingly, undamaged apart from a scratch on one cylinder head. We sat under the stars, silent. I was filled once more with the strangeness of the upside-down sky, and a sense of amazement that we were here at all. I wondered if the truck driver had even seen us.

The next day, stiff and sore, I opened Mondialita's throttle and drove straight east into the morning sun, fears dissolving once again as we were transformed into a red streak of motion. Mondialita flew through the desert. I whooped and screamed with the adrenaline of speed, then settled into an almost hypnotic state of joy.

John Berger wrote that driving a motorbike was the opposite of making poetry, because writing poetry is about slowing down to silence, and on a motorbike, everything is so fast, so instant, so fleeting. I disagreed. As I drove Mondialita as fast as she could go, there was a pulsating stillness within me, a state of hyperawareness and total focus within which I could feel images, emotions and sentences rising up with the clarity of poetry. G.C. held tight to my waist, and I could hear him humming through the intercom.

Suddenly I screamed, wordless and hysterical over the rushing air. G.C.'s hum turned into, 'What! What's wrong!' Some Thing had started to crawl up my neck and over my mouth, inside my helmet. A hysteria that I had never felt before overwhelmed me. I was exploding, caught between my mind telling me that if I crashed the bike at top speed we would be human jam on the road, and my body telling me to rip off everything right now otherwise the crawling Thing would sting my eyes out.

In the calmest voice he could manage, G.C. talked me through what I had to do: pull in the clutch, brake slowly, go down through the gears, pull over, stop. I vaulted off the bike and tore off my helmet and jacket. Something black flew up and away. I was shaking and wanted to vomit. We never knew what it was that came out of my helmet, or how it got there: perhaps inside my jacket, it had been creeping upwards towards shelter or escape since we had set off that morning.

That night we camped wild in the bush for the last time. The sunset was the most magnificent we had yet seen, a trumpet blast of red and orange. As night came, I dreamed of things crawling and scratching in the darkness outside our tent.

At Ceduna the next day, we drank iced teas from plastic packets made in Poland before driving through more farmland, huge fields of grey, dusty earth. Europe felt very far away. G.C. said it felt as if the Nullarbor had chewed us up and spat us out.

The children go back to school today. In Italy it is Ferragosto – the feria, *feast, of Augustus – which since Roman times has been a national holiday. August in Italy is too hot to do anything much, anyway, and whoever can manage it goes to the sea or the hills; not unlike how G.C. and I escaped with Mondialita to India's hill stations. My Italian friends are in eternal disbelief at the barbaric custom of starting the school year now. Part of me agrees with them. Most of me, though, is filled with gladness that the children will be back with their pals, with teachers*

whose actual job and joy is to help them learn; that I will have some time in my kitchen alone, uninterrupted.

In the quiet after the children leave for school, I make a coffee and sit in the gentle Scottish sun. I think of a Syrian friend who called the Scottish sun a liar, because 'he looks bright but is never hot enough', and remember the relentlessly hot outback roads.

The Australian Bight opened up into blue magnificence, proof of forces and timescales that split continents, vastly beyond my comprehension. I thought of the Aboriginal man in the garage shop in Norseman who told us we had to stop here and look for whales. We saw none.

I had taken to reading books when G.C. drove. I liked leaning on his back and holding the pages taut against the whoosh of Mondialita's speed. This would have been suicidal madness in India, but here it soon became normal. We were talking less and less, exhausted by the heat and the glare, the endless, empty tarmac. I remembered the names of places on the coast of Western Australia: 'Thirsty Point', 'Desperation Bay'. So many of those first white people arriving here must have just disappeared and died in the enormity of land. The houses we passed seemed like wee shells set against tides of earth. Perth felt so distant as to be in a different world, the 'Cappuccino Strip' a ridiculous fabrication: a place that would disappear within a few decades if humans didn't work so hard to keep it in being. I was reading our guidebook to Australia again, trying to find stories to answer the riddle of the Dreamtime/nightmare graffiti, but the book didn't help much, beyond reminding me that Aboriginal culture is the oldest continuous culture on our planet. I read on, trying to understand, feeling like a fly buzzing my way through dimensions and histories I could not comprehend while also being part of them. The sun burned new freckles into my face, seeding the shape of future lines in my forehead.

On the road to Adelaide we met dust devils, twisting shapes of powdery air dancing across the land. One was huge and frighteningly close to us: I could see small birds being sucked into it as I accelerated beyond what Mondialita could safely manage. The dust devils were all over the landscape, sucking up the thin soil and spitting it out in a huge grey plume that gently dissipated. We passed a salt 'lake' called Lochiel, a pale expanse of crackled dryness. In its centre, someone had made a Loch Ness monster from truck tyres cut in half and arranged in a snaking row. Growing anything from this land seemed like a preposterous idea, and my mind superimposed the landscape of the thickly planted, fertile Lombard plains where I grew up.

Adelaide too was full of parks. My eyes were shocked by so much sudden green as we walked towards the university area, past moorhens and slow fish in a river. We saw posters for the Adelaide Fringe everywhere, showing some of the same acts I had seen half a world away at the Edinburgh Fringe. With a sudden sharpness I missed Scotland, where I was so much more familiar with the land and its conflicts, where I didn't feel like an ignorant trespasser.

Technical Interlude

Mondialita was suffering after the long, dry road across the southern edge of Australia: her engine had started to cut out whenever it idled, reminding me of the way she had struggled in the high Himalayas. We tried everything we could think of to fix her, but this was beyond any technical abilities we had. We found a hostel and took her to a mechanic. I felt secretly, guiltily glad that we needed to wait for a couple of days until she was fixed, in a city with green parks and a variety of food options beyond our 'Australia diet'.

That evening we sat in a 'pokie' bar, surrounded by slot machines, talking about Mondialita, eating chips and watching Australia beat India at the Adelaide Oval on a screen. The owner was a woman from Bournemouth who had moved here twenty years ago 'for the weather'. She shrugged when we asked about the drought, saying, 'Yes, I'm curious about what will happen if we don't get enough rain this winter. Who knows, eh.' She said she thought Australian farmers copied Britain, laughing at how this was clearly ridiculous. Then she stopped laughing and said, 'But who else can they copy? Can't go listening to the darkies, can they?'

Scotland's late summer light shines golden through the grasses above my head. The membrane between seasons is thinning, allowing autumn to be seen in the ripening rowan berries and rose hips. One month ago I returned from Lombardy, and increasingly I have come back to lie on the earth of this sloping field by the woods and the sea in search of quiet. I need to let all the pandemic stories from Italy out; their weight is both a gift of reconnecting and a grief too wide to handle. I imagine flinging them up into the blue gulfs of sky, letting them wheel about a bit with the birds so that they might resettle in my mind more lightly.

In the middle of all this ripening, this gathering in before shorter days, it seems that everyone is talking of returning: back to school, back to work, back to normal. A friend in Dundee texts me to say that her children's school is closed again because of infections. The streets are still empty, with many shops unlikely to reopen. Nobody I know is untouched by what has happened in these months thick with unexpected change. Families have started up and broken up; people have lost their jobs, their loves, their lives. The familiar things we have longed for now feel strange, exhausting and dangerous. Nobody seems sure where exactly we are going back to, what exactly this place called 'normal' is. The most common expression in conversation is 'who knows'.

Swallows and swifts cluster in the sky: they are readying to return south. Their bodies write loops of urgency in the air: eat, eat, fill up, stay strong for the journey. *The light around me says,* enjoy, enjoy, this gold will not last.

Roseanne Watt describes the seasonal departure of birds in her poem 'Migration Day', writing

[. . .] and all I think is grief

this feels like grief.

This year has brought a heavy harvest of griefs, but I can now glimpse a beauty in this yearning for all the people and things that won't return, however much I try to conjure them: it is one of the shapes of love that shows through loss. Roseanne Watt's words circle in my mind like swallows, looping back upon themselves, speaking for me:

[. . .] The day they left

was blue, and kind and sudden.
And still, some part of me
would beg them stay.

10

The stories we carry

Victoria and New South Wales

The Great Ocean Road took us from South Australia towards Victoria. As we moved further away from the desert, heading south-east, trees slowly became more abundant and filled with extravagantly crested parrots. My eyes, so used to weeks of reddish dust and grey tarmac, felt like wells filling up with colour again. Eucalyptus now filtered its scent into my motorbike helmet, like a blessing of green after the rotting kangaroos along the Nullarbor. I was filled with sudden wonder at where we had got to and what I was doing: *Look, I wanted to shout back across the years at my younger self, Look, it will be OK! You will, one day, drive through eucalyptus and parrots in Australia; you will get through the fear and the mountains and the desert!*

The sea too was a welcome sight, flashing in and out of view as we looped along towards Melbourne after the Nullarbor, and I excitedly looked forward to camping by the great ocean, imagining warm expanses of empty sand and lots of swimming. A quiet beach beckoned, and we unloaded Mondialita, setting up camp in a practised, pleased, efficient silence which lasted until the last tent peg was pushed into the ground and the flies found us.

We were attacked. These were the most ferocious flies I had ever encountered: they bit us through thick denim; they buzzed and clung and stung. G.C. dropped his bag, I flung my motor-bike jacket back on, and we both yelled and sprinted across the beach, flailing like mad human windmills to try and shake off the black tormentors that kept biting us despite the wind and our thrashings. Still yelling and flapping, we made a rapid U-turn back to camp, and within sixteen minutes all our clothes, kit, tent and bags were repacked and loaded on to Mondialita: a new record.

'Ah, the flies, yes,' said the smiling man behind the counter at the next petrol station, 'you'll get used to them. Welcome to Australia!' The man introduced himself as Mick and sold us some antiseptic for our bites, whistling under his breath a tune I recognised as 'Waltzing Matilda'. Was he real, I found myself wondering, or was he a figment of some collective imagination, part of a tourist ideal of an Australian petrol station? Still smiling and whistling, Mick moved away to tidy an arrangement of squishy cups decorated with a panoply of Australian stereotypes: kangaroos, boomerangs, wallabies, koalas. The cups seemed very strange, made of the same material as wetsuits: what liquid could they hold?

'Stubbies!' came Mick's voice, startling us.

'What are they for?' I asked. He tilted his head, amused and slightly pitying.

'For keeping your beer cool, mate!' I bought one with a picture of the Nullarbor road on it. Outside, the toilets had signs saying 'Sheilas' and 'Bruces', written with the font used in Wild West frontier films.

Red and amber leaves have started to appear, surprising me as they do every year: I am not quite ready for summer to end. The changing trees remind me that S and T's birthday is near, and I am grateful for the freedom to have other children in the house again to party and play. I walk through goldening woods to the beach and swim, delighting in my body's motion in the waves, remembering when I was hugely pregnant with twins, barely able to walk, and only felt free when I floated in water. S and T were born as the first leaves turned. Over eighteen months I travelled across half the world; in the space of eighteen months I birthed three babies – a harvest of new stories spinning forwards into the future.

Eucalyptus changed to pine as Mondialita rolled towards Melbourne past huge conifer plantations, hundreds of acres at a time of monoculture, all the trees evenly spaced and at the same height. In places the hillside had been cut clear as far as the eye could see, then another swathe of thousands of tiny pine saplings covered the land. They looked artificial and completely out of place here: like one of the conifer plantations in Scotland blown massively out of scale, another use of this land to grow plants in a way that originated in a different hemisphere.

Continuing my thoughts, G.C. said, 'But I suppose the plantations in Scotland aren't that natural either? I mean, what would have grown before the pine trees, who lived there?' I thought of the Clearances in Scotland, of how the land was taken and used for profit by those who claimed to own it, emptying people away from their homes and forcing them to resettle elsewhere. How many people came to Australia from Scotland because of the Clearances, out of desperation, bringing with them the stories and ways of their land to superimpose on someone else's?

The questions multiplied. By the time we reached Melbourne, I was hungry: for answers, and for almost any food other than Vegemite sandwiches and coffee squeezed from a tube. Thankfully we had friends who were waiting to greet us. Hazel had moved here from Scotland to work in a hospital; after a few minutes of listening to my stories and questions, she said, 'You need to go to the Immigration Museum. But first you need to eat, you crazy skinny nutters.' My eyes widened as she told me that there was a street entirely filled with Italian restaurants.

I spent the next day eating food which was so good, so *right* that my eyes spilled out tears. Bemused Italian waiters hovered up, casting anxious glances at G.C.

'I have not tasted tiramisù or ravioli for over a year,' I explained to them apologetically, slightly embarrassed by how deeply my body wanted the tastes of home. They instantly brought us more food, coffee and shots of grappa on the house. Afterwards, waddling my impossibly full stomach back towards Hazel's flat, I noticed the abundance of red Ferraris parked outside restaurants that logically would not have generated sufficient revenue to pay for such cars. I spotted the well-dressed men loitering on street corners, sunglasses as sharp as their suits and haircuts.

'Ah,' I said stupidly, and walked on. High on some hoardings, someone had scrawled graffiti supporting politicians who had been convicted in Italy years ago of corruption in connection with the Mafia.

In the Melbourne Immigration Museum there were many stories about the Italians who had moved away from poverty and settled in Melbourne, bringing their stories and food, their politics and religion. I looked at their faces, these people who stared back at me looking so very like my family and friends back home. G.C. beckoned me over to a section all about people who had come from Scotland with their differently familiar faces. A sign glibly confirmed that a great many had migrated after the Clearances: 'Settlers often named new places after the homes they left behind: have a look at this map and see if you can spot Glencoe, Glenrowan, Bannockburn!'

I continued to feel the absence of stories about the Aboriginal people whose lands we had travelled through after they had been so euphemistically 'settled' – although in Melbourne, for the first time, we saw plaques and monuments saying that the city 'respectfully acknowledges the Traditional Custodians of the land, the Bunurong Boon Wurrung and Wurundjeri Woi Wurrung peoples of the Eastern Kulin Nation and pays respect to their Elders past, present and emerging'. The names rolled in my mouth like new songs.

P bursts out of school, gesticulating in outrage, shouting, 'Hallowe'en is cancelled! They can't do that! It's not fair!' S and T run out and join the chorus of laments. There will be no

271

guising: the First Minister of Scotland has appealed directly to children, asking them to stay at home.

It is a bit like a pilgrimage, this Hallowe'en ritual whereby children thread their way through the streets seeking sweets in exchange for songs and jokes. It is also, in my mind, not unlike a carnival: sure, the costumes are creepy, the singing and laughter all about grim deathly things, but still – it's a time of excessive sweets and cakes, of staying out beyond bedtime to parade about in the dark, of games and raucousness before the relentless dreich of November. Scotland has taught me to appreciate the timing of Hallowe'en, or Samhain, as it is called in the Celtic calendar: as we tip further into the long dark of a northern winter, this is one night in which we listen to stories about things usually hidden and buried, drawing close to darkness while held in the safety of candles and jokes and costumes. We keek into the world of the dead as nature burrows down into decay, waiting for the light to return.

But none of these musings are in any way helpful right now. My three small people are at the end of their patience: 'Why should we listen to the government? Why do they keep stopping us from fun things? I want to go guising!' Why indeed, I think. Shall we open a discussion on freedoms now, starting with why your freedom to go guising would mean the increase of conta-gion?

I opt for emergency chocolate rations and vague answers: 'We have to listen, dear. You can go guising next year. Let's go home and make a new plan.' We plot a day of dooking for apples, watching creepy cartoons on the telly, making ghost-shaped biscuits, telling scary stories around a fire. Orion's belt rises above us in the cold sky, and I tell the children how in Australia he is upside down. They refuse to believe this. The stories turn *from creepy made-up things to unbelievable real things: how, yes, in Australia the stars are upside down, water spirals in the sink the other way round; how for children growing up in Australia, our stars and water swirls are strange and topsy-turvy; how right now it is moving towards summer there and getting hotter every day.*

Family friends had put me in touch with Kay, an indefatigable environmentalist who grew up in Malaysia and now lived in Melbourne. She welcomed us into her house, bringing us into a kitchen where mugs balanced on books, folders, paper stacked in wobbly piles. She moved in whirling gusts, making us coffee while telling us where the bathroom was, explaining about her work while smiling and asking about our journey. Kay was busy setting up conversations between indigenous people from different countries whose lands and lives were threatened by environmental calamities, to learn from each other's stories and struggles.

'Although, you know, not everyone likes the word "indigenous". It's complicated,' she said, before inviting us to join her on a trip with some of her colleagues from Papua New Guinea: they were going to visit First Nations people on their ancestral lands north of Melbourne, to learn more about the problems they are facing and what solutions they have found.

The trip was intended as a learning exchange for people from Papua New Guinea, whose traditional lands also lay along a river and were threatened by mines, dams and plantations run by Chinese and multinational firms.

'Try to say First Nations rather than Aboriginal. And do

NOT say "tribes", she warned. 'And the sofa bed is made up for you in the living room over there.' I listened, feeling slightly dizzy, and gladly went to sleep early in Kay's living room, ready to leave before dawn.

I woke up to Kay's voice again: 'Grief,' she was saying. 'It's in so many stories of the First Nations people here. They are constantly fighting to reclaim what was taken from them.' G.C. and Kay were in the kitchen getting ready to leave. Groggy, half awake, I stumbled through, clutching at a coffee and at her words. She told us that the land where Melbourne now stands was 'sold' to white men for some wool and iron – but the concepts of land ownership among First Nations people were so vastly different to that of the white European men that the transaction made no sense; many First Nations people now consider it a trick, an invalid claim of ownership.

'It's complicated,' she said again. 'You'll see.' We drove away under trees full of cockatoos screeching at the whitening sky. The seatbelt felt flimsy and strange as I sat sleepily in the back of Kay's car.

We were going to visit people from three different Nations on the banks of the Murray River. A tall woman called Judy greeted us outside a community centre in Deniliquin, her long brown hair in a ponytail that reached her hips. She welcomed us to the land and introduced herself as being of the Baraba Baraba Nation.

Judy explained that all across Australia there were many different nations: 'Like if in Scotland you met someone, you wouldn't describe them as a European, you'd say Scottish? A bit like that? But it's tricky to explain,' she said, smiling. She led us into a low, hot building where children were playing football around a table which was covered in food to welcome us. As we ate, Judy told us that the First Nations had trad-itionally interacted and regulated their lives according to ancient 'Dreaming' stories, which are many things in one. They refer to the Dreamtime, when the world was formed by ancestral beings, and which is still unfolding; they give lore to inform and regulate social interactions; and they contain instructions on how to move across Australia's immense land-scape without trespassing on the land of other nations. This conversation was the very edge, I sensed, of a whole way of making and knowing which my mind had never met before. I could see how this fluid, multilayered way of regulating interactions was almost impossible to reconcile with colonial systems which needed to extract and produce goods, rigidly measuring and enforcing the ownership of land and profit. Maybe this was what the graffiti meant by 'Blackfellow's Dreamtime, White Man's Nightmare'.

Judy took us on a walk and showed us the plants used for medicine and food by her ancestors. A plant close to her feet helped wounds heal faster, and was also called 'Sneeze Weed'. G.C. sniffed it and sneezed seven times in a row, generating much laughter and banter. Another plant was called 'tongue numb', and a few moments after chewing it, I could no longer feel my tongue. Judy grinned widely at my amazement, smile lines lifting around her blue eyes. She was trying hard to preserve traditional Aboriginal knowledge, but said that two centuries of displacement and modernisation had taken their toll and a lot of wisdom has been lost.

'Technically, I mean, in the language of how some people measure things, I am only one thirty-second Aboriginal,' she said. 'But all of my heart belongs with my nation and these lands. The white man tried to breed the black out of us, you see. All this, this trauma, all the loss of land, our culture and traditions gone or going – it's a massive reason behind all the huge social problems we have in First Nation communities today.'

The scale of her people's grievances became depressingly clear. A short, brutal list was distilled for us by Judy and her companions: their land was taken from them by white settlers and hardly ever given back; they were killed by the diseases and violence brought by Europeans; they were forced on to 'missions' which attempted to Christianise them and forbade the use of traditional languages and cultural practices; they weren't recognised as Australian citizens in the census or electoral roll until 1976; for decades, there was a deliberate government policy to 'breed out Aboriginality', with children taken away from Aboriginal parents and brought up in white families under new names.

But the main grievance we heard about on this trip was explained by Sam, of the Yorta Yorta Nation, with many nods and agreements from everyone present: the 'killing' of the Murray River to make the Hume Dam. Traditional gathering places were submerged after the damming of the Murray River early in the twentieth century; the river's cycle of seasonal floods was destroyed, and with it, many of the First Nations' hunting and migration patterns. Sam's voice was angry and loud. Over an evening barbecue – 'Don't worry, we know how to manage fire here' – he told us how his nation had made a legal claim to their land which had been through all the Australian courts but was ultimately denied. A judge had said that 'the tide of history had washed away Aboriginal traditions and claims to the land'.

'Screw him,' Sam snapped. 'We're not going away.' He told

me how they were now learning from Canadian First Nations, who were making cultural maps of their land, showing places used for traditional purposes with their own names and words, 'as a way of fighting back'. I drank my beer, silent, overwhelmed by the stories.

The next day we walked along the cracked riverbanks amidst thirsty trees covered in flocks of pale cockatoos. Ginny, an elder of the Jaitmatang Nation, told us that dams, modern agricultural practices and climate change had devastated the ancient Murray ecosystems. Long grass grew where water should have been. In the gum tree forests of Barmah on the Murray, she showed us a canoe tree – an amazing thing to my eyes – a huge, old eucalyptus whose thick trunk was marked by a patch of thinner bark. It looked like a sunken scar, a missing piece, a flap of skin sewn back over removed muscle. Ginny explained that her people used to make canoes by carefully removing large pieces of thick bark whole, using stone hatchets and wooden levers. The bark would then be shaped into a canoe, leaving the tree scarred but 'still alive for itself and other creatures'. The canoe from this tree would have carried six people easily, she said, and was probably cut about 150 years ago.

At that time the landscape would have been completely different: 'The Murray was alive then,' she said, 'flooding and breathing like it needs to, before the white men dammed it.'

Sadness filled me as the evening grew. It was difficult to see how all this could be undone now, this harm and change. Or maybe I was asking the wrong question – maybe I needed to listen to these new stories and not think in terms of undoing, but of learning. We pitched our tent in a grove of gum trees, sheltered in the calm, fragrant air at their bases while the canopy swayed in strong winds.

'A fire wind, this,' said Judy from her tent. 'G'night, folks.'

As night came, the Southern Cross danced through the leaves. Sam's voice, softened, told the stories he knew about stars, Orion and the Milky Way and the Pleiades, while the darkness stretched above us all.

One of our companions on this trip was Gabriel, an elder from Papua New Guinea. He remembered Scotland with laughter and fondness: 'Here in Oz, people don't talk to me, but in Scotland I always felt so welcome.' He befriended us over the course of our shared journey and told us about the years he had spent in the UK on a post-doctoral scholarship to study and teach agricultural practices and education, saying that he was still in touch with some of his Scottish students. His father was a tradition bearer for their tribe in Papua New Guinea.

'It's OK to say "tribe" if I say it,' he told us, his eyes glinting with laughter. Now he had inherited his father's role, which in his language translated better as 'philosopher' than 'chief' or 'landowner'. He liked to use the word 'guardian'. Gabriel had looked at the changes his people were living through and realised that their oral tradition – the philosophy – was becoming lost, so twenty-five years ago he had started to record traditional chants to preserve their knowledge. He told us that a big nickel and cobalt mine had opened near their tribal lands; it was run by a Chinese company and no local labour was ever used, only Chinese workers 'imported by the company from their country'. Nothing came back to Gabriel's people apart from toxic slurry, which was dumped in the river so that heavy metals now contaminated the water – it was outrage at this that finally moved Gabriel to become active in international environmental work.

Gabriel was shorter than me, with a bushy beard full of tight, greying curls. His bright eyes widened to show the whites all around when he got excited. He had a gentle voice that made people stop and listen.

When we stopped for a coffee break, he became avuncular and told us, 'Listen, apart from all this environmental learning, this is important: don't leave it too late to have kids. Kids are great . . . but grandchildren are special. You want to be alive for your grandchildren.' He said that at some point in everyone's life, 'It is in your blood' that you will 'get the call' of land, homeland and identity – that you will want to settle and put down roots somewhere. 'Nobody will die without that happening.' For him this had happened, strongly, when he became a father. He promised that the same would happen to me, and I would 'make the choice then' of where to stay and build. I thought of all the other bearded men along our journey who had told us that we should settle and have children; Gabriel was the first one who had simply stated that one day we would. I didn't quite know how to react to this: surely it was my choice, to return to Europe and perhaps have babies?

'Ah, yes, but sometimes choices are also meant to be,' said Gabriel. 'Look at you and G.C. You chose him, no? But could you have done anything else?'

The last evening of the trip was spent among peppermint trees that spread out of the ground and up like fingers. We were surrounded by bird calls and the swaying of branches. When night came, Orion and the Southern Cross danced through the leaves. I felt like an aquatic creature looking up through algae to a light-scattered water surface. Three brilliant stars, or planets, stretched like a bird or a boomerang from Orion to the Milky Way. Gabriel told us that in the philosophy of his people, Orion is a man walking home with food for his family: what I was used to seeing as a shining belt and hanging sword was a big bunch of bananas slung up over a shoulder.

November gales whump like angry hands against the windows. It is the evening before Guy Fawkes night, a British celebration which I cannot quite bring myself to appreciate due to its roots in a story that involves burning Catholics. My children celebrate it as Bonfire Night, or Fireworks Night: another excuse to light fires and make brightness against the gathering dark. Neither look likely if this weather carries over to tomorrow. I close the curtains and see the neighbours hurry out to tether their bins, then look for my phone to check the weather forecast.

The phone rings before I find it – Hazel, still in Australia, calling from her early morning. Her voice is brittle, shocked: twenty-eight people have died recently in bushfires. She is trying to get across the scale of the fires, the smoke colouring the sky, the fear: 'Even in Norseman they're evacuating – remember Norseman?' I close my eyes, trying to console her while billowing memories fill my mind and return me to the dry heat, G.C.'s desiccating eyeballs, the fire warnings always at 'extreme hazard'.

Hazel tells me of a friend who lived in an Australian town on the coast where the whole population spent the night squatting in the shallows off the shore 'so they wouldn't burn'. Her kids are sleeping in the school building, which is now their only place of refuge. She asks me to keep an eye out for jobs in

Scotland for her: Australia no longer feels safe. I say goodbye and run to check on my children, their safe breathing as rain whips against our house.

By the morning the storm has passed east, out across the sea. Grey evening comes early. Despite the cold and damp, we manage to make a fragile fire, carefully feeding it twigs. Fireworks flower and the children whirl about with sparklers, little earthbound constellations. The stories I tell them on Bonfire Night are about fire as something beautiful, bringing warmth and safety: a burning controlled by us to meet our needs. I don't tell them, yet, uglier stories of dissenters burned alive, or the ones where humans confuse need with greed and burn up the land which nourishes them. Those stories I leave for later, a burden which I spare my children from carrying for another wee while, until another season.

The sea slowly rose to cover Melbourne's skyline as we sailed out into an unusually calm Bass Strait. We were on a ferry imported from Europe, of the same model that took us to Belgium from Rosyth at the beginning of our journey, in what felt like another lifetime.

Tasmania took about nine hours to reach. I read that it was separated from the Australian mainland about 15,000 years ago, when the gradual end of the last ice age pushed the sea level up and transformed a peninsula into an island. The people who lived here when Europeans arrived had reached the island long before Tasmania became a separate landmass, crossing the isthmus from mainland Australia on foot. I tried to imagine the sea below us as land, and failed.

Mondialita took us on roads where no other vehicle appeared. We camped amidst forests, halfway down the island, and I was amazed at the amount of wildlife that wandered out as we ate our evening rations. A wild echidna snuffled about near our tent looking for ants, and I had to suppress a shout of delight at its appearance, like nothing I could ever have imagined. Was it a reptile, with its scaly spikes? A sort of hedgehog? What are its spikes made of? Why does it lay eggs? Why does it want to eat ants all day? G.C. spotted what looked like the black snout of a small bear crossed with a rodent peeking at us from the undergrowth, but it disappeared as soon as we looked its way. That night a snarling, growling something scuffed at the opening of our tent; we waited for it to leave, and never knew whether it was a Tasmanian devil or not. I had read that Tasmanian devils are carrion eaters, and a pack can make an entire dead cow disappear completely overnight. They even crack the skulls open and chew them. I was glad never to know what had visited us.

We meandered through Tasmania for a week. By the time we reached Hobart, Tasmania's capital, it felt as if we had crossed another planet, devoid of other humans and full of extraordinary creatures. It was strange to walk again on tarmac and sleep in a bed. I looked for stories in the museum; again, most were about white settlers. The British had first used the island as a penal colony, one with a horrific reputation. By the middle of the nineteenth century, the white 'convicts' had been somehow upgraded to 'settlers', but this did not much improve the fate of the island's original inhabitants. A few words stated that 'a combination of brutal policies, new diseases and violence devastated the Aboriginal people of Tasmania, worse than many other Aboriginal nations on the mainland'. Their original language was lost, and lifetimes of stories with it.

We sat outside a pub in Hobart harbour. The pier, the light, the beer, everything was so familiar, like a Scotland transposed to one of the most southerly cities on the planet. I was awash with opposing tides of feeling: on one hand, the sense of ease at having spent weeks in a country where my language and skin tone matched those of most people; on the other, a growing discomfort at seeing how the folk who looked and spoke like me were here because of a not-so-distant history of empire and occupation.

As I dangled my happy, free feet off a harbour at the bottom of Tasmania, far to the north of Australia people were incarcerated in a modern penal colony because they had tried to reach Australia by boat after escaping war and hunger in their countries of origin, rather than arriving by plane or motorbike, escaping their own restlessness. The Australian government had a 'Regional Processing Centre' on Manus Island, in Papua New Guinea, as part of their 'Pacific Solution': a vague name for what was an immigration detention facility, effectively a prison for people who were intercepted by the Australian Navy and classed as 'illegal' immigrants by the descendants of immigrants.

G.C. distracted me with an exclamation: here, at Mondialita's most southerly point of travel, was her flashy younger cousin – a pristine 1985 R100RT, which looked like Mondialita might have if we hadn't dragged her halfway around the world by way of the Himalayas. We had never seen another bike like her on this whole trip, and were amazed to find one in Hobart, of all places. The barman came over with more beer and started chatting about motorbikes, Tasmanian devils and how the

harbour had changed. Now it was taken up by cafes and
galleries, but a large section used to be a jam factory – fruit
grows well in Tasmania. One whole new wharf was built on
land reclaimed by infilling with apricot stones. I wondered if
a forest of apricot trees would sprout up some day between
broken stones.

We had agreed that once we were back on the Australian
mainland, we would head towards Sydney: our savings were
running low by now, and we didn't know what it would cost
to ship Mondialita to New Zealand. But I could not stop
thinking about the conversations with Sam, Kay and Ginny
about the Hume Dam. G.C. was the same: he drove out of
Melbourne in silence, and when he spoke, it was to continue
conversations we were both having about the dam, separately,
in our heads.

'Let's go to see this dam for ourselves,' he suggested as we
boiled up our evening pasta. I nodded. It was on the way to
Sydney anyway – well, sort of.

When we got to the Hume Dam, a friendly engineer showed
us around the huge cement structures, proudly telling us that
although it was finished in 1936, it was still one of the largest
dams in the world and provides water for all of Adelaide, over
1,000 miles away. The engineer spoke of it as a wonder, a gift
that has allowed the Murray Basin to support over two million
people, making the land fertile enough to produce almost half
of Australia's agriculture.

'It's aMAZing, really,' he said, beaming, listing the many
benefits it brought to huge numbers of people. He seemed
kind and looked a bit like one of my Glasgow cousins, which

somehow encouraged me to ask him, tentatively, what he thought about ideas that the Hume Dam contributed to the cycles of extreme drought and bushfires that were growing in frequency and severity. His face expressed complete astonishment. 'How could it not be a good thing? This has changed our lives! We'd still be living like peasants if we didn't have this aMAZing dam!' His freckled hand affectionately patted the massive wall we were looking over.

It was difficult to see how all this could be taken away now. How could such a thing be reversed? How could the river and the land return to what they were without widespread destruction? I also thought that although the First Nations people we had met were proud of their traditions and culture, I was not sure they would be willing – or able – to live as their ancestors did 200 years ago. The dam carved across the land like a scar, a border, a line traced on a living map. As we drove away through acres of fields, past towns named after places in Europe, it seemed an impossible maze to navigate. I wondered again if I was asking the wrong questions, reading the wrong maps.

The Earth has tilted, carrying Scotland to the winter solstice. From today, we start the steady return to the long sunlight of summer. I go swimming in the sea while a slow dawn spreads, and the fact of my body in the water under this sky feels like a triumph beyond all rational proportion, a trumpet blast of aliveness in the middle of so much dying. Shivering, back in my kitchen's shelter, I listen to the radio saying that once again schools will close indefinitely and another lockdown will begin

just before Christmas. There is a calm in me this time round. Like driving a motorbike, I think: if you've done it once, you can do it again. I laugh, sigh, have more coffee, make some more food, write some more words. The thin Scottish sunlight doesn't shine for long: at 3 p.m. it is nearly dark again, just as the children come home from school. We prepare to light another fire in the winter night.

Among the solstice preparations, my phone buzzes with another photo from Hazel in her summer of fires and fear: burning land, red under a sky black with smoke, the sun rising between the two colours. I am jolted by a realisation that this looks like the Aboriginal flag, almost exactly, painted by the burning land – the reverse of those glorious sunsets we had seen spread their wings red over darkening bush. Another image she sends is all lines, graphs showing the steady rise of heat over the past decade across Australia. 2019 was the warmest year since Europeans began keeping records. Rainfall patterns have become harder to predict, fields already scorched before fires touch them. Satellite images show farmland covered in ash. I see videos of First Nations people calling for their knowledge to be listened to, saying that the land needs to be managed differently, and white farmers saying that these ways would result in economic ruin. I watch them obsessively, suddenly hungry to hear Australian accents again. Beneath the voices hums a rage born of hurt and fear without resolution.

What are the stories that can help heal? How can we find ways to tell of things that are so complicated and sore that they are left buried, unspoken? I think of Sam's anger, Judy's tired kindness, Bob in the outback garage: the stories we carry, about ourselves and each other, which cannot be challenged. I see now, returning in memory to journey with Mondialita, my own

286

patterns of anger and fear repeated all the way up to this summer when I had to think before answering G.C.'s 'do you still choose this?'

Of all the stories, one of the most helpful to me has been the dance between Odysseus and Penelope: the wanderer constantly ready for new adventures but also desperate to return home, and the faithful wife waiting at home but also finding ways to weave and unweave her own fate. After years of thinking that I hated Penelope, the truth now seems wider: there is no need to choose between one or the other of these archetypes, or even between different aspects of them. I can be, I have been, both of them. Feeling trapped back in Waiting Penelope mode this year has sharpened my desire to never return to that place of corrosive anger. To help me, I summon up Mondialita in my mind, remembering the freedom and growing and joy she brought: a talisman against feeling left behind and powerless.

I tear little pieces of paper, on which I write all these thoughts down, trying to order them into a solstice ritual of naming what has grown stronger over the past season, what has broken, what must be left behind. It is not easy to do. The words burn quickly into sparks.

The road towards Sydney surprised us with Glenrowan, not so much due to its improbable name in a land where no rowan trees were in sight, but because of the enormous statue of an armed man with a bucket on his head which loomed above us as Mondialita took us down the main street.

'Whaaaaat is that!' G.C. exclaimed. The bucket turned out to be a sort of helmet with a slit for a visor. The rifle between the man's hands only got bigger as we approached. It was a statue to Ned Kelly – Irish convict, hero, gangster, freedom fighter, depending on whose stories you believed – immortalised in a song I suddenly sang from start to finish in front of the statue, to G.C.'s surprise. It tells the more hagiographic version of the Wild Colonial Boy's life, as a brave defender of the poor (he robbed the rich / he helped the poor) who was also scary (a terror to Australia was / the Wild Colonial Boy) and fought against nasty sheriffs who, tragically, kill him in the end (a bullet pierced his brave young heart / from the pistol of Fitzroy / and that was how they captured him / the Wild Colonial Boy).

'How do you know that crazy song?' asks G.C., as some pedestrians give me a slightly bemused round of applause.

'Oh, my mum used to sing it to us as a lullaby,' I said.

'A lullaby? Jeez . . .'

I remember how morbidly fascinating I found the story even as a small girl. Instead of falling asleep, I would sit up and ask streams of questions: 'But why did he rob the rich? Why were the sheriffs bad? What does "pierce" mean? Why was he wild?' I sing 'The Wild Colonial Boy' to my children in the morning instead, to make breakfast interesting. It works well, especially now that the children are old enough to understand that part of their family comes from Irish immigrants who happened to escape hunger by going to Glasgow instead of Australia.

My mother's cousin's husband on the Connelly side – or was it the Madills or the McGuinnesses? So many names, so many cousins – has recently retired and developed an interest in gene-

alogy. This has led him to trace a pair of my ancestors to Ireland, where they got married in Donegal in 1845, then disappeared from Irish records to reappear in Glasgow a year later, alongside thousands of other people escaping the potato famine in Ireland. Some of these ancestors went on to have children, and slowly moved away from the starvation which made them leave home, building new lives in Scotland. Others ended their days in the poorhouse or in prison – the fate which would have awaited the Wild Colonial Boy had he not opted for a final shoot-out with the sheriffs. My children and I look at the world map in our kitchen after breakfast, comparing the distances between Ireland and Glasgow or Melbourne. I wonder if I have very distant relatives somewhere in Australia, descended from ances- tors who followed a different journey of migration, whose stories evolved down a different path.

G.C. had a real, living relative in Australia, Aunty Helen, who was waiting to welcome us in Sydney, where we were now heading. We were almost there, embarking on the final stretch of a journey we had started in another hemisphere over a year ago. I couldn't find words to contain the mixture of relief and sadness that swirled about me: reaching New Zealand meant gladness, but also the end of travelling with Mondialita. I wasn't ready to return home; I was completely ready. Above all, I was glad that New Zealand still lay between now and having to end our journey.

'The Blue Mountains aren't really mountains, are they,' G.C. commented, distracting me back to the present, 'more a series of deep valleys cut into a plateau which was worn down by how old this land was.' He had a point, especially when I compared the Himalayas or the Alps to the gentle slopes we were driving through. They were covered by a blue haze that the heat raised up from gum trees, and the air smelled like a very clean flavour of heaven. That night, we savoured our last wild camping in Australia: tomorrow the road would take us into Sydney.

We took turns driving the last stretch of highway, both silent. We stopped in front of the Sydney Opera House. Getting off Mondialita, rocking her on to the centre stand, taking our helmets off: I noticed how all these movements were now one fluid sweep of practised ease. A sudden gush of exhilaration rushed out of me in a whoop: we had done this! Together! Whatever happened next, this would always be something that had happened! G.C. was grinning so much that his eyes almost disappeared. We danced about, laughing with a brittleness that contained tears. A kind and confused man took a photo of us, posing triumphantly in our tattered clothes and straggly hair.

Helen enveloped us in welcome, with a wonderful openness, and immediately started to tell us hilarious stories about growing up in New Zealand amidst her huge and raucous Māori family. She fed us abundantly and then announced that she was going on holiday the next day, insisting that we use her home and mobile phone, 'so you can sort whatever needs sorting'.

In between visits to Sydney's beaches and sights, we investigated our options and, after days of circular discussions, returned to the same conclusion: we couldn't afford the exorbitant quarantine and import taxes involved in getting Mondialita across the Tasman Sea to New Zealand – and even if we had wanted to sell her, we couldn't because of Australian customs regulations and the promise written in our *carnet de passage*. Unless we decided to stay in Australia and work for six months – which we very much did not want to do – our only feasible choice was to return Mondialita to Scotland now, shipping her from Sydney to Dundee via Singapore and Folkestone. This was it: the end of her journey with us after 23,000 miles.

After the first shock of sadness, practicalities took over and were again a form of distracting consolation. Arranging to ship Mondialita back home would have been many times more difficult without Helen's gifts of space and time. We managed to get a custom-made Kawasaki motorbike crate from a mechanic in Parramatta who asked only for a crate of beer as payment, in solidarity as a fellow motorbike enthusiast. I watched Mondialita being boxed up for her sea voyage home, hoping she would be alright without us. She would take eight weeks to get to Scotland: time for us to travel down New Zealand before flying back to join her.

Being 'just' pedestrians again was strange. We walked around the cargo port in Botany Bay, watching kite surfers and imagining what it would have been like before the British Empire landed and decided to make it a penal colony. I kept on spotting blue lizards, and ibis birds with black heads and tails wandered about the town centre with us. Again we were drawn to Sydney Opera House: it seemed impossible that such a vast building could give the impression of sailing off into the harbour, but this one did, surrounded by small boats and bathed in beautiful light.

I wished we too could sail out of the harbour like Mondialita, but it was no longer possible to get a commercial sea passage across to New Zealand, so we had to fly. Two months in Australia suddenly seemed like a flash, our whole trip condensed into a shining sphere of experience that rolled around in my brain, for ever there to return to.

11

Free to return

Aotearoa New Zealand

*H*ogmanay, New Year's Eve: the night bordering one year and the next. Through the brief day's light, I hum words to an old, old tune from Shetland which is traditionally played through this night of fires and celebrations:

It's the dawning of the turning of the year
It's the coming of the growing of the light
It's the leaving by of what is past and done
It's the turning round and facing to the sun

We prepare yet another fire outside, to celebrate with a very small group of friends. Gathering indoors is still illegal under Covid regulations. There is ice underfoot, and the children slip about dangerously close to the flames. We are all tired, very ready to leave by what is past and done from this year.

It's the coming of the greening of the earth
It's the leaving of the time of dark and death

It's the sharing of the good that we have done
It's the turning round and facing to the sun

Our plane flew towards the dawn, and after Australia's immensity disappeared into the sea behind us, New Zealand appeared: a bank of low clouds. Aotearoa – the country's mellifluous name in Te Reo, the Māori language – is often translated as 'long white cloud'. We were welcomed off the plane by G.C.'s uncle Chris, and taken straight to a huge family party celebrating a thirtieth birthday. There were cousins, aunts and uncles who had not seen G.C. since he was a boy; they handed me beers and cake as if they had known me for ever and wrapped us in easy rejoicing. We were surrounded by people with the same eyes and nose and hair as G.C.'s, and familiar names like Douglas and Sheena. It felt like a Scottish homecoming on the other side of the world.

G.C. told me that when he was growing up, he was fascinated by stories of Uncle Chris who, years before, had emigrated to New Zealand. The Christmas when G.C. was five, this famous uncle came back on holiday and arrived at the family home in Fife driving an astonishing gold motorbike, dressed in leather and sharing the saddle with his new wife, Joy. She had a wide grin, long black hair in braids, and explained to G.C. that her skin was brown because her ancestors came from a hot place where the sun always shone. She spoke with a funny accent and claimed never to have seen snow in her life. G.C. had a fairly vague concept of distance at the time and asked her if New Zealand was farther away even than Aviemore, that impossibly distant and magical place.

He held his breath when she explained that it was much farther, that it lay on the exact opposite side of the world. She said that if he went out to the garden and dug a deep enough hole, down through the bubbling lava at the centre of the Earth, he would come out in New Zealand. G.C. told me that he then spent an afternoon in the mud, crouching in his wee wellies and digging with a trowel, but found only worms and stones. I loved this story, recognising in it the seed of an idea, needing a long and careful germination, that was planted in his mind and led towards us both being here today.

Uncle Chris and Aunty Joy hosted us in the house they had built themselves near Whangārei. The atmosphere was of gladness and peace, one of those rare homes where silence is as welcome as talk. There could have been no better place to stop and consider how far we'd come. Joy was Helen's sister, and gave us her own tales of growing up in a vast Māori family. As one of seventeen siblings – 'We were known as the Tribe Up the Hill' – she deeply appreciated quiet and her calm, gentle, practical husband. She had planted swan plants outside the house, and Monarch butterflies loved to lay their eggs on them. There were butterflies hatching out of their pupae every day we were there, an unfurling of jewels into the air. Whenever someone ate an avocado in the house, Joy would take the stone and lob it out of a window, so it would grow into a tree. I was amazed by the abundance and fertility of this land after months of Australia's thin soils.

Chris and Joy brought us evening beers as we studied maps, working out how to move on south-east without Mondialita. Chris quietly said that he could lend us his truck – which he referred to as a 'ute' – for a few days. Tears came to my eyes and I couldn't speak, overwhelmed by the open, simple hospitality after long travels, and the sudden ease at being with family. I was also missing Mondialita, and realising that our journey was coming to an end. Chris silently passed me another beer, and Joy touched my hand before starting to tell us stories about the North Island. If you looked at it on a map, she said, you could see that it was shaped a bit like a fish; Māori stories told that it had been caught and hauled out of the ocean by the hero Maui as he sat on the canoe which was the South Island.

'The ute will be more practical for you than a canoe, though,' Chris said, smiling.

He said that a ute is 'the quintessential Kiwi vehicle': in Scotland we would call it a pickup truck. There were many of them on the road as we set off the next day, and I felt that we blended in very well, at least until we opened our mouths to ask for directions. We quickly worked out that the open back of the ute was the perfect place to eat food and pitch our tent, and I felt slightly disloyal to Mondialita as we delighted in our new transport arrangements. She was somewhere on the ocean by now, the wide blue we had crossed by plane, returning slowly home.

Aunty Joy had said that one place we had to go to was Te Rerenga Wairua, the northernmost point of North Island. She explained that its name meant 'the place where spirits leap off': it was where departing souls gather before leaping into the ocean and heading towards the afterlife, following the paths of the Māori ancestors who had first arrived in Aotearoa by boat, guided by low white clouds.

The sky above the astonishing ninety-mile beach was cloudless, and we were the only humans visible. It was like a gigantic, sunny version of beaches in the Western Isles of Scotland, complete with a solitary lighthouse to guide ships in the darkness. I lay face down at the end of a cliff and thought that it would be a good way to leave this life: a swoop and a leap towards the next adventure.

We needed to decide the shape of this adventure, though, and work out how much time and money we had left. We were helped by my brother who, eighteen months after helping us set off, joined us for the end of the journey. We drove back south to pick him up from Auckland airport. He stepped out of arrivals, hair as madly regrown as mine, truly and unbelievably there. Seeing Lorenzo again, more than anything else, made our planned return to family feel real, and right, and timely. Chris and Joy included him in their warm welcome, bought us all Kiwi fish and chips and beer, and told us that Cousin Shona had offered us her car to finish our road trip south.

So many habits had become instincts after nearly eighteen months on the road, especially those involving shopping. When we went to buy food for the journey, G.C. and I approached the supermarket till with combined baskets containing exactly two apples, one packet of pasta, one tin of tomatoes, one onion. Lorenzo sailed over steering a trolley laden with vast amounts of beer, loaves of bread, bags of fruit and packets of chocolate biscuits. I looked at him with a full blast of Older Sister Disapproval and he stared at our baskets in horror: 'Are you guys crazy? We have a car! With a boot! Go get more stuff!'

He was right, and so we did. Having a boot full of food and drink made every meal a luxury. I thought of people we'd met who so love motorbikes that they scoff at cars, saying that car drivers move in a modified cage, strapped in and buffered from danger. A road trip by car is like watching a film through a screen; the biker isn't watching a film, she's in it, buffeted by the winds, soaked by the rains, awash in the elements. All this was true; but it was also very nice to be protected from the gathering antipodean autumn by a car which easily carried me and G.C. as well as an abundance of food, my brother and all our bags.

We sat by a campfire the next evening, drinking beer and eating snacks, amazed at our good fortune. On Joy's recommendation, we had spent the day visiting the Marae at Waitangi. She had told us that it was where Māori leaders signed the Treaty of Waitangi, giving a measure of authority to the British in return for certain acknowledgements of native rights. The treaty itself was still hotly debated, largely because it had been proven that the Māori translation from the English was not correct, involving errors with such important concepts as 'sovereignty'. Joy had also told us that the Māori people were themselves immigrants, settlers in these islands, and there had been conflict between different Māori people long before the white settlers arrived and became a common enemy.

'We're not a unit,' she had said, 'remember that. No people are a unit; it's always complicated.'

There were many carvings at Waitangi, traditionally made by Māori men, surrounded by weavings made by women from flax. I had seen flax plants growing on the Waitangi grounds, at the Bay of Islands, and marvelled at how many things could be made from them. Some of the weavings told stories, myths of creation and transformation that humans tell to make sense of what happens in the world. They described movement from Te Kore (nothingness) towards existence, and from Te Pō (darkness) to Te Ao (light). I thought of the Dreamtime stories from Australia, Gabriel's careful caretaking of his people's philosophy, the many European stories of light and being coming from dark and nothing.

Tiny green points are appearing in the dark January earth, the promise of bulbs slowly keeking out, visible proof that Scotland's side of the planet is turning back to the sun. The longing for spring is like an itch under my skin: I want to plant seeds, clear out rooms, swim in the sea as often as possible to wash away the winter. I think again of the selkie story, so loved and returned to by the people living by the seas of northern Europe, and the many layers of possible meaning in a tale that centres around the changing of skin, the moving from the daylit earth to the darkness underwater; the shift from one state of being to another.

I swam everywhere I could in Aotearoa New Zealand, and rejoiced in ancient trees. Lorenzo, a keen and able birdwatcher, was basically in heaven. He could not get over the biodiversity, the sheer amount of natural reserves available to explore, along with the care that people gave to the environment: in Italy we had grown up surrounded by farmers who shot songbirds for sport. We saw many signs explaining what the Department of Conservation was doing in an attempt to reverse the mistakes made by settlers in the past, especially the damage brought by introduced species, creatures like starlings, sheep, cats, dogs, rats and sparrows. All of these were commonplace in Europe, but here were invasive aliens, altering a delicate ecology which had evolved in its own direction without big apex predators. So many birds were flightless and seemed fearless, totally indifferent to our presence. Seals with their pups, too, stayed still on their rocks and didn't run away from our approach.

In Gisborne we stood at the furthest eastern point of our whole journey, facing out towards Fiji, Midway, the Bering Strait and the international date line – an arbitrary border into yesterday. We had all got up before dawn, to be among the first on the planet to greet the new day and celebrate by swimming in the Pacific. In a charity shop, I found a copy of *The Golden Peak*, a book by Kathleen Jamie describing her travels in north Pakistan. It flooded me with memories, which gushed up with the force of water barely held back. I wondered how long it would take for this journey to fully percolate within me.

We learned the Māori/Te Reo names for some animals, and I relished the new sounds: parakareka, kōtare, the amazing pukeko with its vivid purple breast and white tail that twitched with every step. Bellbirds astonished us with their loud, clear, liquid songs. Kaka parrots woke us up every day with their loud congregations in the branches above us. One morning, after squeezing out of our tents, we realised that a falcon, a kārearea, was sitting in a tree just above us, eyes alert, looking out for its morning breakfast. Apparently they are able to prey on the likes of pigeons and magpies, and sometimes even gulls and herons. It seemed undisturbed by our exclamations of amazement. Enormous fern trees were everywhere – Joy had told us that they were very common in the North Island, where water is abundant. The fern tree leaves open up by uncurling, and the shape of the young leaf in formation is an important symbol for the Māori people, indicating new life and birth. The fully extended leaf is the national symbol of Aotearoa New Zealand.

From Wellington we sailed south and into the Marlborough Sounds. Dolphins raced the ship, leaping in the sunlight, a blessing on our passage to South Island. We spent a few days camping on the shores of magnificent fjords, in more of the well-kept Department of Conservation sites that we used all over the country. They were usually in stunningly beautiful or remote places and had little honesty boxes where we paid our camping fees. I began to feel that we were moving through oneiric landscapes, in a world of transcendentally beautiful scenery where we interacted with no other humans. Waking up in the tent, I reflected in amazement that Delhi, Istanbul, and Aleppo also existed on this same planet.

We drifted through the Abel Tasman National Park and Golden Bay, then down the west coast of the South Island, past rising ranges of mountains and over fast-flowing rivers of glacial meltwater. One April morning near Glenorchy I woke to find frost on the ground and on our tents. I dragged myself out, shivering, to see Lake Wakatipu shimmering with autumn mists and golden dawn light. A kayaker slipped through the pale fog, his paddling the only sound and move-ment in a scene so perfectly composed that I laughed out loud with delight. The stunning views made the cold mornings worthwhile, but I knew – we all knew – that our dreamlike wandering was coming to an end as summer moved into autumn. We spent a day exploring the loch, and the surreal colours of the beaches caused by the iron-rich soils in that part of Aotearoa New Zealand. I was full of the awareness of endings, knowing that we were moving closer towards our agreed destination: Stewart Island, off the most southerly point of the South Island. The temptation was strong to hoard every iron-striped pebble, pack away each autumn leaf, fold the whole landscape up to take away with me. I forced myself to throw the pebbles into the lake instead, a splashy music of relinquishment.

As the Feast of St Bride approaches once more, I note any hints of spring greedily, measuring every second of extra light and each new millimetre of green shoot like a jeweller weighing diamonds. The children are still not back at school, and there is no indication of when they might return. Now, though, there is a precedent against which I can set this new chapter of restrictions and see how we have all adapted and changed. There is a strength that comes from having weathered a season of fear and loss – a winter of the spirit, even though it unfolded over months which were summer in the world outside. I see a beauty now in the domestic chores that I once found so restrictive: there is something like the taut balance of a poem in the measuring of resources required to ensure that everyone has food when they're hungry, rest and work when they need it, games and cuddles, clothes that fit. Folding away towels as sleet falls outside, I think again of those lines from Kathleen Jamie's poem 'St Bride's':

> So this is women's work: folding
> and unfolding, be it linen or a selkie-
> skin tucked behind a rock.

Yes, I think. Yes – that's it. Folding and unfolding towels, memories, stories, days and seasons. Finding ways to regularly retrieve your selkie-skin so you can always return to whatever nourishes you. And the trick – which seems increasingly feasible, although never easy – is to never stop looking for adventure in the folds of daily living. Adventure, which shares colours in my mind with magic, unexpectedness, beauty, freedom – those fine travel companions. I realise that unfolding the sticky tar of last summer's rage has helped it to become more akin to a fire which fuels me instead of a corrosive pain; a protective mantle rather than a scarring acid. On the wall by the pulley there is a photo of myself, G.C. and Mondialita in front of Sydney Opera House. I smile at the restless glee in our younger faces: hello, *I whisper,* you'd never guess what happened after you came home.

Aunty Joy had told us that the further south you go in Aotearoa New Zealand, the colder it gets, and 'the more Scottish people liked it and settled there, because the climate reminded them of home'. Most Māori people lived in the North Island. The road signs proved her right again: Bannockburn, Clyde, Mosgiel, all the way to Dunedin.

The street names of Dunedin seemed to be in all the wrong places.

'Like an Edinburgh re-dreamed by people with no sense of direction,' said G.C., looking at me with a laugh. It seemed to me that the statue of Rabbie Burns was frowning at the ridiculousness of Grange Street being next to Leith Street, Clyde Street crossing the Water of Leith. Walking through sheets of battering rain that stung our faces, we laughed at how the

Scots had indeed crossed the world to find a climate miserable enough for their comfort. The Settlers Museum was full of portraits of mournful old men with names like Reid, McLean, McGregor.

In Dunedin's jumble of names, I found myself wanting to be back in the city I had come to love as a student, years before, with G.C.

'We'll be going back soon,' he said, reading my face. 'Not long now.'

Today's restlessness has taken me on a cycle around Edinburgh, thinking about Aotearoa New Zealand and finding reminders everywhere of the journey with Mondialita: a line of shops selling Punjabi clothes and Bollywood DVDs, a branch of the (British) Hong Kong and Shanghai Bank, no less than three Australian-themed pubs in the space of one street. But the most compelling is a large black rock lying by the riverfront of the Water of Leith, the site of the old Edinburgh docks. It looks like a meteorite, plunged out of the sky and buried into the embankment. Parts of it are polished and shimmer with a dark sheen, like wet seal pelt. A tiny plaque, almost illegible, reveals that it is a sculpture by Sylvia Stewart, and explains that 'this volcanic magma rock was brought here from the Water of Leith River near Dunedin, New Zealand'.

I sit beside this rock from the other side of the planet, filled with a gladness beyond words for the wealth of love and fortune that made my journey with G.C. and Mondialita possible. All the networks of family and friends, which I remember treating like a burden to be shed before departure – I now see that they were the threads from which my freedom was woven. My motor-

bike clothes were like a selkie-skin, allowing me to dive into a different way of being which altered my relationship with the world and with myself. Mondialita changed me, allowed me to explore the edges of my strength and fear. Now that she is burned away like paper in a bonfire, I still find her – the feeling of freedom that came with her. It surfaces in the new ways I have found of slipping away: into memories, into story, into the sifting and weaving of words; into the sea and into the earth as I feel it under my fingers while planting, anxiety tapering away from me into the soil so that I become just another living thing among the plants, removed from my constantly thinking human brain, breathing in and out under the sky. I find in these things a deep freedom, a state of being where self, thoughts and emotions are subsumed into a vaster otherness and the boundaries between world and self are thinner.

On my cycle back home I stop by an enormous tree and pull myself up and up until my muscles burn and I am held, swaying, between stretching branches and winter clouds. I climb down and undress to slip into the sea. The scurrying concerns of my heart are shocked away by the water's cold, my tiny human body held up by swaying depths.

Our boat left Invercargill, on the southernmost tip of South Island, with a single toroa – royal albatross – flying in our wake. It followed the ferry and swooped past us, amazing to me in its huge size and ability to effortlessly shave over the waves.

'They nest along the fringes of the Antarctic,' said Lorenzo excitedly. 'We are that far south!'

We'd started this journey on Orkney, an island off an island on the wild North Atlantic; soon we'd reach Stewart Island, or Rakiura, an island off an island in the wild South Pacific. Our trajectory spinning away from Scotland was finished, and every step onwards from here meant a step back towards home.

The ferry pulled into the harbour of Oban, where there was a street named after Charles Traill. At the turn of the nineteenth century, this adventurer, sailor, and unsuccessful gold panner from Orkney arrived on Stewart Island by way of California and Australia.

Across the bay behind Oban lay Ulva, an island with magnificent and varied bird life because all introduced rats had been wiped out. We immediately got on to another boat to get there. Lorenzo was so excited that he dropped his camera tripod into the bay, but with characteristic enthusiasm he jumped into the sub-Antarctic waters and managed to get it back. He warmed up over a campfire on the beach, surrounded by fearless birds who had evolved without any natural predators. A weka bobbed up to him and stole his sandwich.

Back in Oban, we ordered beers outside a pub by the harbour, raising them to the stars. That night was cloudless, clear. Under the Southern Cross, we confirmed the decision we'd already taken: to choose the freedom of returning home.

'Well,' G.C. said, 'I guess we should toast the conclusion of our journey.' I clinked my glass, feeling a quiet sense of triumph.

'Yes,' I answered. 'Here's to journey's end – and the beginning of What Next.'

There is always a What Next: stories don't end, they move on. They grow, and new things are made with each telling.

The day of St Bride has returned with the earth's turning. Once more the snowdrops nod their reminder to start thinking of P's birthday. I am not hungover today. The dread and anxiety I felt one year ago because of Brexit has been subsumed into vaster worries caused by the pandemic – and yet there is a core of something glad within me which has grown in strength over the past twelve months. I feel it, daily, lifting me from fear and returning me to the spirit of adventure that started off the journey with Mondialita: a lightness, a looking ahead with excitement to what might come next, despite all the very real griefs and dreads.

The Rail Bridge has not moved or changed, a giant solace of strength as I drink my morning coffee. Its interlocking girders remind me of the stories and connections which link us all, and our journeys. Sometimes a ponderous freight locomotive rumbles across with its long load of carriages. The London train, sinuous in silver livery, glides by on its way to and from Aberdeen.

The coffee cools as I sit, looking, thinking, remembering when I returned to Scotland from Aotearoa New Zealand with G.C., and how over the next two years we lost Mondialita and gained three children. Settling here, by a busy river estuary which used to mark the border between hostile peoples and is now wreathed with bridges, has meant that there are always journeys to imagine vicariously until we can take off again. This evening, when the day's work is done, the dishes cleaned and the children asleep, I will sit again and watch the lights on the bridges, and the ships beneath them, and the restless tides. I will think again of Cavafy, and the ending to his poem 'Ithaka':

Ithaka gave you the beautiful journey.
Without her you wouldn't have started out.
She has nothing else to give you anymore.

And if you find her poor, Ithaka hasn't fooled you.
You'll have become so wise and experienced
you will understand, by then, what these Ithakas
    mean.

Acknowledgements

My abiding gratitude goes to the many people across the world who have given me welcome, shelter and sustenance. You showed me the best ways of being human, and your gifts have stayed with me.

For my friends, fireworks and cartwheels of thanks. To the incomparable Cheering Section, Rachel Farrier and Fiona Couper-Kenny, for always being there. To Ilaria Bignotti, Besitonissimissimi. To Federica 'Fege' Rossella, Amica, grazie. To Andrea D'Agostino, for all the words exchanged. To Dawn Macnamara, for your kindness and support in the Baby Years and beyond. To Ben White, for years of staunch friendship. To Niamh Murphy, Vicki McWalter and Gowan Calder, for fire and celebration even in dark times. To Roxani Krystalli, for always noticing joy and beauty. To my fellow Poetistas and Poetry Zoomies, for the glee and delight in fine wordsmithing. Thank you to the many other lovely friends who have kept me nourished with listening, coffee, drams, walks and laughter. And to Calum Morrison, greatly loved and missed, gratitude for the drams and coffees and conversations.

This book has been years in the making, and it could not have grown to completion without the support of other writers and book-nurturers. To all of them I am deeply grateful. Claire Askew was unstinting in her assurances that it would be 'my turn next'. Kathleen Jamie, Melissa Holbrook Pierson, Chitra Ramaswamy and Malachy Tallack gifted precious words of encouragement. Francis Bickmore gave keen and kind insights at a critical point in the journey. Jenny Brown, with her generosity, enthusiasm and wisdom, is the very best of all literary agents.

Earlier iterations of some parts of the journey with Mondialita have been published by Granta (*Four Syrian Borders: a motorcycle journey*, 2018) and Gutter Magazine (*The Freedom Papers*, 2018). I am grateful to them for their support.

Much gratitude to Roseanne Watt, Liz Berry, Kathleen Jamie, Sharon Olds – for their craft in the world, and for their generosity in allowing me to quote their words. Thank you also to Soraya Chemaly, Caroline Criado Perez and Rebecca Solnit, writers whose work enlivened this book and keeps inspiring me to be brave.

I am grateful to Creative Scotland for trusting me with a grant from their Open Fund: I would not have been able to focus on finishing this book without this support.

Thank you to the good people at John Murray Press, especially Kate Craigie and Abi Scruby who helped to start and finish the editing of *Free to Go*.

For my family, love and appreciation vaster than language. Gavin – thank you, Compañero, for all the adventures and all the corners between things. Lorenzo, Yoda Best: grazie, Fratello. Rita and Giovanni, thank you for the love and care throughout the years; for the journeys, the stories and the homecomings. Jack and Jinty, your unwavering support and warmth are a wonder, and I am very lucky to have you in my life. Nonno, your love and stories and coffee-making live on. And to my beloved children: grazie 'infinitamente sempre sempre' for all the love and cuddles and games; for your curiosity and joy; for helping 'Mamma's Motorbike Book' with proofreading and drawing; for being the most brilliant humans I have ever met.